Signals and Instructions

1776–1794

Signals and Instructions

1776–1794

EDITED BY

JULIAN S. CORBETT, LL.M.

UNITED STATES NAVAL INSTITUTE

1971

Published by Conway Maritime Press
7 Nelson Road, Greenwich, London S.E.10

First Edition 1905
New Impression 1971

In the United States of America
UNITED STATES NAVAL INSTITUTE
ISBN 0 87021 877 8

Library of Congress Catalog Card No. 71-156308

Reprinted in Great Britain by
Lewis Reprints Limited
Port Talbot, Glamorgan

PREFACE

WHEN three years ago the Society issued its volume on *Fighting Instructions*, a gap in the series had to be left unfilled. It was found impossible to reconstruct satisfactorily that important period in the history of sailing tactics during which the old system of Instructions was superseded by the Signal Book system. The material that was necessary for the purpose seemed to have disappeared beyond recovery. The attention which the volume called to the subject led to several isolated pieces of evidence being brought to the notice of the Council and the Editor, and the *Barham Papers* shed further light, especially as to Kempenfelt's share in the reform. But all this did little more than show more clearly the high interest of the transition period and how little we knew of it. The new material raised new problems rather than solved the old ones. At last, however, three collections of documents became accessible all relating to this period, which have made it possible to tell the whole story in quite minute detail.

The first was the *Bridport Papers*, acquired by the British Museum, containing the tactical orders issued by Lord Howe between 1790 and 1794, and covering the last stage of the transition. Secondly, there were the *Rodney Papers*, generously presented to the Public Record Office by the admiral's descendant, Mr. Harley Rodney, containing amongst other things the actual copies of the Instructions which he amended and used in his campaign of 1780.

With all this new material in hand, incomplete as it was, it was felt that an attempt to deal with the period was justified; and this work was already in the press and was about to be issued when the accidental discovery of a long-forgotten chest in the United Service Institution brought everything to a standstill.

For it proved to contain a voluminous collection of Signal Books and Instructions, some originals and some copies, made by Admiral Sir Thomas Graves, K.B., a cousin of Lord Graves and Nelson's second at Copenhagen. There were nearly a hundred documents of various kinds, forming an almost complete series of the signals and instructions used in the War of American Independence. Throughout that war Graves was continually in active employment as a lieutenant and captain, and finally as flag captain to Commodore Affleck. He served in the Channel and on the North American and West Indian stations, where he was present at most of the chief actions, and thus had exceptional opportunities of collecting his material and tactical experience. From the first he seems to have been an ardent student of signals and tactics, and to have been heart and soul with the forward party. In the ardour of his studies he succeeded, whether purposely or not, in preserving for posterity a series of documents which embodies for us a practically complete history of the transition which naval historians have so long sought in vain. The admiral died in 1814, and in course of time his representatives patriotically presented his collection to the United Service Institution. A few of the documents found their way to the shelves of the Library, but the bulk of them remained forgotten and uncatalogued. It would seem that they have remained buried with a few other items in the chest, which had never been opened, certainly since the Institution removed to its present premises about thirty years ago. Their previous treatment is unexplained.

As will be seen, the new light which this priceless collection threw on the tactical history of the time was of the most startling kind, confirming beyond question and amplifying inferences that had been drawn from the previously accessible material. So rich indeed did it prove that it was found necessary to stop the work in the press and to reconstruct it entirely. In coming to this decision the Council felt that the importance of the new matter fully justified the cost and delay involved, and that subscribers would prefer to have the volume as complete as it could be made, even though the process of reconstruction entailed the regrettable delay in its issue which has occurred.

In the somewhat arduous task of recasting the book the Editor has been happy to find an invaluable collaborator in Mr. W. G. Perrin, the librarian of the Admiralty. His unrivalled knowledge of signal-books, untiring research, and fertile suggestions have greatly lightened the task and added much to the completeness of the work. He has also been good enough to read the proofs and to prepare the bibliographies, and to him the thanks of the Society and the Editor are specially due. To Sir John K. Laughton the Editor is again indebted for the detection of many errors and inaccuracies, as well as for ready help in other directions.

The Society is also under obligations to several gentlemen who have placed documents at its disposal or have assisted in bringing them to light, and the kindness of each will be found acknowledged in its proper place in the notes to the documents.

The Editor also desires to express his thanks to the librarians of the United Service Institution for the promptitude with which he was informed of the discovery of the Graves Collection and for the special facilities they afforded for its thorough examination.

Besides dealing with the transition period it has been thought well to add in appendices all that has been gleaned for the other periods covered by the Society's former volume. For the Seven Years' War some not unimportant new matter has come to light, mainly from the Duff Papers, which were kindly placed at the Editor's disposal by Mr. Robert Fraser Duff; and for the earlier periods a few new documents have been found by Mr. Perrin in rearranging the Admiralty Library.

On the whole the Society may now fairly claim that it has succeeded in making accessible a sufficiently complete series of documents to render possible a real study of the development of sailing tactics. In no period are we without practically complete light except for the latter part of the Seven Years' War. The question of how far the Additional Instructions of 1778 were founded on the work of Anson, Saunders, Hawke, and Boscawen seems to be the only one of any importance that is still obscure, nor can it be cleared up until there comes to light a copy of the Printed Additional Instructions which we know were being issued in 1760.

J. S. C.

January 1909.

CONTENTS

APPENDICES

GENERAL INTRODUCTION

I

THE period covered by the present volume—that is, from the beginning of the War of American Independence to the 'glorious First of June'—has always been regarded as the period of the great tactical transition. So much we knew, but little more. We knew it was the time when the old system of Fighting Instructions perished, and the new Signal Book system began; but the process by which the reform was carried through was wrapped in obscurity, and the names to be honoured for it were forgotten. Naval historians, who had to deal with the question in passing, were forced to be content with what they could make of two facts—the first, that Rodney broke the line on April 12, 1782, and the other, that Clerk of Eldin wrote a work on tactics. True it is that more deeply-read students knew of scattered allusions to the share of Kempenfelt and others; but these were scarcely noticed, and to Rodney and Clerk the credit was given.

How entirely misled we have been by building rashly on these two 'ounces of fact' the documents which follow will show. For the long series of Instructions and Signal Books which have come to light since the publication of the Society's former volume on the subject enable us at last to trace with certainty step by step the process of development, and to do justice to its real authors. At last we can see the transition period clearly for what it was—a period of tactical ferment in the service in which such men as Howe, Kempenfelt, Hood, Rodney, McArthur, and Knowles were striving to give form to the ideas with which they were in labour, and of which Anson and his school had sown the seed. Had the close of the Seven Years' War been more fertile in great and equal actions, there is no doubt we should have seen the fruition long before; but as it was it required a new war against a redoubtable enemy to quicken the dormant grains.

We can see moreover why it was that the service seems to have treated with an apparently obscurant coldness the work of Clerk of Eldin. The first part of his *Essay*, after circulating in manuscript, was privately printed in 1782. By that time it will be seen the tactical reform from within the service was in full swing, and many of his ideas must have been perfectly familiar to the leading spirits in the Navy. The need at least of a scientific study of tactics, with which Clerk enunciates his *Essay*, was fully recognised, and the invaluable work he did can only be regarded as one expression of a deep and widespread movement.

Kempenfelt at least had no doubt on the subject. 'Sir,' he wrote to Middleton, in August 1779, 'That we have no regular system of tactics you know; also that tactics are as necessary for fleets as armies. Of two fleets if one acts by a regular system of tactics when the other has none, I needn't say where the advantage must lay (*sic*). Our enemies have theory, we were superior in practice. They are in a way to remove the difference in the last, and how will the comparison then stand between us?' And again, in January 1780: 'I believe you will with me think it is something surprising that we, who have been so long a famous maritime Power, should not yet have established any regular rules for the orderly and expeditious performance of the several evolutions necessary to be made in a fleet. The French have long set us the example. They have a formed system of tactics which are studied in their academies and practised in their squadrons. . . . We should therefore immediately and in earnest set about a reform. Endeavours should be used to find out proper persons, and encouragement offered for such to write on naval tactics, as also to translate what the French have published on that subject. They should enter into the plan of education at our marine academies.'[1]

From this letter of Kempenfelt's we get a hint that the inspiration of the movement, however much it owed to Anson and Hawke, came at last from France. We know that after the peace Kempenfelt went to that country and employed his enforced leisure in making a profound study of French naval institutions. And if we turn to 'what the French had published' the hint leads us to certainty.

The standard French work at this time was the *Tactique navale ou traité des évolutions et des*

[1] *N.R.S.* xxxii. (*Barham Papers*), pp. 295, 309–13.

signaux, par M. le Vicomte de Morogues, Capitaine de Vaisseau. Its author, Sébastien François de Bigot, Vicomte de Morogues, was the founder of the famous Marine Academy at Brest, but is best known to us for his fine performance as captain of the Magnifique at Quiberon in 1759. The book was first published in 1763, at the close of the Seven Years' War, and dedicated to Choiseul, the great war minister who, nursing his revenge, was then absorbed in regenerating the French navy. In his introduction the author tells us he had been pressed to write the book by many distinguished officers and had reluctantly consented. But the work needed no such apology. It can still hold its own as perhaps the most scientific book on naval tactics ever written. For philosophical grasp of the eternal principles of the subject it is far beyond that of Clerk of Eldin, and it is not to be believed he did not know of it. Its fame soon spread beyond the land of its birth. In 1767 an English translation of all the theoretical part of it was published, perhaps under the auspices of Hawke, to whom it was dedicated. It is entitled *Naval Tactics, or a Treatise of the Evolutions and Signals, with cuts, lately published in France for the use of the cadets or gardes marines of the Academy at Brest, and now established as a complete system of the Marine Discipline of that Nation, by Mons. de Morogues, Captain in the Fleet, and translated by a Sea Officer.* With it was printed an older English essay on tactics which had long remained in MS. It is called *Instructions in Sea Discipline written by a deceased officer for his son, then growing up, who has had a command in two successive wars and done well.*[1] The Essay gives many hints as to the activity of thought in the service at a time which we have been taught to regard as tactically dead.

The author mentions Captain Cornewall, the hope of the service, who was so unhappily killed in Mathews's action off Toulon in 1744. He must have written on the subject, for we are told he was not only brave 'but made special study of the various discipline and government of the fleets of all nations, out of which he made excellent observations and comparisons with improvements.'[2] In his notes to Morogues the translator also confirms what is stated in the Society's previous volume as to Norris and Vernon originating the Additional Instructions.[3]

Another work, which had scarcely less influence on British naval thought, was *Le Manœuvrier ou Essai sur la théorie et la pratique des mouvements du navire et des évolutions navales*, by Bourdé de Villehuet, an officer in the French East India Company's service. It was issued with a high commendation from the Académie in 1765 and dedicated

1 Neither the translator of Morogues nor the author of the English essay has been identified. The latter speaks of serving with Rooke at Vigo and Malaga and also with the elder Byng at Cape Passaro in 1718. He cannot, therefore, have been Sir Charles Knowles or Capt. Cornewall, the only two officers of the period who are known to have left MSS. on the subject.

2 *Op. cit.* p. 90, *note.*

3 *N.R.S.* xxix. (*Fighting Instructions*), pp. 205-7. He also adds one not found elsewhere, which shows that Vernon originated the idea of making a signal overnight to be executed at daybreak. Most of his remarks on Norris are taken word for word from the pamphlet cited *ibid.* which was attributed to Lestock, and this was probably his main authority. See especially p. 55.

to Choiseul. As its title indicates, it is mostly devoted to what we call seamanship, but the fourth part is concerned with Naval Evolutions. Though less illuminating on fundamental principles than Morogues its methods of handling a fleet are more fully elaborated, and it ends by heralding the final reform with an explanation of the system of numerary signals devised and practised by that all too little appreciated genius Mahé de la Bourdonnais, under whom the author must have served in India.

Kempenfelt certainly possessed a copy of this work, for when about 1781 he was urging the adoption of a numerary system he translated the whole of the chapter on signals and sent it up to Middleton.[1]

It was not, however, till 1788 that Kempenfelt's wish to have a full translation was fulfilled. In that year it appeared in English form as *The Manœuverer or Skilful Seaman, being an essay on the theory and practice of the various movements of ships at sea as well as of naval evolutions in general. Translated by the Chevalier de Sauseuil, Member of the English Society of Arts.* It was dedicated to Prince William Henry, Duke of Gloucester. In his Preface Sauseuil tells us he was assisted by 'a British naval officer of experience and capacity' who did not wish his name to appear. He also adds notes and drawings by 'another able British officer' who, he says, had translated the greatest part of our author for his private use, and added many very ingenious and

[1] See *N.R.S.* xxxii. (*Barham Papers*), pp. 343-8. The matter in these pages is chap. vi. of part iv. of Villehuet's work. Kempenfelt's translation differs verbally from Sauseuil's.

useful observations with fine drawings of his own to illustrate them, and these he regarded as 'of too great importance to be omitted.'

Paraphrases of the fourth or tactical part of Villehuet's work, combined with that of Morogues, continued, as we shall see, to form the substance of English text-books till the sailing era ended with the Baltic Fleet in 1854.[1]

The extent to which the earlier and partial translation of Morogues—that is, the anonymous one dedicated to Hawke—was used in the service up to and during the War of American Independence is not known. No mention of it has been found in the correspondence of naval officers, and copies appear to be very rare. But at the outbreak of the war a new edition of Morogues was called for, and issued at Amsterdam under the title *Abrégé de l'art des armées navales ou éléments de tactique navale avec un traité des évolutions et des signaux par un capitaine de vaisseau au service de France*, 1779.

This was the very year that Kempenfelt was crying out for translations of the French text-books, which doubtless he had collected when abroad, and there can be little doubt he knew Morogues as well as he did Bourdé de Villehuet, for much of his subsequent work is obviously inspired by him. Still, the only treatise that is mentioned in his correspondence is the earlier work of Père Hoste, upon which Morogues' was founded. In any case, Morogues must have been well known to the leading spirits in the service; for on September 20, 1780, that promising young officer, Lord Robert Manners,

[1] See *English Works on Tactics*, App. E, *post*, p. 376.

who had lately been made captain of a ship of the line under Rodney in the West Indies, wrote to his brother, the Duke of Rutland, for a copy. 'Pray send me,' he says in his postscript, 'a "Delphin Horace," Morogues "Sur la Tactique Navale," a "Court Calendar," or any other book or new pamphlet;' and he gives 'the old seaman's direction, Windward Islands, Jamaica, or elsewhere.'[1] The suggestion may well have come from Hood, to whom Manners was always 'his dearest Bob.'[2]

This is the only direct mention of Morogues' work that has yet come to light in the correspondence of naval officers. Yet its influence upon British naval thought is as conspicuous as it is unconfessed. It is impossible even to avoid an uneasy suspicion that many of Nelson's best-known aphorisms, which we cherish with honest national pride, were drawn by him from the pages of Morogues. In any case it is certain that in the older and stronger British instinct for maritime warfare the seed of Morogues found a more fertile soil than in his own service. In England his deeper meaning was better understood than in France, and was more quickly and more thoroughly transformed into practical results.

II

In the case of Rodney, as is only to be expected, the influence of Morogues is specially marked. It is true that, like the rest, he nowhere

[1] *Duke of Rutland MSS.* (*Hist. MSS. Com.*), vol. iii. 36.
[2] *Ibid.* p. 53.

mentions the book in his correspondence, but there can be little doubt that, seeing how much and how recently he had been in France, he must have been familiar with it. And, if we compare the chief alterations which he grafted upon the old instructions with the principles that Morogues develops, his debt to the Frenchman becomes as clear as that of Kempenfelt.

Morogues starts in the most modern fashion by laying down the law that the weapon is the basis of all tactics, and that it is only in relation to changes in the weapon that tactics can change. From this point of departure he steers us through the development of tactics from the earliest days of galley warfare up to the adoption of the close-hauled line ahead as the tactical outcome of the broadside sailing vessel.

Then he deals with Hoste's elaborate evolutions for handling the line and shows the necessity for simplifying them, laying down the Nelsonian maxim that movements in the presence of the enemy ought to be the least possible. But simplification of evolutions, he urges, will not in itself suffice. Without constant tactical exercises to give the necessary skill and precision they will be useless. The bane of the old English school, as we know, was the idea it inherited from the Elizabethans that a captain had done all that was required of him when he could handle his ship in a seaman-like manner. But for Morogues, as for Anson before him, this was not enough. They must learn to think and act in squadrons. Fleet and squadron drill, he says, is as necessary in a fleet as in an army, and, other things being equal, the best-drilled force will win. They are almost Kempenfelt's words.

From this point Morogues proceeds to the essential difference between fleets and armies. That difference lies in the extreme difficulty of obtaining a decision at sea owing to the facility with which a fleet may avoid one if it wishes. 'We have no longer,' he laments, 'decisive affairs at sea—that is to say such as the end of a war absolutely depends on, nor even general actions, except where both sides desire it equally. Nothing but superior tactics and manœuvring can secure such ends, and for these the first essential is a good and simple system of signals.'[1]

Coming to the tactics which he recommends, we see at once that the main ideas underlying them are concentration and mobility. After dealing with the meaning of the close-hauled line of battle, and the comparative advantages of engaging to leeward and to windward, he says: 'If the ships in the line are not formed so closely as those of the enemy, several ships will have each to sustain the fire of two others; whereby they will be reduced to inferiority. Thus we see the advantage of large ships of the line and heavy guns. The enemy is beaten by a more numerous and much more powerful artillery.'

Then after dealing with the subsidiary advantages of the big ship—its superior command, its

[1] Compare Jervis's remark in commenting on Keppel's action off Ushant. 'I have often told you that two fleets of equal force never can produce decisive events, unless they are equally determined to fight it out, or the commander-in-chief of one of them bitches it so as to misconduct his line.'—Jervis to Jackson, July 31, 1778. *N.R.S.* iii. (*Hood's Letters*), p. viii.

superiority in a sea-way, and its superior defensive protection—he sums up the dominating tactical argument for preferring a squadron of heavy ships to an equal force of lighter ones.

'A fleet which has a greater number of heavy ships need not preserve such close order as that which has fewer of them. It may moreover be less numerous without being less powerful.

'A fleet in less close order manœuvres in certain circumstances more easily than a fleet more closed up. And if it is less numerous its movements are more prompt, signals are better taken in, the formation is preserved with more exactitude, and the ships run less risk of separation.

'The result of the preceding reflections is that the fleet which has a greater number of heavy ships will be more powerful than a more numerous fleet, if the difference does not fall in the number of guns or of the crews. That does not exclude a certain number of ships of the second and third rate necessary in all fleets.'

Summing up his theory of naval warfare in general, and tactics in particular, it is this: Firstly, that the paramount means of securing the end of warfare is a crushing decision against the enemy's fleet. Secondly, that, given the gun as the weapon basis of tactics, and given the ease of avoidance at sea, such a decision can only be gained by superior concentration of fire and superior mobility. But here a dilemma is involved. Superior concentration can best be obtained by close order, but close order means loss of mobility. The dilemma, however, is not insoluble. The way out is to use big ships and big guns, whereby you can secure at the same time both superior concentration, and, having fewer units, superior mobility.

There were, of course, other ways of securing concentration well known to Morogues—such as by cutting the line and doubling—but, as we shall see later, both these methods were regarded as imperfect. The shortened line was the method of his choice. His views are echoed by Boisnormand de Bonnechose, in his *Essais historiques et critiques sur la Marine de France*, in which he summarised the lessons of the War of American Independence. 'At sea,' he says, 'the gun decides the fate of battles. It is a case of mobile batteries coming to engage others. Thus the advantage should be with him who knows how to mass most fire in a given space, or with him whose gunners shoot straightest.' He also advocates firing at the hull and not the rigging (except in chasing), in order to destroy the enemy's gunners. Suffren he claims as an exponent of his theory, and assures us that that fine tactician learnt to mass his big ships in van, centre, or rear, as being the only practicable way of bringing a superior concentration on part of the enemy's line.[1]

It is not to be supposed that so sound an idea, rooted as it was in the essence of gun tactics, did not have an immediate effect in England. It can plainly be seen in the Instructions and Signal Books we are considering. Let us begin with Rodney's Instructions of 1779. In the original printed form

[1] Pp. 270, 275. The work was published anonymously in London in 1813. But the latest date it mentions is 1789, and it was obviously written before the Revolutionary war.

of 1778, as he, Byron, and Keppel received it, there appears a new article relating to engaging a numerically inferior enemy. The old article on the subject, which was No. 1 of 1759 (Boscawen's), is also there, numbered 24. It merely provided for equalising the lines by falling out the superfluous smaller units which were to act as supports to the rest. The new article, No. 26, gives these vessels a definite function, in the following words: 'Upon meeting an enemy of inferior force, ships of the squadron as shall be over and above the numbers of them are to quit the line . . . . and rake the enemy's van and rear.' This Article Rodney clearly disapproved. For after adding a few words to the old Article 24, he struck out the new one No. 26, and in its place he inserts two new articles, one for the three-decked and heavy ships to draw out of their places in the line and form in the rear or van of the fleet, and the other for closing up the line of battle. And these are followed by three more new ones for attacking the enemy's van, centre, or rear. Here clearly we have Bigot de Morogues' idea of concentration by closing up the line and massing the heavy ships on part of the enemy's line.

How strongly the idea was in Rodney's mind is further evidenced by his well-known criticism of Graves's action: 'His mode of fighting I will never follow. He tells me that his line did not extend so far as the enemy's rear. . . . If the enemy had extended their line to any considerable distance, by contracting his own he might have brought his nineteen against the enemy's fourteen or fifteen, and by a close action totally disabled them before they could have received succour from the remainder.'[1] The same line of thought pervades the notes he made some time in or after 1782 to Clerk's *Tactics*, as for instance: 'It is well known that attempting to bring to action the enemy, ship to ship, is contrary to common sense, and a proof that that admiral is not an officer, whose duty it is to take every advantage of an enemy by which he will be sure of defeating the enemy and taking the part attacked, and likewise defeating the other part by detail unless they make a timely retreat. During all the commands Admiral Rodney has been entrusted with he made it a rule to bring his whole force against part of the enemy's, and never was so absurd as to bring ship against ship.'[2]

Take, again, the following note: 'I suppose every admiral will carry his fleet down in a slanting line . . . . and, if the enemy's line is extended, will bring his whole force against part of the enemy's, which was the case on April 17, 1780, when the British of nineteen sail of the line would have been opposed to only fourteen of the enemy.'[3] Or this, in relation to the same action: '[The enemy were] standing on in a very extensive line

[1] *N.R.S.* iii. (*Letters of Sir S. Hood*), p. 46.

[2] Clerk's *Naval Tactics*, third edition, 1827, p. 18. The 'naval officer' who edited this edition says he received from General Robert Clerk a copy of the *Naval Tactics* as printed January 1, 1782, 'which copy contains a number of valuable marginal notes in his lordship's [Rodney's] own hand.' *Ibid.* p. 273. This was only 'Part I.,' relating to Clerk's proposed attack on part of the enemy's rear in engaging from to windward. Part II. containing the attack from to leeward by breaking the line was not then written. *Ibid.* p. xii.

[3] *Ibid.* p. 170.

of battle, which gave the admiral an opportunity of bringing the whole British fleet against a part of the enemy's. . . .'[1] Or this, again, for the tactical employment of heavy ships when the enemy is seeking to avoid action: 'And, in case the enemy retreats, the heaviest ships should be placed in the van, to attack the enemy's rear; which, as the heaviest ships advance along the enemy's line, will leave an easy conquest to the fleet that follows.'[2]

All this, of course, is on the lines of Bigot de Morogues, and it was to a reform of the existing system and not to its abolition that Rodney looked for improvement. 'The naval instructions,' he wrote, 'want a thorough reformation, but it is not in the power of every commander-in-chief to make what additions he pleases.'[3]

Possibly the most remarkable feature of Rodney's idea of concentration is that it did not at once take its place in our tactical system. Rodney himself did not use it, for his grouping of three three-deckers in the centre of his line on April 12, 1782, was hardly a departure from established practice. In the system of Howe and Kempenfelt it had no place. It is found in no battle order of this or the next war. Thus, while recent research forces us to deny to Rodney any tactical initiative in the matter of breaking the line, we may at least restore to him

[1] Clerk's *Naval Tactics*, third edition, 1827, p. 92, and cf. note to same effect, p. 88.

[2] *Ibid.* p. 40. See also his letter written in December 1781, on the eve of sailing for his last campaign. 'Much depends on three-deckers.' *Hist. MSS. Com.* IX. iii. 114*b*. The same idea underlay Don John of Austria's formation at Lepanto with his heavy galeasses advanced to take or give the first shock.

[3] *Ibid.* p. 16.

the credit of his own special idea. Nor is that credit small. For, though long neglected, it received in the culminating hour of sailing tactics the supreme endorsement of Nelson. This fact has received little attention, except from French officers who were at Trafalgar. Yet it is true that Rodney's form of concentration did in effect form part of the famous Trafalgar memorandum, in which all the harvest of the transition period seems to have been garnered, and in which every one of the latest schools of tacticians was drawn upon for its best. Unlike any previously known order of battle, that which Nelson drew up for his own grand division shows all his three-deckers massed in the van, exactly in accordance with the signal which Rodney was the first to introduce.[1]

III

While Rodney was thus working aloof, and therefore in vain, upon the old lines—seeking salvation by weaving the latest French theory into the old Fighting Instructions—an entirely new school was growing up at home which looked to the Signal Book as the basis of its system. But before dealing with it, it will be well to get a clear idea of the authority of the various signal codes that it brought into use, the process by which they were produced,

[1] The French believed that Graves used this device on Sept. 5, 1781. An account issued at Cap François, Nov. 27, says: 'The English fleet was soon near enough to be perceived forming the line . . . and placing its heaviest ships in the van.' Beatson, vi. 286. In fact Graves did not do so.

and the extent to which they were binding in the service.

Admiral Henry Raper, writing in 1828, puts the matter quite clearly. In the preface to his *New System of Signals* he says: 'The general Sailing and Fighting Instructions [meaning the old ones of Queen Anne's time] continued till after the commencement of the war of 1793 to be the only signals established by authority for general use. They had, however, before that period become too limited for the increased demands of the service, and each admiral therefore issued his own plan of signals to the ships under his immediate command. This gave occasion for the exercise of different schemes, and by engaging experienced officers to turn their thoughts to the subject was the means of introducing many improvements. In this manner appeared the new numeral method by which signals, which till then depended on the particular part of the ship where they were displayed, were now exhibited wherever they could be best discerned.'[1]

Here he touches the dominant note of the new school. Its moving spirits were Howe and Kempenfelt. But it was Howe who struck the first blow at the old system; of this we already had a hint from Sir Charles Knowles.[2] It was not, however, till the rediscovery of the priceless *Graves Collection* that we could know the character of the blow—how shrewd and bold it was, and how far in advance of

[1] H. Raper, *A New System of Signals*, 1828. Raper was signal lieutenant to Howe on June 1, 1784, and afterwards special signal officer to the Portuguese squadron. (See *post*, pp. 74, 344.)

[2] *N.R.S.* xxix. (*Fighting Instructions*), p. 235.

such men as Rodney. It was nothing less than the entire suspension of the established Fighting Instructions and the substitution of a signal book and instructions of his own.

It was in July 1776 that Howe took up the American command, but in that year he contented himself with the issue of an excellent set of instructions regarding the organisation of the fleet in two or three divisions according to its strength (a subject with which the reformers were much concerned, as we shall see), and some standing orders dealing in a very advanced way with watches, sanitation, inspection of kit, night rounds, and similar matters.[1] In the following year he took his bold stride forward. He was about to undertake the operation of transferring his brother, General Howe, and the bulk of his army from New York to the Chesapeake, and on July 1, 1777, he issued a set of 'Additional Instructions respecting the conduct of the Fleet preparative to and in action with the enemy.'[2] Both in scope and arrangement they differed entirely from anything that had yet appeared. They were accompanied by a regular printed Signal Book, to which they were explanatory, and which, as Howe enjoined in a note, was to supersede the signals provided in the regular Fighting Instructions. 'All signals,' the note runs, 'contained in the General Printed Signal Book which are likely to be needful on the present occasion being provided for in this signal book,

[1] *Instructions and Standing Orders.* (Copy) issued to Capt. Chaloner Barnaby of H.M. Sloop Merlin, from H.M.S. Eagle, Sandy Hook, July 12, 1776. *Graves Collection*, R.U.S.I.

[2] *Graves Collection*, R.U.S.I.

the signals in the General Printed Signal Book will only be made in conformity to the practice of some senior officer.' [1] Now as there was at this time no General Printed Signal Book apart from the General and Additional Instructions and their Index, it is clear that it was a direct blow at the old system that Howe was delivering, and that so long as he had a free hand and no senior officer arrived on the station he meant to rely for the tactical handling of his fleet on a signal book and not on a set of regular tactical instructions. It was this system which, as we shall see, finally broke the old tactical fetters, but it was to take nearly twenty years of ceaseless effort to get it finally established.

The fact that Howe thus early tried to bring in the system under which Nelson fought and which exists to this day does not exhaust the interest of his work of 1777. Not only do his orders of that year adumbrate the new system, but the explanatory instructions actually contain the germ of his famous attack by breaking the line in all parts by which the problem of decisive action at sea was finally solved. With this point we must deal more fully in its place. Suffice it now to remember that when Howe in hostility to the Government resigned the American command and went home in September 1778 he had already set on foot the first element of the reform—that is, that tactics must rest on a signal book and not on cut and dried instructions. Towards the

[1] *Graves Collection.* It is a thin quarto, rebound, with a modern label 'Lord Howe's Signals.' Its authorship is fixed by a MS. copy made by Graves, which is similarly labelled, and the date by the fact that the signals correspond with those in the Instructions of July 1, 1777.

second element, the establishment of a numerary code, he had done nothing. Knowles tells us he gave the Admiral such a code, but Howe did not adopt it. He still fettered himself by retaining the old system of giving each flag a meaning in accordance with the place in which it was shown.

With his resignation Howe's work was arrested for the time. When he reached home he became what we can only call the centre of a strike of the most capable flag officers on the active list against an unpopular and unsuccessful government. So serious was the general refusal to serve that in order to find a commander-in-chief for the Channel poor old Sir Charles Hardy had to be pulled from a well-earned retirement of fourteen years at Greenwich Hospital. It was then that Kempenfelt came upon the scene. Though left in neglect since his fine performances as flag-captain on the East Indian station during the Seven Years' War, he was regarded in the service as perhaps the most accomplished and scientific officer on the list, and in deference to service opinion he was appointed Hardy's first captain or chief of the staff in May 1779. In this way the old system was attacked from a new direction. Fresh from his theoretical studies in France he brought to his duties a philosophical intellect ripened by long and active service and profound thought. Of the trials and difficulties he encountered in his effort to get new wine into the old bottles we have lately read in the *Barham Papers*. The *Graves Collection* with some other recent discoveries enables us to see exactly how he went to work, not only to introduce the best French ideas, but also to harmonise his own views into a working partnership with those of Howe.

His first attempt was made at the end of the first defensive campaign in the Channel, when Hardy had retired to recruit at Spithead, and a final effort by the Franco-Spanish fleet was daily expected. The *Graves Collection* gives us the Admiral's Order Book of September 1779.[1] It contains orders for the better organisation of the fleet, an order for introducing the French sailing order, and, above all, the French order of retreat. From this point the work went on under successive commanders-in-chief in the Channel, with whom Kempenfelt remained as first captain, but always, it would seem, in touch with Howe. The path the reformer followed will appear later. For the present it is enough to indicate the general lines on which he was working.

Like Rodney both Howe and Kempenfelt were seeking for concentration of gun power, and looking to French writers for enlightenment. Though they did not adopt Morogues' idea of massing the heavy ships it is clear they had in mind concentration by a closed-up line. But to pin themselves to any particular form was, as we shall see, contrary to the free spirit in which they were working. Their object was to place in an admiral's power the means of executing any known movement or device that might fit the moment. 'The choice to be made,' wrote Howe to his late flag-captain Roger Curtis on September 10, 1779, 'of the expedients, which any set of signals

[1] See *post*, p. 124 *et seq.*

has provided for, will constitute, as we know, the ability of the flag-officers.' So from the French they revived the old 'order of retreat,' the sailing order in three lines, and the manœuvre of doubling the enemy's rear or van. At this time Kempenfelt must have been at work on the new Instructions and Signal Book which we know he completed and used in 1780 and which formed the basis of Howe's final code. And it is clear from the same letter that he must have asked to see Howe's new signals. 'I should be glad to know,' Howe's letter began, 'what part of our signals have been adopted. I should then be able to form an opinion of the principle upon which that great machine (the Grand Fleet) is to be put in motion. Our signals were adopted rather for a single squadron; and though most of the articles might be applied to a larger force the necessary continuation of the signals being different the propriety of their use under different circumstances will vary also.'[1] And on March 9, 1781, Kempenfelt wrote to Middleton: 'The plan I followed in the signals I made was not that I most approved of. That which I would have adopted, though most evidently the best, I could not get any of the admirals or officers of note to approve and countenance. I therefore followed in a great measure Lord Howe's mode, he being a popular character. The night and fog signals we use are almost entirely his, and both extremely defective. I would have used the French night signals, which are by much superior to anything of the kind that

[1] Barrow, *Howe*, p. 142. Howe probably wrote 'adapted' not 'adopted.'

has yet appeared.'[1] And a few days later quoting Villehuet, 'Signals should be simple, clear, and easily discernible. I don't know any more perfect than those invented by Monsieur de la Bourdonnais.'[2] It is clear, therefore, that though Kempenfelt treated Howe's opinion with great respect, he believed he had much yet to learn from the French.

As a final testimony to the influence of the French authorities there is Lord St. Vincent's letter written off Ushant in 1806 to Lord Howick, who had asked for his views on Clerk's treatise: 'I would not for the world subtract from the merits of Mr. Clerk, which I have always admitted; yet . I perceive evident signs of compilation from Père le Hoste down to Viscount de Grenier. In truth it would be difficult for the ablest seaman and tactician to write upon the subject without running into one or all the French authors.'[3]

IV

Still the fact remains that the tactical devices which Kempenfelt and Howe borrowed from France

[1] In the Signal Book issued by Kempenfelt in May 1782 (in the editor's possession), the whole of the established fog and night signals are cancelled.

[2] *N.R.S.* xxxii. (*Barham Papers*), pp. 340, 343.

[3] Brenton, *Earl St. Vincent*, ii. 238. Ekins long ago suggested Kempenfelt's indebtedness to France. 'Admiral Kempenfelt,' he says, 'who was a man of talents and acquirements, is thought to have practised the "order of retreat" to protect his convoy from superior force. This mode of retreat is fully described and explained in the *Traité des évolutions navales*, by Paul Hoste. From this circumstance it may be presumed that he had consulted and profited by that useful treatise; and to him it is more than probable the system of Mr. Clerk would not have appeared new.'—*Naval Battles*, p. 101. It is clear from this that Ekins knew neither Morogues nor Villehuet.

were but an insignificant part of their system. Their reform went far deeper and wider—mere changes in methods of attack were not its characteristic. It was something far more drastic, as must be explained later. First, however, as the characteristic feature of Rodney's system was improved methods of attack, it will be well to consider once more the most famous of them.

With the insight we now have into the way the minds of the most active tacticians in the service were working, we can do so with a better chance of fixing its true place in the history of tactical development. We can see, to begin with, why it was that Rodney's manœuvre of 'breaking the line,' at the time he executed it in 1782, appeared to have made so little impression. 'Sir George Rodney cut through the rear of the French line' is all Hood has to say in reporting the battle privately to Middleton. In his 'Journal' he says nothing at all.[1] Rodney himself does not so much as mention it, either in his official despatch or in his private letters to Lady Rodney and Stephens, all written immediately after the battle. In his Narrative he merely records the manœuvre, but with no hint at its being a particularly creditable or new one.

The fact is to the men of that time there can have been nothing surprising in it. Practised by our admirals of the seventeenth century, and provided for in Hoste's system, it had never been forgotten. Where the enemy gave an opportunity

[1] *N.R.S.* xxxii. (*Barham Papers*, I.), p. 160. See also his letters to Jackson, *N.R.S.* iii. (*Letters of Sir Samuel Hood*), p. 102. His journal is *ibid.* p. 120.

by leaving a gap in his line it had always been regarded as the obvious thing to do. It was tried against Rooke in 1704, and against Byng in 1756, but in each case was parried. And, steeped as Rodney and his like were in French ideas, they could not possibly have claimed it as a new invention. The sole reason why it was not tried more often was its danger, as they all must have known perfectly well. They all must have been familiar with it from the French text-books. In his chapter on 'Battle Tactics' Morogues has thirteen articles, and two of them are devoted to breaking the line in line ahead either at one or several points, with special signals for each form of the movement. All these were reproduced in the English translation, together with Morogues' diagram illustrating the manœuvre and the method of parrying it.

Similarly in Ozanne's illustrated work on the same subject, though he devotes only about half a dozen plates to battle tactics, two relate to cutting the line, one from to windward and one from to leeward; but he adds the note, 'As a rule we only cut the enemy's line when a superiority or a decided advantage in the action leaves no fear that he will in turn cut off our vessels which have cut his line, in order to sever them from their fleet, an incident to which this manœuvre is subject.'[1]

It was certainly the danger of the manœuvre and not oblivion of it that caused it to be practised so seldom. The belief was that it could be parried,

[1] *Marine militaire . . . suivie de manœuvres qui ont le plus de rapport au combat, &c.* Par Ozanne l'aîné, Dessinateur de la Marine. Plates 28 and 29.

and even turned against the fleet that attempted it, by a simple manœuvre. 'The General,' says Morogues following Hoste, 'will prevent the enemy cutting the line or render his attempt useless by making the preparatory signal, and immediately it is repeated he will make the signal to tack, and if any of the enemy's vessels have already passed through the line, they will be cut off.' This was Evolution 62 of Morogues' system, and he explains it thus fully: 'The fleet will keep well closed up to prevent the enemy breaking through. But if, in spite of its care, the enemy cuts the line, immediately some of his vessels have penetrated and before many have got on the other tack, the fleet will tack together. In this way, by getting on the same tack as the vessels that have broken through, those of them which are passing the line at the time the movement is made will be between two fires and will quickly be disabled, and those which passed through first will themselves be cut off and severed from the rest of their fleet.' Still he does admit the manœuvre (Evolution 57) as a means of forcing action on an unwilling enemy who is to windward.

It was thus used by Rodney, but it is to be noted that he did not attempt the movement till he suddenly found that a shift of wind had opened a gap in the enemy's line. Almost at the same moment and from the same cause a similar gap opened opposite the 'Bedford,' the sixth ship astern of him, being the rearmost of his own squadron (as the fleet was then formed in reverse order) and flying the broad pennant of Commodore Affleck, with Thomas Graves for his flag captain. Affleck also led through, apparently as a matter of course, and was followed by the whole of Hood's squadron.

Beatson, who wrote the first critical account of the battle, gives us a strong light upon the way in which the manœuvre was regarded in the service at the time. His testimony is important, for from his comments on the previous action of 1780 it is clear he was in close touch with the men of Howe's and Kempenfelt's school, who saw in reformed signals the condition precedent of improved tactics.[1] The section of opinion which he voiced regarded Rodney's penetration of the French line as an accident of wind, and refused to countenance the popular view that a new departure in tactics had been made. It specially protested against false deductions as to the value of the manœuvre based upon the erroneous supposition that Rodney broke through a connected line of the enemy's ships. Indeed, Beatson and those who thought with him were persuaded that Rodney's success was not due to the manœuvre in question; they doubted if it was even a fortunate evolution, and in any case decried jumping to any hasty conclusion that it was worthy of imitation.[2]

To the French it was certainly no innovation. For it is to be observed that De Grasse was as ready for the movement as De Guichen had been on April 17, 1780. In that action De Guichen believed that Rodney intended to break his line in order to cut off his rearguard. 'In effect,' wrote the French admiral in his official despatch, 'the English

[1] *Naval and Military Memoirs*, v. 61–3.

[2] *Ibid.* v. 470. For Beatson's criticism and the manœuvre in British text-books see *Appendix D*, p. 372.

admiral manœuvred so as to execute the plan, and attempted to pass through a great vacancy . . . . in our line, and had already doubled one of our ships when the Comte de Guichen made signal for the rear to tack.' Thus, he says, Rodney's attempt was parried.[1] So now De Grasse did or tried to do the same thing, and made the regular signal as Bigot de Morogues had laid it down. According to 'an honourable gallant admiral,' to whom Ekins was indebted for all his best professional criticism, 'Mons. de Grasse, after the action of the 12th of April, justified himself . . . . by pleading his compliance with the Ordonnance du Roy, which specified a particular line of conduct in similar circumstances. The case was this—Rodney's fleet, being to leeward of the enemy, was enabled by a shift of wind to lay through the enemy's fleet. The ordonnance said that the French fleet was then to tack together. De Grasse made the signal for that purpose, which was not obeyed by Mons. de Vaudreuil, the second-in-command, and his squadron, under the pretence that no man in his senses would have ordered such a manœuvre under an enemy's fire.'[2] The fact indeed would seem to be that clever as the parrying manœuvre looked on paper it would not work when the enemy was engaging as closely as Rodney was, for it exposed every ship to be raked by the enemy opposed to her as she went about.

It is thus abundantly clear that the idea of the manœuvre was familiar to both the French and the English services. All that was remarkable about it

[1] Mundy, *Rodney*, ii. 296, *note*.
[2] Ekins, *Naval Battles*, xiii.

in Rodney's last action was that so far as is known it was the only time, since tactics had been reduced to anything like a system, that it had been practised successfully.

V

Thus the case stood until the discovery of the documents given below: that is to say, that although it was known that the French had signals both for making and parrying the manœuvre, it was believed that the English had none. Now, however, it is necessary entirely to rewrite this chapter in the history of naval tactics. For on the evidence of the various Signal Books in the *Graves Collection* we have to face the fact that a signal for making the manœuvre had been introduced into the Channel Fleet by Sir Charles Hardy while Kempenfelt was his first captain, introduced, that is, as early as the winter of 1779–80, considerably more than two years before Rodney's famous action was fought. We also know on the evidence of an original Signal Book signed by Kempenfelt that under his influence the signal was continued and that when Howe returned to active service as Commander-in-Chief in the Channel early in 1782 it was established both for his own fleet in the Channel and for the East Indian Station. We also know that apparently under the influence of Channel men Graves introduced the signal after his action in 1781, and that Rodney did not do so, though Pigot did when he superseded him, and Hood the moment Rodney left him in command of the fleet. And what is still more striking, we know that Sir Charles Douglas, Rodney's first captain, and Affleck, who made the manœuvre independently, were both Channel Fleet men who had been serving under Kempenfelt's system. Finally it is beyond dispute that even if Rodney did not know of the innovation when he sailed for the West Indies in 1779, he certainly must have known of it before he sailed the second time in 1782. More than this there is evidence that as early as 1779 the value of the manœuvre and the neglect to revive it was the talk of intelligent ward-room officers. In the *Graves Collection* is a set of the Additional Instructions which Byron issued to Captain John Graves, of the Savage sloop, on March 3, 1779, at St. Lucia, and which Thomas Graves took over from him when he succeeded to the command of the vessel on his brother's promotion a fortnight later. In going through these instructions the young student of tactics (it was he who made the *Graves Collection*) has scrawled his contempt for them in the margin, and at the end he has written in disgust, 'Is it not wonderful that there are no signals for breaking the enemy's line, which may be advantageously done by the fleet to windward bearing down on the rear of the enemy, or when on different tacks to cut off the rear of the enemy to leeward.'[1] And be it remembered this was the

[1] It will be seen this cannot have been suggested in any way by Clerk of Eldin, whose proposed attack by cutting the line was from the leeward, and even so did not appear till much later. Graves's comment, if not written at the time, must have been not later than March 29, 1780, when he received Rodney's edition of the Instructions. Graves had been serving in the Preston, 50, Commodore William Hotham (Lord Hotham), under Lord Howe on the North American Station.

man who was Affleck's flag-captain when he broke the line in 1782.

Consequently we are forced to this remarkable conclusion, that so far from Rodney having revived the manœuvre he must have excluded it deliberately from his own modifications of the Fighting Instructions. All the evidence in fact points to the conclusion that so far from Rodney being the parent of the manœuvre—a claim which he himself never made, so far as is known—he rather shared the views of the school which Beatson voiced, and condemned it as a dangerous and unsound form of attack only to be practised in very special circumstances. There is indeed no evidence that Kempenfelt gave it any warm approval. It is true that his Signal Book of 1782 contains a signal for breaking the line when engaging on opposite tacks, but the instructions contained no article relating to it. His method of engaging on opposite tacks, as will be seen presently, was quite different, and it is probable he merely introduced the signal for breaking the line as part of his plan of placing every possible movement within reach of a fleet commander. The problem of breaking a well-formed line remained in fact insoluble till Howe matured his variation of the manœuvre which the French parry would not meet.

The real lesson of April 12 was not to teach any new set form of attack. It was something quite different, as was pointed out long ago to Ekins by his anonymous friend 'the honourable and gallant admiral.' His comments on De Grasse's failure to parry are used not to uphold the idea of breaking the line, but to impress the heresy of the old system of Fighting Instructions, of trying, that is, to reduce naval tactics to a set of formal rules. 'One disadvantage,' he says, 'of being compelled to perform certain operations is that the enemy may anticipate all your motions by being possessed of your rules of action.' But this was not his main objection. 'The recipe for a good admiral,' he goes on, 'is found in the person who combines theory and practice, is blessed with a clear head and a heart in the right place.'

Beatson, who published his *Naval and Military Memoirs* in 1790, shows us that this view was actually current at that time. In criticising De Grasse's failure to restore order to his line he says: 'French sea-officers are supposed to be more particularly instructed concerning the movements of ships in fleets than those of Britain, and their directions in certain cases, which are most likely to occur, are clear and definite. But in an uncommon and improbable situation such as that which happened about 10 o'clock on April 12 [i.e., when an irregular change of wind opened the French line] these plans and instructions became useless; and nothing could have collected the fleet in the best defensive position but the comprehensive understanding of a real thorough-bred seaman conversant in the motions of fleets, who could direct every movement of his ships by a clear and extensive system of signals.'[1]

[1] Vol. v. p. 472.

VI

This utterance of Beatson's in which he repeats his judgment on the action of 1780 is well worth noting. His words exactly express the essential difference between Rodney's school and that of Kempenfelt and Howe. They reveal to us, as the documents given in this and the previous volume abundantly confirm, that the two schools were working side by side—the one seeking improvement in a better though still formal system of tactics, the other in giving fleet commanders absolute freedom of movement and all that was necessary to secure that freedom.

It is here that lies the greatness of Kempenfelt as a reformer. A careful study of the instructions he drew up will make plain what has been said of him above: that his idea was not to add to the established list of technical devices, but to provide a simple system of signals and evolutions whereby an admiral could order and perform securely any manœuvre which his tactical abilities might see the moment called for. Under his system, as under both the earlier and later systems of Howe, the Fighting Instructions entirely disappear. Their place is taken by 'Instructions Explanatory to the Signal Book.' The idea is not to provide the admiral with ready-made tactics, but to insure that any movement he orders will be clearly understood by his subordinates and carried out in a prompt and uniform manner. That he studied deeply the French system is certain; but with the clear eye of a real master of war he was able to see what was good in it and what was bad, and the outcome of it all was that he sought and found not a system of tactics but a system of evolutions. In his eyes this was the secret by which precision and uniformity could be attained without formality and without loss of mobility and freedom.

The idea that highly developed perfection of evolutions did not connote a highly formal system of tactics was not confined to himself. It was the note of the period of culmination. St. Vincent stood by regular evolutions as heartily as he despised regular tactics. When Brenton once asked him if he had been at all guided by Clerk of Eldin in his great action he replied: 'Sir, I never once thought of him. Lord Hawke, when he ran out of the line and took the "Poder" sickened me of tactics.' Mathews's action off Toulon in 1744 in which Hawke founded his reputation must have been Jervis's earliest naval memory. He was only nine at the time, and the tale of Hawke's bold breach of the Fighting Instructions that was in every one's mouth had made a lasting impression on his mind.

Such a habit of thought was of course far from Kempenfelt. It was not in his scientific spirit to reason thus tumultuously from an isolated fact. Where he saw in the French system tactical ideas that commended themselves to his reason and experience he was ready enough to adopt them, as is witnessed by his reintroduction of 'doubling' and 'the order of retreat.' But the pith of his work was not this. It was in freeing tactics from its fetters.

His genius was fully recognised at the time,

though, until the publication of the *Barham Papers* enabled us to see into his mind, we had missed the full significance of contemporary eulogy. The passages in which his praises were sung are many, but they have been taken for little more than the usual panegyric that follows the tragic death of a deserving officer. As a captain he was regarded, says Beatson, 'as the most experienced in the service with respect to fighting in the line of battle and the manœuvres of a fleet. His abilities were known and admired by all the naval powers, and he was justly esteemed to be as brave and able a sea officer as this or any other nation ever produced.' His reputation was founded as flag captain to Sir George Pococke in the East Indies during the Seven Years' War, and in relation to these campaigns Ekins quotes the following contemporary 'character of Kempenfelt': 'The nation is indebted to the late Admiral Kempenfelt, from whose genius and labour the art of manœuvring a great fleet was put in practice and brought to a degree of perfection never known before. Signals were also methodised and were at once rendered distinct, comprehensive, and intelligent.'[1] Gardner in his *Recollections* calls him 'the ablest tactician in the navy,' and 'a man that has never been surpassed as an able tactician.'[2]

VII

The way in which the great reform was carried out was characteristic of English methods; for it

[1] *Naval Battles*, p. 29.
[2] *N.R.S.* xxxi. pp. 16 and 24.

was not effected by logical or direct process, but, as Admiral Raper hints in his book, on a side wind—as though nothing were in hand but an alteration in the system of signalling. Under the old system of Fighting Instructions each article that contained an evolution provided a corresponding signal of usually a single flag, whose signification was determined by the place in which it was shown. Such a system of course restricted an admiral's tactics to the set movements provided for in the articles. All, that is, that he could do was to put one of the articles in operation, and to that extent alone could he signal any movement at all. If anything else were wanted he had to send a boat. Thus it constantly happened, conspicuously in Byng's action at Minorca and Rodney's of April 17, 1780, that the admiral found himself dumb at the critical moment. An unforeseen movement was required which was not contained in any of the articles, and for which there was consequently no signal. All he could do was to signal the article which most nearly contained the directions he wanted to give, and the result was usually an increase of the confusion.

To get over the difficulty it was decided to adopt what was called a numerary system of signals. A list of every conceivable movement and order was drawn up in a Signal Book, the items being numbered in succession. There was also provided on French models a table for signalling numbers with two flags and a 'hundreds' pennant. Everyone, who was working at an improved system, except possibly Rodney, was agreed that a numerary plan was the best; but, as may be seen from the

Barham Papers, there was a considerable difference as to the best system to adopt.[1] The French had two: firstly, the simple digit system of La Bourdonnais, with two flags, one for units and one for tens; and, secondly, the tabular system used by Orvilliers, in which the numbers were arranged in a chessboard table and indicated by two flags, one for the row and one for the column. Both systems had pennants for 'hundreds.' These were the methods favoured by Kempenfelt. Howe, however, preferred a modification of the tabular system, by which the signals were indicated not by consecutive numbering, but by page and number.[2]

It is one of the many debts which we owe to the *Barham Papers* that they enable us to trace almost step by step how the transition was really set on foot. We may take it as actually beginning with the letter, already quoted, which Kempenfelt wrote to Middleton on August 14, 1779. As Sir Charles Hardy's first captain he was then in the crisis of a defensive campaign against the allied forces of France and Spain, and he found the fleet to be destitute of the tactical efficiency which a few days before he had laid down as the essence of a naval defensive.[3]

It was during the following autumn and winter, as we have already seen, that he prepared his first signal book and explanatory instructions. The instructions are lost, but two copies of the signal book exist. One was made by Lieutenant Waters

[1] *N.R.S.* xxxii. (*Barham Papers*), 343–9.

[2] See *post*, pp. 45 *n.* 51 *n.*

[3] *N.R.S.* xxxii. (*Barham Papers*), August 9, 1779, p. 294.

and is now in the Admiralty Library. The other, made by Thomas Graves, is in the *Graves Collection.* It is this code which he refers to in his letter of February 22, 1781, to Sir Charles Middleton as having been in use the previous year.[1]

The code was not a numerary one. It is on the old plan of flags varying their signification with their position. But, nevertheless, he did try to get in the thin end of the wedge by numbering all the signals consecutively and providing a numerary table ; and his correspondence of this time reveals how earnestly he was trying to get one of the French systems adopted. So soon as he knew the allied fleet had retired into Brest he was expounding to Middleton two methods of numerary signalling, particularly recommending that which his adversary, Orvilliers, had been using.[2] 'I could,' he says, 'in a few days (less than a week) arrange our signals according to both the above methods, could I have those days to myself without interruption.' During the winter he continued to urge the importance of reform on French lines.[3] From Middleton he must have received all encouragement, for on

[1] *N.R.S.* xxxii. (*Barham Papers*), p. 337. Neither copy of the Signal Book is dated, but we must assign it to 1780, because they have certain three-striped flags with the colours horizontal, and Kempenfelt, in his letter to Middleton of February 1781, says he has changed them to vertical. These copies also have the chequered pennants which he says he has altered to stripes of the same colours. For the probable nature of the Instructions see *post*, p. 119. The 'Explanatory Observations' as to making signals at the beginning of the Signal Book are identical with those of 1781–2.

[2] *Ibid.* October 17, 1779, p. 301.

[3] *Ibid.* January 18, 1780, p. 309.

April 6, 1780, he had completed the draft of a new system. 'Those movements and evolutions,' he wrote to Middleton, 'which I put into your hands this morning, are so frequently practised in a fleet, that some rule which is proved to be the best should be laid down for the execution. . . . There may, perhaps, be some obscurity arise from the manner of expression. I should be glad [if] you would mention such as you meet with. It is rough wrote; I intend to correct it.'[1]

It is probable that the instructions issued by Admiral Darby to the Channel Fleet in February 1781 and by Kempenfelt himself in 1782 were the outcome of this draft. It must have been quickly approved by Middleton, for he at once sent the set of books out to Rodney. Writing from St. Kitts on July 24, 1780, Young, Rodney's first-captain, says: 'I have delivered the signal books to Sir George for his perusal, though I am apprehensive these are books he will pay little attention to. But I think the colour of the flags well adapted, all but the chequered ones, which I would recommend not to be introduced.'[2] On July 31 he writes again: 'I probably may have omitted acquainting you that I received the signal books and delivered them to Sir George, with whom they may continue for a length of time and never be looked at or studied.' He repeats his objections to chequered flags and suggests substitutes that can be distinguished better at a distance. But he warmly approves the general idea: 'I wish,' he says, 'most

[1] *N.R.S.* xxxii. (*Barham Papers*), April 6, 1780, p. 322.

[2] *Ibid.* p. 69. The translator of Morogues also condemned chequered flags. *Naval Tactics*, 1767, p. 38. See *supra*, p. 4.

sincerely that an established code of signals were adopted for the use of His Majesty's fleet.'[1]

How long Rodney kept them or what attention they received from him we do not know, but no trace of their influence is to be found in his instructions.

Meanwhile, if we may believe a story told by Barrow in his *Life of Howe*, Kempenfelt had been practising afloat the code he had elaborated at the end of 1779. In the following summer he was first-captain in the Channel Fleet under Hardy's successor Geary and 'was constantly in the habit of exercising the ships by his signals. . . . . One day a fleet of ships supposed to be that of the enemy hove in sight. The signals were resorted to; but . . . . somehow or other were not managed so well as when made at their leisure. Geary at last grew impatient and going up to Kempenfelt, and laying his hand gently on his shoulder, exclaimed with good-natured earnestness, 'Now, my dear Kempy, do for God's sake, do, my dear Kempy, oblige me by throwing your signals overboard and make that which we all understand, "Bring the enemy to close action!"'[2]

From Rodney when he came home he received probably little more encouragement. His system at any rate was not established by the Admiralty, and when Rodney at the end of 1781 hoisted his flag to proceed once more to the West Indian command he took with him the old General

[1] *N.R.S.* xxxii. p. 72.

[2] *Op. cit.* p. 141. The incident may well have occurred in the attack of July 3 on the Port-au-Prince convoy. See Beatson, v. 131. See also Ralfe, i. 218, where the story is told in different words.

and Additional Sailing and Fighting Instructions only modified by his own alterations.

Still, it was becoming clearer every day that some system would have to be established. Not only was the existing uncertainty confusing, but the Navy Board protested that, 'in consequence of the present unsettled state of additional signals and the variety of demands made by commanding officers on that account, the number of flags necessary . . . and the very great increase of the expense of that article exceeds what was ever known,' and they submit 'a general mode should be adopted.'[1]

But the time was not yet ripe. When Darby, who had been second in command in the Channel all along, succeeded Geary in August, Kempenfelt's domination continued, and during the winter he issued the second edition of his Signals. Except for a few changes in the flags it differed hardly at all from the first, and was still far short of what he was aiming at; but it was the best which the conservatism of the service and his arduous duties in the fleet would permit.[2] In a letter to Middleton of March 9 of this year, after explaining the advantages of a numerary code, he says of the code he had just had accepted: 'Had I remained ashore this winter, which my health very much required, I think I should have been able to have rendered the signals much more perfect and useful by the helps I have received from others and my own observations.'

[1] *Navy Board, Out-letters*, 2208, February 1, 1781. For this information I am indebted to Mr. Perrin.

[2] A copy of this issued by Darby at Spithead, February 11, 1781, to Captain Graves, H.M.S. Bedford, is in the *Graves Collection*.

And then he proceeds to explain: 'The plan I followed in the signals I made was not that I most approved of. That which I would have adopted, though most evidently the best, I could not get any of the admirals or officers to approve and countenance. I therefore followed in a great measure Lord Howe's mode, he being a popular character.'[1]

VIII

Nevertheless Kempenfelt's ideas continued to force their way and to dominate all the most advanced thought in the service except Rodney. Officers from the Channel Fleet were spreading them, as we shall see, to the ends of the earth. By the beginning of 1782 he found himself practically within reach of his goal. In the previous autumn he had received his flag, but so indispensable was he to Darby that he was continued as first-captain. Early in 1782, however, he at last got a command. Lord North's administration, against which the best men had struck, was tottering to its fall. Every one knew that Howe would soon be in the saddle, and Barrington consented to take command of the Channel Fleet, or so much of it as was ready for sea. Kempenfelt was made his second-in-command, and together they established the last or third edition of Kempenfelt's code. This we know from a recent discovery. It is a printed folio *Signal Book for the Ships of War* signed by Admiral Samuel Barrington and delivered by him to 'Captain Keppel, Commander of His Majesty's ship

[1] *N.R.S.* xxxii. p. 340. He refers to Howe's code of 1777.

Fortitude.[1] Subsequently Barrington's name has been erased and Kempenfelt's substituted. This fixes the date of issue exactly. On April 5, 1782 Barrington with Kempenfelt for his vice-admiral put to sea for a cruise off Ushant with twelve of the line, of which the Fortitude (Captain George Keppel) was one. He returned to Spithead on the 26th, having cut up a convoy destined for the West Indies and captured the two ships of the line which formed its escort. By that time Lord North had resigned, Lord Keppel was First Lord, and Howe had then come down to assume the command of the Channel Fleet in person for his memorable defensive campaign. Proceeding eastwards himself, and taking Barrington with him, to secure the temporary command of the North Sea against the Dutch, he detached Kempenfelt with a squadron of nine of the line to watch Brest. This squadron also included Captain Keppel's ship. Kempenfelt sailed on May 3, and it must have been then that he reissued the Signal Book. On May 6th he issued a paper of additional instructions of no great importance which has been fastened into the book with sealing wax. His orders from Howe are dated April 30, and they contain this passage: 'While you remain on this service you will establish such signals and instructions for the government of the ships under your orders as you may think fit.'[2]

He was thus given a free hand to try his system,

[1] In the Editor's possession.

[2] *Admiralty Secretary: In-Letters*, 97. It was probably in pursuance of this authority that he has cancelled the whole of the fog and night signals which Howe had adopted against Kempenfelt's judgment.—*N.R.S.* xxxii. (*Barham Papers*) p. 341.

but his code was of course regarded as still in an experimental stage. It is clear that for the moment Howe was using in the North Sea the old fighting instructions. For in the 'Explanatory Observations' prefixed to Kempenfelt's Signal Book was one providing, as Howe had done with his in America, as follows: 'All the signals contained in the General Printed Signal Book, which are likely to be needful, being provided for in this Signal Book: the signals, as appointed in the General Printed Signal Book, will only be made, when in company with other ships not of the fleet under the Admiral's command, and unprovided with these particular signals.'

Besides the extra leaf of instructions and the cancelling of Howe's fog and night signals the book contains many alterations, one or two being of importance. This is explained by a letter he wrote to Stephens, secretary of the Admiralty, on May 4, in which he says, 'I have been constantly using all possible despatch for perfecting the necessary signals and instructions for the conduct of the squadron to be in readiness for putting to sea.'[1] The result of this work was the Signal Book in its corrected form and the shorter set of instructions which are printed below.

An examination of the Signal Book proves it to mark the exact point of transition. Though it contains all Morogues' signals and some others (of which more presently), it is still in the old form and on the old system. That is to say, the system of signalling is a single flag varying its signification with the

[1] *N.R.S.* xxxii. (*Barham Papers*) p. 341.

position in which it is shown. Consequently there is no logical order in the signals, all the various significations of each particular flag being grouped on the page devoted to that flag. But Kempenfelt was still persisting, and, as in the earlier editions, the signals were also numbered consecutively up to 421. At the end too is a numerary table,[1] headed by a statement that the Admiral would occasionally use it, and that such intention would be intimated by hoisting the Royal Standard as preparatory flag. To familiarise his captains with the new system, he had a signal 'to signify that the numerary signals are going to be made for practice and not for execution, when the ships are to note down the number of each signal made in the order they are made.'

Here we may conveniently note some of the more important changes over and above those which he had introduced as Hardy's first-captain in 1779, such as those for doubling, attacking rear, centre, or van, breaking the line, order of retreat, the French sailing formation, and the rest from Morogues' evolutions. Of these, none perhaps advanced fleet tactics more than the adoption of the French sailing formations in two or more columns. The order which had become the rule in the British service was the 'Fourth order' of Hoste and Morogues,

[1] It is on the 'chess-board' plan. The board had 100 squares, each containing a number. Thus by means of two flags—the superior indicating the column, and the inferior the row—any square could be indicated. A substitute flag was provided so that one set of flags would do. Hundreds were indicated by pennants. This was not the simple digit system of La Bourdonnais which Kempenfelt himself preferred (see *ibid.* i. 343), and which was established in 1799.

and it was used by Rodney to the last.[1] In an anonymous English text-book entitled *A System of Naval Tactics* which was published in 1797, and purported to embody the results of the transition period,[2] the formation is thus described: 'The fleet is divided into six columns, two for the van, two for the centre, and two for the rear. Each commander is in the middle, ahead, and to leeward of his two columns. The commanders, ranged upon the two close-hauled lines, have their squadrons astern of them upon two lines parallel to the direction

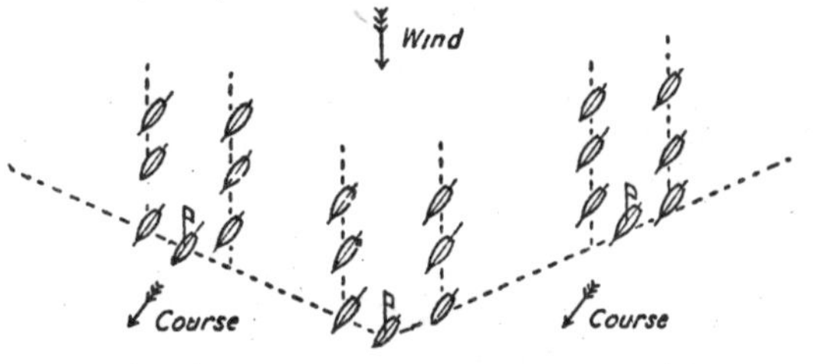

of the wind: the first ships of each column being with respect to the commander of their squadron the one on his starboard, the other on his larboard quarter.' The text-book condemned it as requiring too much time to reduce to the order of battle, and as being liable to be broken in sailing, in that the proper bearings were difficult to maintain. Moreover, it bore no relation to the battle order. As Ralfe tells us, the fleet was arranged 'without regard to the station of any ship in the line of battle. It therefore took several hours to form the

[1] See his 'Order of Sailing,' copied by Graves into his new Signal Book, February 1782—*Graves Collection.*

[2] See *post*, p. 75.

line of battle, whereas when the ships are stationed in columns the line is formed in a few minutes.'[1] Though Rodney retained this clumsy formation, an attempt to remedy it had been made at the opening of the war by providing an order in two bow-and-quarter lines. Kempenfelt abolished it entirely in favour of the simple formation of divisions abreast, each in single line ahead, with the ships in their battle stations, which thenceforward became the rule.

Still more characteristic of his method is his drastic modification of the new battle signal for superfluous ships to fall out and rake the enemy's van or rear.[2] Rodney, it will be remembered, had cut this out and substituted his attack by massing the heavy ships. What Kempenfelt did, as usual, was to free the movement from any special tactical situation, and to give an admiral the means of executing it whenever he chose and with any part of his force. The signification runs: 'For particular ships or divisions to rake the enemy's van.' The next signal is left blank as though for raking the rear, but he has not filled it in. Thus for the first time there appears in the Signal Book a plain signal for 'Crossing the T.'

Equally characteristic of his open mind is his latest introduction—a signal for long range firing. This signal is a MS. addition and was probably regarded as so heretical that he added an apologetic note. The signification runs—'To fire single round

[1] Ralfe, *Naval Biography*, ii. 232, *sub nomine.* Sir Charles H. Knowles, whose contributions to the new system were dealt with in the society's previous volume. *N.R.S.* xxix. pp. 133–7.

[2] See *supra*, p. 13.

shot leisurely at the enemy, as soon as within reach, aiming at their masts, the guns to be pointed by some of the best marksmen,' and the note is: 'N.B.—This method of firing may be useful when the squadron is to leeward and the enemy bear down to attack, or when he passes you on the contrary tack, or in any other manner within reach. Not to fire short, the distance should be first tried with a single shot or two.'[1] The rest of the signals can best be studied in their final arrangement as printed below (p. 171).

IX

For Kempenfelt was not yet content. He was still working hard at his code. On June 5 he rejoined Howe at Spithead, who, having achieved his object in the North Sea by getting the Baltic trade safely home, had returned to Portsmouth to deal with the last great effort of France and Spain to secure the command of the Channel. With Barrington and Kempenfelt for his chief flag officers he put to sea to meet the combined fleet on June 29, and it is well known how brilliantly he performed his defensive task in spite of the unequal speed of his fleet and the bungling of his captains over the new code when he first sighted the allied fleet.[2] But Howe persevered patiently. On August 13, as he cruised to the westward to receive the ocean convoys, Capt. Henry Duncan entered in his journal, 'The

[1] This signal was adopted by Hood on April 27, 1782, together with that for breaking the line. See the Signal Book of 1782, *Graves Collection*, 'For a particular ship to fire single guns well directed at the enemy.'

[2] Barrow, *Life of Howe*, p. 129.

admiral called all the admirals and captains on board and explained to them his intention and manner of attacking the enemy if we should find it necessary to engage them. Exercised the fleet frequently during the cruise.'[1] In the action with Cordova his efforts were fully rewarded, if we may judge by the reports of his squadronal commanders. 'I have the greatest satisfaction in informing your lordship,' wrote Barrington, 'how much I am satisfied with the good conduct of Commodore Hotham and all the captains of my squadron who kept the finest close connected line I ever saw during my service at sea.' Milbanke made a similar enthusiastic report.[2]

The code Howe used on this occasion we are now able to determine with certainty, and it tells us that not only had he again cut himself free from the old Fighting Instructions in favour of Kempenfelt's plan, but that he had been persuaded to adopt the numerary system as well. We know at least that some time between June and his sailing for the relief of Gibraltar in September he and Kempenfelt elaborated together a new edition of the Instructions and the Signal Book. In all probability this was done in June before they sailed, for they did not return to Spithead till August 15 and on the 29th Kempenfelt was drowned.

The result of their last collaboration was a new Signal Book and the Explanatory Instructions printed in the Society's volume xxix, at page 239, from the copy in the Admiralty Library.

[1] *Journals of Henry Duncan, N.R.S.* (*Miscellany*), xx.
[2] *Admiralty Secretary; In-Letters*, 97. Oct. 22, 1782.

It was there conjecturally entitled 'Lord Howe's First Code, 1782.' We now know that this attribution is correct, except that, though the code itself was founded on Lord Howe's of 1777, its perfection was the work of Kempenfelt. A MS. copy, containing both the Instructions and the Signal Book, is in the United Service Institution. It is labelled 'Rear-Admiral Kempenfelt's Signals, 1780.' A note by Admiral B. W. Page, who made the copy in 1784, explains that the service always regarded it as 'the compilation and much of the invention of the gallant and most noble Admiral Richard Kempenfelt.' It also states, somewhat inaccurately, that it was used by Sir Richard Bickerton who went out to reinforce Hughes on the East Indian station in February 1782. Page also says Kempenfelt compiled the signals for the British Navy in 1780, but his untimely death retarded their use. The discovery of Kempenfelt's Signal Book of May 1782, however, reveals to us that they did not exist in this completed form so early. Indeed Page himself explains that the signals Bickerton took out in February 1782 were 'differently arranged.' In all probability what he took was the Signal Book which Barrington issued in April as it stood before Kempenfelt altered it in May.

Page's MS. copy of the Signal Book, to which the second edition of these instructions belonged, is with them in the United Service Institution; a printed copy, as stated in the previous volume, is in the Admiralty Library.[1] Its main points of interest over and above the inclusion of Kempenfelt's evolutions are that the numerary system has been adopted

[1] *N.R.S.* xxix. (*Fighting Instructions*), pp. 234–8.

definitely in place of the single flag system of the old Fighting Instructions, and that this has enabled the signals to be placed in logical order, instead of being grouped under the corresponding flag. All the groups which relate directly to tactics are printed below, so that the arrangement and general bearing of the new tactical system can easily be understood.[1]

X

Thus then at last we can fix the exact period of the transition when the old and the new were in force side by side—in the West Rodney's last development of the old system, and in the Far East and in home waters the first development of the new.

It proved an immediate success. While Rodney in the West was failing to secure the fruits of his tactical skill for lack of means to handle his fleet,

[1] The 'page' system was adopted with a 16^2 'chessboard' table. Its use is thus explained in the printed copy of *Lord Howe's Signal Book*, 1782, in the Admiralty Library: 'These signals from the admiral when under sail will be made with two flags shown one above the other; the upper flag denotes the page in which the order is pointed out by the other flag.' Besides 'substitute,' 'answering,' and 'annulling' flags, there were sixteen, each denoting two pages of the Signal Book, viz. pp. 18–49. Each page was divided into eight transverse sections, in which the significations were written, and each section was denoted by one of the sixteen flags in the margin. He thus obtained 256 signals numbered 41 to 296. At the end were two smaller tables of 10^2. No. 1 'for use of squadrons that have not the new flags, to express any number in the new Signal Book with such flags as they have.' No. 2 'for ships to express numbers, *e.g.* number of enemy sighted, soundings, latitude and longitude, &c.' There was also a letter table for paroles. The 'page' system is taken directly from the French. It is identical with that of the code printed at Brest in 1781, entitled *Mouvements généraux à l'usage de l'armée du Roi, commandée par le Comte de Grasse*, 1781, which De Grasse used in his action with Rodney. A MS. copy is in the *Graves Collection*.

at home Kempenfelt was snapping up a convoy under the nose of De Guichen and a superior fleet, and Howe, in the Channel, by sheer perfection of manœuvring, was baffling the efforts of the vast combined fleet of France and Spain. In August the tragedy of the Royal George deprived him of Kempenfelt's assistance, but the work went on, and in the autumn, as we know, Howe gave the final demonstration of its value in his unrivalled tactical feat of relieving Gibraltar in the face of the Spanish fleet.

But it must be said that it was only where Rodney's conservatism was supreme that the old form of the Fighting Instructions was strictly adhered to. On the North American station certain noteworthy modifications had been introduced. When Byron took over the command from Howe in 1778 he went back to the regular form. At least he certainly issued a copy of the old Additional Instructions when he moved down to the West Indies, and it was under his own modification of these Instructions that he fought his action off Granada on July 6, 1779.[1] But when Arbuthnot took his place on the station he brought with him a new set. In form it was a compromise between the Instruction and the Signal Book System: that is to say, it was in signal-book form, with the usual three columns—for signals, place where shown, and significations; but in this case the articles of the Instructions took the place of the significations. This

[1] *See* Additional Sailing and Fighting Instructions, dated Princess Royal, Gros Islet Bay, St. Lucia, March 3, 1779, *Graves Collection.*

arrangement, of course, made signalling much clearer and quicker; but no tactical advance appears. Indeed, in matter it was distinctly reactionary. A number of articles, including several of recent introduction, are omitted. Among the omissions are six articles (Nos. 6–11) for manipulating the line, the 15th for two separate lines of battle by divisions, the 18th for attack in general chase, and the all-important battle articles, No. 21—to lead down against opposite numbers, and No. 22—to engage in reverse order on coming up.

It was under this book that he fought his action with Des Touches in March 1781.[1] But some time before the fleets met he had practically restored the omitted fighting articles by a long series of Additional Signals. These signals show a strong trace of Channel Fleet influence, particularly in the introduction of answering and annulling flags, and in the signals for raking the enemy's van or rear. The influence was possibly that of Graves, who, with Affleck under him, had recently come out with reinforcements, after serving a campaign with Kempenfelt.

When, in July 1781, Arbuthnot went home on sick leave, his successor, Digby, had not arrived; so Graves, his second, took over the command. He continued Arbuthnot's instructions and his additional signals, and it was under them he fought his action with De Grasse on September 5. As a tactical failure it is notorious from the severe criticisms of Hood and Rodney. Graves's own view is less well known, but it is now clear what it was. In his eyes

[1] See *post*, p. 235 *et seq.*

the fiasco was entirely due to the fact that his captains, and particularly Hood and his squadron, were too hide-bound in the stereotyped tradition of the old Fighting Instructions to interpret his signals intelligently, or to act with a reasonable initiative. It will be remembered that, on September 5, with 19 of the line he caught De Grasse with 24 to leeward, and at anchor in the mouth of the Chesapeake. To save himself from a catastrophe De Grasse slipped and stood eastward out to sea in confusion, forming line as convenient. Graves, instead of signalling 'General Chase' or one of its modified forms, so as to attack the French before they could form, continued to stand in shore, so as to extend his line parallel with theirs. He then wore his fleet together, and brought them on the same tack as the French. Drake, the Rear-Admiral, was now leading and Hood had his squadron in the rear. Then, instead of making the signal for each ship to bear down and engage her opposite, Graves signalled for the leading ship to lead more towards the enemy, meaning apparently that every ship should follow her example and keep the line parallel to the enemy as the fleet bore down. In spite of his setting the example with his own ship, the fleet as a whole continued to follow the leader, with the result that, as usual, his line came down obliquely on the enemy, and his van ships were cut to pieces before ever his rear got into action at all. Why Hood of all people did not show more initiative, it is difficult to understand; but he chose to keep the line as it was formed, obliquely to the enemy. It may be he hoped still to see a concentration on De Grasse's centre and van, or that he was so much out of heart and temper at the chance that had been missed that he would do nothing but obey the order for the line literally.

What Graves meant is clear enough. Immediately after the action, when he hoped to renew it, he sent down a frigate with verbal orders to keep the line parallel with the enemy.[1] Next day, finding himself unable to renew, he issued a tactical memorandum on the subject, which is of no small interest.[2] It practically amounts to his reading Hood a lecture on the theory of the line, and reproving him for adhering to its letter instead of acting boldly in its manifest spirit.

The signal for the line, he says, is not to be understood as rendering the signal for battle ineffectual 'by too strict adherence to the former.' It is merely to be regarded as 'the line of extension,' to develop the full fire-face of the fleet, and captains 'are desired . . . to keep as near to the enemy as possible whilst the signal for close action continues out.' Had Nelson written these remarks we should know them like household words, but Graves is a dog that won himself a bad name. He concluded with an injunction that captains were to see they kept a line parallel with the enemy without regard to any particular point or bearing, and the same day he issued a new signal with that signification.

[1] Log of the *Royal Oak*, one of his seconds.

[2] A copy of it is printed in *N.R.S.* xxxii. (*Barham Papers*), p. 127, with Hood's comment. The date is there given as November 6, *i.e.* when Digby had already come out to relieve Graves. November 6 must therefore be the date the copy was made. In Thomas Graves's Signal Book, 1781 (*Graves Collection*), the date is September 6.

That the rebuke was not without some justification appears from the contemptuous note which Hood wrote on the back of his copy of the memorandum. 'It is the first time,' he begins, 'I ever heard that too strict an adherence could be paid to the line of battle'; and he ends: 'According to Mr. Graves's memo. any captain may break the line [*i.e.* his own line] with impunity when he pleases.'[1] It is all unworthy of so great a sailor as Hood; but if his temper could not bear a rebuke from the man who had just missed the last chance of retrieving the fortunes of the war, who can blame him? Yet was it entirely lost? Had Hood but acted with one-half of the spirit that Nelson showed at St. Vincent would De Grasse have been able to get back to the Chesapeake? And if he had not, what then?

The picture which the incident presents of Hood as the fanatical devotee of the letter of the law, and Graves as the enlightened expounder of its living gospel, is not a little disturbing. There seems no way to explain it except on the supposition that Hood felt himself such a master of tactics that the line must always be his servant, while Graves feared it as a weapon too rigid and heavy for the strength of his wrist. But however we regard it there is nothing left for us but to place Hood as a tactician in the school of Rodney, and Graves in that of Kempenfelt, though he lacked the genius that was necessary to practise successfully his master's principles.

Still he had not yet done. On September 24 Digby arrived to take over the command, with an

[1] See *post*, p. 260 *n*.

order for Graves to take his flagship down to Jamaica. So critical, however, was the situation that it was agreed the ship could not be spared, and Graves must remain. Digby thereupon generously begged him to retain the command for the present. It was under this *régime* the Channel ideas were still further introduced. Digby had been second-in-command during the whole of Kempenfelt's administration, and Affleck had now a broad pennant, with Captain Thomas Graves for his flag-captain. Consequently on October 15, two days before the reinforced fleet sailed from Sandy Hook to carry Clinton's army to the relief of Lord Cornwallis in the Chesapeake, a further set of signals was issued. Six of them are aimed at giving the fleet squadronal freedom, and three are devoted to 'forcing through the enemy.'

Thus we are brought to the incontestable conclusion that by the end of 1781 there was a signal for breaking the line on every principal station except that which Rodney commanded.[1]

On the North American station the tactical ferment which had begun under Graves went on to the end. The last manifestation is the first activity of McArthur, who afterwards became Lord Hood's

[1] If we may take Beatson as voicing the average opinion of the time, it differed entirely from the modern valuation of Graves. Speaking of Digby's arrival he says : 'The officers of the fleet, as well as of the army, were desirous that Admiral Graves should continue in chief command . . . and no one was more solicitous for his stay than Rear-Admiral Digby himself. In compliance with this desire Admiral Graves continued to direct and superintend the naval operations, with the same assiduity and vigour which had marked his conduct before. . . .' His record under Howe in the next war earned him the title of Baron Graves.

trusted secretary and the biographer of Nelson. The claim which he made in his 'Memorial of Service' to have been the actual author of the numerary system finally adopted by Lord Howe, and used on the First of June, has hitherto been treated with scepticism, but two recent discoveries prove that it was literally true, and that he was indeed one of the minor figures of the transition period. When, after Cornwallis's surrender, Graves, on November 10, 1781, proceeded, in accordance with his orders, to Jamaica, Digby succeeded him. Now one of McArthur's claims was that in 1782 he presented a new numerary code to Digby, and that it was used by his orders in a small cruiser squadron under Captain Salter for three months. In this there is nothing incredible. It was then, as McArthur tells us, the duty of clerks and admirals' secretaries 'to watch signals.' Moreover his statement is corroborated by the existence in the *Graves Collection* of a Signal Book issued by Digby to Captain Graves, of the frigate Magicienne, on October 5, 1782. It is a printed form on the old system with the signification column left blank and filled in in MS. But at the end, as in Kempenfelt's book, there is a numerary table on the chessboard plan which could be used alternatively for the old system. The special signal for putting the numerary code in force was the Royal Standard, as in Kempenfelt's book. It also has a smaller numerary table for use by private ships, as they only had the old set of flags. At the end is a table of signals numbered for use with the private ship code.

It is quite possible that this was the code

McArthur claimed to have presented to Digby, but if so he was certainly under heavy obligations for it to Kempenfelt.

XI

Such were the last attempts to develop our tactical system on the old plan of Additional Instructions which had lasted about half a century. Henceforward the plan of Kempenfelt and Howe was to hold the field, but with the peace of 1783 the movement was arrested before the new system had been regularly established.

In that year Howe became First Lord, and further progress might naturally have been expected; but during the strenuous period of his administration, when he overhauled the Navy from top to bottom in anticipation of an early renewal of war, other calls and the violence with which his reforms were assailed seem to have delayed the work. When in July 1788 he gave way before the storm and resigned, the old General and Additional Instructions remained at least nominally in force. Consequently in October 1789, when the outlook towards Spain grew threatening, he was again pouring out his anxiety, apparently to his friend Sir Roger Curtis. 'The looseness,' he wrote, 'of our present system of tactics in the Navy—if any system may properly be said to exist—is such that I cannot say I have quite made up my mind upon the plan I would recommend for publication. The digest you have made of those which have yet appeared in practice and your additions to them, invite me to resume that train of thinking.'[1] The result of the invitation was the Signal Book of 1790, mentioned in the Society's previous volume.[2]

In taking up the work again where he and Kempenfelt had left it at the end of the last war, what caused Howe most anxiety was the complete want of any system for the handling of large fleets. 'I have deemed it very possible,' he continues in the letter above quoted, 'that this country may have to put to sea in a future war from thirty to forty, fifty and even sixty sail of the line in one collective body. . . . It has not appeared to me that we have any common opinion amongst us how such a force is to be trained and conducted to act with uniformity and effect.' He believed that nothing but practice could ever produce a satisfactory system.[3]

It is a problem that is still with us, and it was one that had been exercising Kempenfelt up to the time of his death. As early as 1780 he had tried to get Sir Charles Hardy to adopt a definite organisation for the fleet in squadrons and divisions. But Hardy would only reply 'that we did very well last summer in the manner the fleet was then divided, and he did not therefore see any occasion for altera-

[1] In the editor's possession is a small MS. volume entitled *General Index to the Signals by Day.* It contains a prefatory note signed 'R. C. 1789.' It is a numerary code clearly founded on Kempenfelt's, though the numeration differs. It omits the signals for 'doubling,' while retaining that for 'preventing being doubled.' It also retains breaking the line. The principle battle addition is 'to attack the enemy's four headmost ships when passing them to windward on a contrary tack,' a form of engaging condemned by Clerk. It is just possible that the code to which the *Index* refers was that which Curtis submitted to Howe this year.

[2] *N.R.S.* xxix. pp. 252–3.

[3] Barrow, *Earl Howe*, p. 143.

tion.' As usual Kempenfelt consoled himself by explaining his ideas to Middleton. They amounted to a revival of the seventeenth century practice of varying the complexity of the organisation with the size of the fleet. His system may be tabulated thus:—

No. of Ships.	*Organisation*	*Flag-officers.*
15 to 27	3 squadrons	1 admiral, 2 commodores.
27 to 45	3 squadrons, each in 2 divisions	3 squadronal admirals. 3 other divisional flag-officers.
Above 45	3 squadrons, each in 3 divisions	3 squadronal admirals, each with their vice- and rear-admirals, or commodores acting as such.

As yet, it will be observed, there is no suggestion of a light or observation squadron, such as Orvilliers employed two years later. Bigot de Morogues formulates the same basis of organisation as Kempenfelt, but he too says nothing of a light squadron.

In 1782 there was a chance of putting these ideas into practice, when immediately after Kempenfelt's death Howe sailed to the relief of Gibraltar with thirty-four of the line. The fleet was organised exactly as Kempenfelt had laid down, in three squadrons of two divisions each.[1]

[1] *Admiralty Sec. In-Letters* 97, where is given the organisation used in the action against Cordova, October 20. *Van*, 12 ships, Barrington, No. 4; Hotham (2nd), No. 9. *Centre*, 11 ships (Nos. 13 to 23), Howe, No. 18; Hood (2nd), No. 23. *Rear*, 11 ships (Nos. 24 to 34), Hughes, No. 26; Milbanke, No. 31. Flag officers are in the centre of their *divisions*, except in the centre squadron, where Howe takes the centre of the *squadron* and of the fleet, Hood, his second, taking the rear of the squadron.

The peace prevented any further developments, but a few months after his letter to Curtis Howe was able to continue the work of reform. In anticipation of war with Spain over the affair of the Nootka Sound the Channel Fleet was mobilised under his command, and from midsummer 1790, when he hoisted his flag, we may date the inauguration of the new order. Though the fleet consisted of no more than thirty-five sail of the line, he had under him six flag officers and was thus able to give the force its full organisation.

The Signal Book that was then used was that just referred to, which Howe was completing in collaboration with Sir Roger Curtis. Its most striking feature is that it has discarded the signal for 'breaking through the enemy's line,' which had appeared in all the new Signal Books up to 1789, and in its place we have for the first time a signal for Howe's great manœuvre of breaking the line in all parts, to which we must return. In the United Service Institution is a MS. copy formerly belonging to Lieutenant John Walsh of the Marlborough, entitled 'Earl Howe's Signals by which the Grand Fleet was governed 1790, 1791, and 1794.'

About '1794' Walsh is mistaken. He went on half-pay after 1791 and clearly did not know the Signal Book had been altered. In 1791 and 1792 McArthur had greatly increased the convenience of Howe's code by providing it with a proper index. In this form it appears to have been printed and issued by the Admiralty in 1792. But Howe must have been still dissatisfied with it. For in 1793 McArthur produced for him a new edition with the signals entirely renumbered and a few added of his own devising. This was the code which Howe used on the First of June 1794, and the 'Admirals' Day Signals' from it were printed by Admiral Jackson in his *Logs of the Great Sea Fights* from Captain Schomberg's MS. copy. The edition of 1792, however, continued in use in the Mediterranean till both codes were superseded by the new Signal Book of 1799. Still the fact remains that Walsh's book was certainly used in 1790, for its squadronal and divisional signals exactly correspond to the organisation which Howe adopted in that year; that is, there are distinguishing calls for the three squadrons under himself, Barrington, and Sir A. Hood, and also for the two divisions into which each was divided.

On the whole, therefore, we may safely confirm the long held estimation of the importance of Lord Howe's peace cruise in the autumn of 1790 and those of the following years; and in the 'Bridport Papers' we are able to follow step by step the way in which was elaborated the system on which Nelson was to work.

XII

In order to appreciate fully the importance of those four memorable years it is necessary to recall the circumstances in which the final development was achieved.

On June 22, 1790, Howe received a commission, dated May 13, to take command of a fleet to be employed in the Channel Soundings. He hoisted the Union at the main in the Queen Charlotte, with Sir Roger Curtis for chief of the staff, and towards the end of July was directed to proceed to Torbay. Thence on August 18 he put to sea with thirty-five of the line, organised, as we have seen, in three squadrons each with two flag officers, and also in two divisions, according to Kempenfelt's rule. Until September 12 he remained at sea constantly exercising fleet tactics. It was at this time he issued the remarkable instructions of July 10, which are given below, and which have so long remained unnoticed. The importance of the occasion can hardly be exaggerated. For the first time we see a great fleet being trained in peace time with a proper organisation. We see what was practically the final abandonment of the old Fighting Instructions, and the definite substitution of a well-ordered Signal Book with explanatory instructions for evolutions. Tactics are brought back at last to a clear scientific basis, and the line to its true position of service instead of mastery. And finally we see the introduction of the famous manœuvre of breaking the line in all parts, which after a century of effort practically solved the problem of decisive action at sea. With the origin of this manœuvre, so long ignored by naval historians, we must now deal.

For now at last its origin can be distinctly seen. From Walsh's copy of the Signal Book of 1790, it is clear it formed no part of that code as Howe originally drew it up. Internal evidence shows it to have been an addition to the simple signal 'to engage,' written in when or after the book was ssued. The form which the addition took in the Signal

Book of 1793 runs thus: 'If having the gage of the enemy the admiral means to pass between the ships in their line for engaging them to windward, or being to leeward to pass between them for obtaining the weather gage. N.B.—Commanders not able to perform the evolution may act as they please.' Now, although there is no direct evidence of the date at which the addition was made, it is clear from the Additional Instructions issued by Howe, July 10, 1790, that the idea was then already in his mind. As originally issued they contained no suggestion of the manœuvre. It only occurs there as a MS. addition to Article VIII., which was an article directed simply to rendering more effective the well-known attack, which had so often miscarried, by each ship steering independently for her opposite number in the enemy's line. As printed the article, like the corresponding signal, was incomplete, a blank being left for the insertion of the particular method Howe meant to employ. Since similar blanks occur in all the signal books used by Howe, it is probable that secrecy was his motive for not permitting his new ideas to appear in print. In any case before the Instructions were issued it was filled in with words permitting his captains in bringing up against the enemy to take their stations to windward or to leeward of their opponents as they saw 'most suitable for closing with them to advantage and to disable them most speedily.' This meant of course that they were at liberty to pass through the enemy's line or not as they pleased.

It may be doubted whether at the moment Howe realised that he had discovered a new form of attack which solved the problem. But from this point it was but a step to the final stage, and some time during his two autumn cruises he must have added the famous signal which he himself first used on the First of June, 1794, and which received its apotheosis at Trafalgar.

For the moment, however, he was not permitted to carry his great reform further. On September 12 he returned from his evolutionary cruise, and at the end of the month was about to proceed to sea to continue his experimental work when news reached him that the differences with Spain had been settled and that he was to strike his flag. The order seems to have caused him deep pain. He called it his 'professional annihilation' and seems to have lost all hope of carrying his reforms to perfection.

The work, however, went on under Lord Hood, who by this time had reached to the position of Howe's recognised rival in the service. In 1791 he had command of the 'Russian Armament,' and McArthur was his secretary. In the previous year, as the result of his experience with the 'Spanish Armament,' McArthur had perfected his code presented to Digby in 1782, but the Admiralty did not accept it, and issued Howe's last code to Hood. After the tension with Russia had passed and Hood was at Portsmouth he tried again with something less revolutionary. 'Finding,' he says in his *Memorial of Service*, 'that some scruples of delicacy intervened in the adoption of any new plan of signals which would supersede that of Earl Howe's numerary code, the memorialist therefore made a new arrangement of his Lordship's day signals by simplifying the form of the Indexes . . . and engrafting in the body and instructions many new ideas and instructions of his own. In this new arrangement plates or engraved plans were originally introduced by the memorialist explanatory of the principal evolutions, together with instructions illustrative of them ; and the whole, with a paper containing the memorialist's observations and reasons for making so many material alterations, were transmitted by the late Admiral Sir Hyde Parker to Lord Howe, who was pleased in the most flattering manner to approve of the alterations made *in toto.*' At the same time he says he prepared a new code of Night Signals, 'principally compiled from some undigested manuscripts put into his hands belonging to the late Admiral Kempenfelt, but the lamented death of this officer some years before prevented his having brought them to greater perfection. These day and night signals were approved by the Lords Commissioners of the Admiralty and were ordered to be printed under the inspection and superintendence of the memorialist, and were accordingly issued for the first time to the ships belonging to Lord Hood's squadron.' The Admiralty also approved the day signals and had them printed under McArthur's supervision at the end of 1792.[1]

From July 10 to August 14 Hood was out continually practising evolutions, his custom being to fall his flagship out of the line and drill his fleet by the amended signals. Further amendments of the instructions appear to have been established by

[1] 'Memorial of John McArthur,' *Adm. Sec. Promiscuous*, M. 4. Dr. Burney's *New Dictionary of the Marine*, p. 477.

him, for on July 20, that is ten days out, and immediately before beginning his evolutions, he issued 'a memorandum relating to the separate and additional instructions.' No copy of these instructions has been found.[1]

McArthur claimed that 'the signals used on this occasion, prepared, classed and arranged after some years of labour, have from that time been universally used in the Service.' But this was certainly putting his claim very high. That he made a new arrangement of Howe's Signals 'by simplifying the form of the indices' is true enough. A copy of such an index is in the possession of Vice-Admiral Sir Wilmot Fawkes, and in McArthur's own hand it is inscribed 'Lord Howe's Signals classed under general Heads, Alphabetically subdivided and adapted for a commander-in-chief's ship. The whole arranged for Lord Hood in the Russian

[1] *Admirals' Journals*, 125. Hood constantly records the times the evolutions took. On July 24 the lee division formed line of battle on the starboard bearing in 17 minutes, and tacked together in 8 minutes. On the 27th the line was formed, centre and rear having to tack together, in 43 minutes, and he inverted the line in 1 hour and 45 minutes. The usual method was to send several vessels out to chase and then signal for the line of battle. On August 9 he made the general signal for line of battle on the starboard bearing, and 'the line was formed perfectly correct from the obtuse angle in 12 minutes.' This means that the fleet was 'in order of retreat' at an angle of 158 degs., with the Admiral at the apex, and the two divisions of the fleet thrown back on the starboard and larboard lines of bearing. Line of battle was formed on the starboard division. The manœuvre is shown in a set of ten diagrams of each day's evolutions in the Record Office (*Adm. Sec. Miscellaneous*, 582), entitled 'Principal Evolutions of the New Arrangements of Lord Howe's Signals, prepared by John McArthur and Exercised by Admiral Lord Hood's Squadron in the Summer of 1792.' It was an exhibit to his Memorial above mentioned.

Armament, Summer 1791, by John McArthur, Secretary.' But it is clear from internal evidence that the code to which it refers was practically the same as that of the Walsh copy, used the previous year; nor can any alteration or addition of importance be detected except those which Howe himself had introduced during his cruise, particularly on August 26.[1]

At the end of the year Howe had a hint he was to be employed again, and once more he was busy with every kind of detail for remedying defects in the service. On February 6, 1793, he kissed hands on his appointment to the Grand Fleet and hoisted his flag at the end of May. On July 14 he put to sea with secret orders to commence hostilities. All his journals are missing, so that we cannot tell what work he did on this occasion. It is certain, however, that as the result of this cruise he produced his final code, which was used on the First of June, 1794, and at Camperdown.[2] It shows no important tactical departure from the Walsh and McArthur form, which continued in force in the Mediterranean and was used at St. Vincent and the Nile.[3]

A printed copy of this final code of Howe's is in the Admiralty Library and it is conjecturally dated on the cover 1792/3. Much of it is in MS. The numbers of the signals have been put in by

[1] See *Bridport Papers*, *Add. MSS.* 35194, and *post*, pp. 317, 339.

[2] Printed in *N.R.S.* xvi. (*Logs of the Great Sea Fights*, vol. i.), pp. 9–20, from Capt. Schomberg's MS. copy. This copy must have been made some time after the Signal Book was issued, for it contains two or three signals which are not found in the printed Admiralty copy.

[3] See *Nelson's Signals*, *N.I.D. Historical*, No. 1, p. 23.

hand, and all the important battle signals have been left blank and subsequently filled in in MS.[1] The Signal Book was accompanied by an Instruction Book and an Additional Instruction Book.[2] Neither of these has been found, but the references to the Instruction Book show that it resembled that of 1782, as modified in 1790, while those to the Additional Book relate mainly to the performance of evolutions. The numerary system for flagship signals is that of La Bourdonnais, which Kempenfelt had always wished to adopt—that is a simple two-flag system for units and tens, with pennants for hundreds. But there is also a 'chess board' table on the old plan for private ships to use in communicating with the admiral. A special list of private ship signals is attached and arranged in alphabetical order under subject headings on McArthur's plan.

Howe's famous signal for breaking the line in all parts is one of those entered in MS. It is No. 34 and is almost in the same words as in Walsh's book. It runs thus: 'If when having the weather gage of the enemy the admiral means to pass between the ships of their line for engaging them to leeward, or being to leeward, to pass between them for obtaining the weather gage. N.B.—The different captains and commanders not being able to effect the specified intention in either case are at liberty

[1] The two-flag signals which were left blank and appear in MS. are: 11, 12, 24, 27–9, 31, 34, 36–42, 177. Of the single-flag signals Nos. 5, 15, 16, 18, and 28 are in MS. For their signification see *Logs of the Great Sea Fights*, vol. i. 9–20.

[2] Signal 179 is 'To denote attention to an article in the Instruction Book'; 180 is the same for 'an article in the Additional Instruction Book.' The reference numbers do not agree with any of the known books.

to act as circumstances require.' There is no reference to either Instruction Book, but it is obvious Howe's idea was still rather to secure a decisive action than to secure concentration by cutting off part of the enemy's line.[1]

We can, however, be in no doubt as to his own mature opinion of the manœuvre, for he himself has placed it on record. To the end he regarded it as one involving great risk and not lightly to be undertaken. In his last letter to Sir Roger Curtis, one he wrote a week or two before his death, he says 'Some occasions in *our* profession . . . . will justify if not require more hazard to be ventured than can be systematically defended. In our action of the 1st of June, the pushing through the enemy's line from *to windward* (with respect of each ship against her opponent), much risk of injury to each other was obvious. It would have been less had *every ship* (which was not able to secure her adversary by close action to windward) gone through the enemy's line as we did. But admitting the risk of mutual injury to be as great as I believe many officers supposed, the times and peculiar circumstances of the country at that period . . . . called loudly in my opinion for some conclusive issue of the contest.'[2] It was exactly Nelson's frame of mind when he made his risky attack at Trafalgar.[3]

1 See also *N.R.S.* xxix. (*Fighting Instructions*), p. 255. The editor there conjecturally assigned this book to 1790. The testimony of the *Bridport Papers*, however, proves that this was an error. From them it is clear that the book was not used in 1790, and cannot have been issued before 1793.

2 Barrow, *Life of Howe*, p. 379.

3 The following passage from Codrington's notes to Barrow's *Life* throws further light on Howe's intentions as well as his diffi-

It remains to deal with his final ideas on the organisation of a battle fleet. With his last Signal Book complete he put to sea again on May 2, 1794. Besides the huge convoy above mentioned he had under his flag a fleet of 32 of the line organised as before on Kempenfelt's plan, which had become constant, that is to say he had six flag officers each in command of a division of the three squadrons. Howe himself had his station in the centre. There was also the new regular dual organisation of a starboard and larboard grand division. All units ahead of the Admiral—that is all the van squadron and the first or starboard division of the centre squadron—formed the starboard or van division of the fleet. The rest, led by the Admiral, formed its rear or larboard division. The instructions for the manipulation of this organisation were the same as those he had issued on July 10, 1790, given below (p. 319). But on this occasion he made a highly interesting innovation. This he did in the general letter, also given below (p. 342), dated April 20, immediately after he hoisted his flag. For the first time on record in a British Fleet a regular advanced

culties. He is relating a conversation with Lieutenant Floyd of the Gibraltar after the battle, who said, 'Our captain is the stupidest man possible. Having been signal midshipman with Lord Howe I took the opportunity of saying, "Captain Mackenzie, you have not been accustomed to signals. Will you allow me, as I have been signal midshipman in the Queen Charlotte, to go over the signals with you?" He said, "I shall be very much obliged to you." I dwelt particularly on the two signals, "each ship to engage her opponent," and "engage to leeward," which we always understood Lord Howe would use . . . After the action, although there were only two signals made before bearing down, Captain Mackenzie asked me if either of those signals had ever been made.'—Bourchier, *Memoirs of Sir E. Codrington*, i. 27.

squadron was formed under a flag officer. It consisted of four 74's under Rear-Admiral Pasley, who commanded the first division of the van squadron. Three units were from Pasley's own division, and the fourth was the last ship of the fleet. On September 28 it was reconstituted with some different ships and was called the Reserve.[1] Another order relating to it is dated Nov. 5. In the order of battle which Howe drew up next year it disappears, and its place is taken by two frigate squadrons.[2]

But the idea took root. It reappears in an 'Order of battle and sailing' issued by Sir William Parker in the Mediterranean fleet on March 31, 1798. In that case it consisted of 5 sail out of a fleet of 23 and was accompanied by the following instruction. 'As line of battle ships may occasionally be required to look out or for other particular service, the ships marked thus * are selected for that purpose . . . to haul out two leagues in the wind's eye of the flagship.' On April 12 the same year Jervis, having been reinforced to 31 of the line, issued a fresh 'order,' in which the detached squadron was increased to 7 sail. It will thus be seen that Nelson in the Trafalgar memorandum was following in this respect a well-established practice.[3]

With regard to nomenclature it appears that a confusion of thought existed in 1794 between the ideas of an advanced squadron and a reserve. This confusion seems to have ceased the following

[1] 'Order of Battle and Sailing.'—*Bridport Papers, Add. MSS.* 35194, f. 55.

[2] *Ibid.* January 21.

[3] The above details are from two original documents sold by Messrs. Hodgson, April 3, 1908.

year when in addition to the advanced squadron Howe constituted a true reserve. The occasion was the arrival of a Portuguese squadron to serve with our Channel Fleet, and the order which Howe issued in regard to it is the last document in the present volume. In our old wars the practice had been on such occasions to constitute the foreign squadron as one of the three squadrons of the fleet. But taught possibly by his knowledge of the difficulties which Orvilliers had experienced during the late war in incorporating the French and Spanish squadrons into a workable whole, Howe kept the Portuguese outside his own organisation and formed them into a reserve.

XIII

The process of transition was now complete. We have the high authority of Admiral Raper for asserting that, as all the evidence implies, Howe's Signal Book and Instruction Books of 1793–4 finally ousted the old General and Additional Instructions.[1]

There is, indeed, one piece of evidence that the Howe-Kempenfelt system was actually established in 1790; for there is a Navy Board entry of July 2 of that year concerning 'the present scheme of signals, by Earl Howe, approved and to be established.'[2]

[1] *A New System of Signals by which Colours may be Wholly Dispensed With*, by Admiral Henry Raper, 1828, *Preface*. He was Howe's signal lieutenant in 1794, and was afterwards appointed signal officer to the Portuguese squadron.

[2] *Navy Board Out-letters* 2215, a reference for which I am indebted to Mr. Perrin.

The effect of the whole movement upon the Service was condensed in the anonymous handbook, already referred to, which was published in 1797, and entitled *A System of Naval Tactics combining the Established Theory with General Practice and particularly with the present practice of tho British Navy*. The work is divided into three parts. Part I. is a paraphrase and rearrangement of Morogues with many amendments. 'M. Morogues,' says the author in his Preface, 'is the most copious author upon the subject, and his system is the practice of the present day. Of his work, therefore, a more full translation now first appears with every subsequent improvement on the same basis correctly methodised.' Part II. is a full exposition of the new order of sailing put forward by Bourdé de Villehuet in his *Manœuvrier.* He called it the 'order of convoy,' and its characteristic was that it disregarded the old plan of moving the fleet on its course in line of bearing. Under the new arrangement the ships were disposed in one, three, or six columns and sailed the course desired in each other's wake. Part III. was 'the present practice of the British Navy, compiled from official documents with the assistance of several experienced officers.' It consists, in the spirit of Howe and Kempenfelt, entirely of directions for performing evolutions in order of sailing and battle. Nothing is said of tactics proper. The established order of sailing, it says, is a combination of Morogues' 'Fifth order,' that is in three or six columns, and Bourdé de Villehuet's 'Order of Convoy.' 'There are, however,' the author adds, 'several regulations to which it becomes subject in our Navy.' The most important of these was the rule that 'the leading and other ships of the squadron bear from each other respectively *in the direction of the wind*, but the ship of the admiral or first in command is not to be regarded as a leading ship of either squadron, although he will probably be at the head of one of them.'

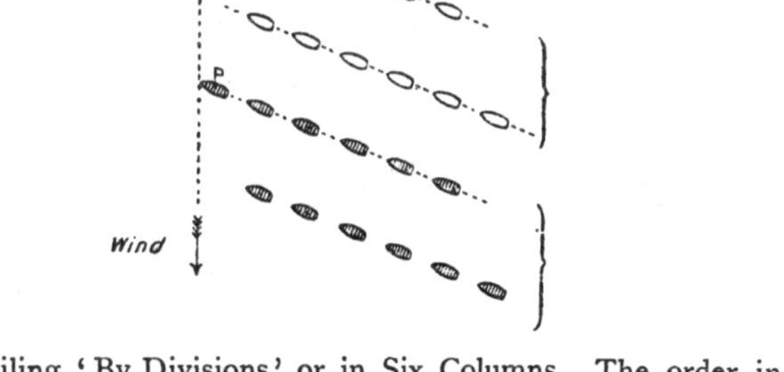

Order of sailing 'By Divisions' or in Six Columns. The order in Three Columns or 'By Squadrons' had the rear divisions in the wake of their respective van divisions.

This was Lord Howe's improvement of Kempenfelt's order. (See *post*, p. 146, art. 10.)

The author also gives as the special British formation the sailing order in two 'Grand Divisions,' by means of the organisation by which one division of the centre squadron could be attached to the van squadron and one to the rear squadron, as devised in the final instructions of 1790.[1]

[1] See *post*, p. 333.

Another noteworthy peculiarity of the British Service is stated to have been that the 'close-hauled' line was not the true *ligne du plus-près* of the French, that is six points from the wind. The English established it at *seven* points from the wind, so as always to have a point in hand 'to enable leewardly ships to keep in their allotted stations.'

Perhaps the most interesting feature of the book to us now is the way it puts us in possession of the then received views regarding breaking the line. Howe's method of breaking it in all parts is not

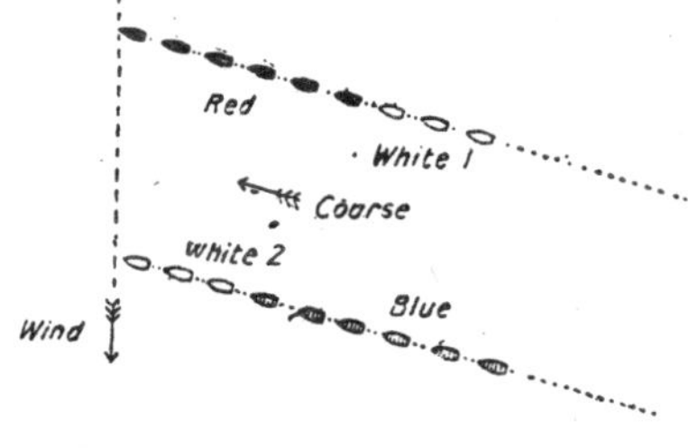

Order of sailing in 'Grand Divisions' or Two Columns.

mentioned. Indeed, it appears to have been kept a profound secret, for in Sir Charles H. Knowles's Signal Book, which he printed and submitted to the Admiralty in 1798, the signal is added in MS. Breaking the line in line ahead even is only dealt with in Part I. as an amplification of Morogues. But the whole drift of Morogues has been changed. The manœuvre is treated in two ways: firstly, as a method for a lee fleet to gain the weather gage or for a numerically superior fleet to defeat Torrington's manœuvre—that is the manœuvre by which an inferior fleet seeks to avoid being doubled-on by engaging the extremities of the superior line; and secondly, as a method of forcing a lee fleet to action. This section is a pure translation from Morogues. The other is not. The passages in question are reprinted from the English text-book below (p. 373).

The whole work, as embodying the conclusions of our late eighteenth century school, shows how quickly we had outrun the French when once we began to move, just as we ourselves had been outrun by the Dutch at the end of the seventeenth century. The French service showed no progress whatever beyond the point of Choiseul's revival. In the same year, 1797, an official book of instructions and signals was issued for the Republican Navy, and it is little or nothing but a reissue of Morogues, without any of the improvements of the English text-book.

The final step was taken in 1798. In that year the Admiralty decided at last that a regular official code, binding on the whole Service, should be established on the French plan, as Howe and Kempenfelt had so long urged in vain. Howe himself had retired in 1797, and was now a complete invalid, but the work was entrusted to Captain James Gambier, who was a particular favourite of the veteran admiral's, from his having been the first to break through the line and carry out his intention on the 1st of June. He had received the gold medal and had just joined the Board of Admiralty. As evidence of how fully Howe's system had won acceptance in the Service, Gambier was strongly advised by his colleagues to base his work upon it. 'I am of opinion,' Admiral Lord Hugh Seymour wrote to him, 'that Lord Howe's signals, which are now well understood and much approved by the Navy in general, should be followed as much as possible.'[1] Nelson, in acknowledging Howe's congratulations on the battle of the Nile, endorses this view. In describing his manner of attack, he says, 'This plan my friends readily conceived by the signals for which we are principally indebted to your lordship.'

The result of Gambier's work was the famous code of 1799 under which Trafalgar was fought. He had completed it by May,[2] but it does not seem to have been established for some time afterwards; for as late as September Howe's Instructions of 1790, as modified in 1793–4, were issued by Vice-Admiral Sir Roger Curtis to the squadron with which he was then sailing to take up the command of the Cape Station.[3]

The golden period which we must associate chiefly with Howe's name may be said to have culminated with Trafalgar. After that its vitality was spent and stagnation began to set in. The last work ever produced on sailing tactics in England was the *Naval Tactics and Sailing Trials* of Sir George Biddlecombe in 1850. He was then master

[1] Lady Chatterton's *Memorials of Lord Gambier*, i. 342. Seymour had served in all the fleets in which Howe's system had been elaborated.

[2] A copy in my possession formerly belonging to Prince William Henry is dated May 13, 1799. So also a copy in the Admiralty Library, and another in the Record Office.—*Adm. Sec. Misc.* 585.

[3] A copy is in the United Service Institution 'given on board the Lancaster, September 1, 1799, to Hon. Captain Stopford, H.M.S. Excellent.' Curtis sailed with his flag in the Lancaster September 26. The Excellent was one of the squadron (Ralfe's *Nav. Biog.*). In this copy the signal blanks are filled in with the numbers of the 1794 book.

of the royal yacht, and afterwards Master of the Fleet in the Baltic in 1854. It purports to be an original work, and merely acknowledges 'material assistance afforded in the arrangement of it by a work published by David Steel.' This is the *System of Naval Tactics* of 1797, and on examination the tactical part of Biddlecombe's work proves to be little but a reprint of it. It is true he adds improved methods of performing evolutions, and a half-seen method of executing Clerk's attack on the rear ships of the enemy, but all he has to say on tactics from a scientific point of view is yet another rehearsal, as with all his predecessors, of what Morogues had written a century before in his immortal Introduction.

Biddlecombe's book, in fact, with all the skill and knowledge of that very distinguished and capable officer, embodies the decadence of the school of Howe and Kempenfelt. By the irony of destiny the last word of their art was to fall to a sailing-master.[1] As with all strategical and tactical reforms, Kempenfelt's, for all its health, had dormant in it the seed of decay. In seeking to break down tactical formulas and to secure tacticians a free hand by giving fleets the utmost nimbleness, his school appeared to devote their reforms to evolutions rather than to tactics, and in doing so they

[1] That it was the last word is curiously marked by his rule for doubling, p. 129: 'The ships sent to double the enemy ought not to be ordered upon that expedition but in weather when there is a commanding breeze; and none but the best sailers or screw propellers.' In 1857 he published his first work on *Steam Fleet Tactics.*

unwittingly started a process which forced evolutions to such a growth of pedantry as quickly to choke tactics altogether. When the great British Fleet sailed in its glory for the Baltic in 1854, the process was complete. The Navy could still repeat, as part of some venerable ritual, the once living words of Morogues; but their meaning, which for Kempenfelt had been a stirring inspiration, was long cold. The heresy of smart evolutions had become the real religion of the service, and Biddlecombe was its prophet.

LORD HOWE.

North American Station, 1776–8.

THIS unique series of orders is one of the chief surprises found amongst the Graves Collection. Until its rediscovery we had no hint that they had ever existed, nor that at that early date Howe's mind was already seething with the reforms which he was unable to perfect and establish till nearly twenty years later.

The series consists of four documents, all MS. copies:—

1. Instructions and standing orders for the discipline of ships: dated July 12, 1776.

2. A new Signal Book: undated.

3. A complete new set of Sailing and Fighting Instructions: issued with a copy of the Signal Book under date July 30, 1778.

4. A set of Additional Fighting Instructions for use with the Signal Book: dated July 1, 1777.

From these particulars it is clear the documents must have been issued in the order given above—that is to say, that Howe, immediately after his arrival on July 4, 1776, to take up the command of the station, must have established the standing orders for discipline and internal administration; that some time before July 1, 1777 (the date of the Additional Instructions), he must have issued his new Signal Book, and with it his new Sailing and Fighting Instructions, although the original of the particular copy that survives was not issued till 1778; and that finally, on July 1, 1777, he issued the Additional Instructions. The first document—that is, the 'Instructions and standing orders'—has been copied into a paper folio-book, and consists of twenty articles in all; but, as they do not relate to tactics, it would be out of place to print them in full in this place.

It has been thought well, however, to include the first half-dozen of them, which relate to 'divisions,' watches, and sanitation, as showing how curiously primitive the routine of the fleet must have been at the beginning of the transition period, when Howe set about trying to introduce his reforms. It is startling, for instance, to find that no such thing as 'divisions' then existed, and Howe's order enables us to understand better Kempenfelt's lamentations on the subject in 1779.[1]

The Signal Book is a paper quarto, arranged on the 'page' system—that is to say, the significations of the signal flags still vary according to the place where they are shown, but for convenience of reference the signals made with each flag are gathered in a regular order on a separate page and numbered. From this of course it was but a step to a numerary page system with two flags, one denoting the page and the other the section; but this advance was not yet.

It was this Signal Book that really marked the first step from the old system to the new. It contains ten 'Explanatory Instructions' as to the making of signals, and the last enjoins that 'all signals contained in the general printed Signal Book which are likely to be needful on the present occasion being provided for in this signal book, the signals in

[1] See particularly his letter to Middleton, *N.R.S.* xxxii. (*Barham Papers*), p. 305.

the general printed Signal Book will only be made in conformity to the practice of some senior officer.'

Thus, as it were, with a bold stroke of the pen, Howe cut himself free from the old fighting instructions.[1] To complete his bold revolt he issued in place of the old set of instructions a new set of 'Explanatory Instructions,' and this is the third document of the series. It is a MS. quarto volume, entitled *Instructions for the Conduct of the Ships of War explanatory of and relative to the Signals contained in the Signal Book herewith delivered.*

The volume contains an entire set of instructions corresponding in a general way with the various sections into which the old instruction books were divided, *i.e.* 'sailing,' 'fighting,' 'fog,' and 'night.' In all there are four groups of articles, arranged under the following heads:—

1. 'General instructions and directions for the conduct of the ships of war when sailing or in chase by day'—6 articles.

2. 'Instructions respecting the order of battle and the conduct of the fleet preparative to and in action with the enemy'—21 articles, printed below.

3. 'Instructions for the government of the ships of war during a fog'—3 articles.

4. 'Instructions respecting the conduct of the fleet in sailing and order of battle, &c., by night'—10 sailing articles and 11 fighting articles.[2]

Of these four groups only the second, or 'Fighting instructions by day,' is printed below. It will

[1] Another copy of this Signal Book, also belonging to Graves, has long been in the Library of the U.S.I., but it was without date. It was one of the very few items of the Graves Collection that escaped the premature burial.

[2] At the foot the whole are dated 'Given on board H.M.S. the Eagle at Sandy Hook, the 30th of July, 1778.'

be seen that these Fighting Articles closely resemble the instructions which Kempenfelt caused to be issued to the Channel Fleet in 1781, and which in an amplified form Howe himself used in 1782. The sailing instructions also are almost identical with Kempenfelt's.

The fourth document is the most remarkable and significant of all. It has been saved for us by being copied into the same paper folio as the Standing Orders. Each article deserves the closest study, for here, it may be said, the soul of tactics has been brought to life again. Officers are reminded in each case that tactics are not merely fleet movements to be used as instruments to secure victory, but that such movements are only more or less imperfect expressions of the principle that the object of all tactics is to develop the utmost power of our weapons against the enemy, while giving him the least possible power of using his against us. It was this line of thought that brought Howe to the eighth article, where for the first time he foreshadows his immortal form of attack, which was finally to solve the problem of decisive action at sea—a whole generation before Nelson consecrated it at Trafalgar.

To complete our view of the way in which his mind was working it is necessary to note the principal tactical signals in his new code. Those which are referred to in his 'Fighting Instructions' are given in the footnotes to the articles in which they occur. The others are as follows:—

For particular ships or divisions to attack any number of the enemy's ships of war, seeming to be kept separate for any purpose from the body of the fleet.

To denote that the signal made herewith is to be carried into execution after the close of day.

An annulling signal.

To board the enemy on coming up.

To engage the centre, van, or rear division of the enemy; particular ships or divisions to whom the signal is addressed will be specified.

To engage the enemy in line of battle, formed as the ships are able successively to come up with them.

To form the prescribed order of retreat.

To form the line in two divisions, equal and parallel.

INSTRUCTIONS AND STANDING ORDERS

For the General Government and Discipline of Ships of War.

[MS. copy. Graves Collection.]

Preamble.

Whereas an uniform system of discipline established in this squadron would be productive of many essential benefits; the subsequent regulations, prepared in that view, are to be conformed to, and continue in force till further order.

1st.

A public orderly book to be kept.

Every ship is to be provided with a publick orderly book, wherein is to be entered all orders and directions issued for the current daily services; likewise such parts of all general orders, given from time to time, and extracts of these instructions as may be necessary for the information of the inferior officers and ships' companies in the duties required of them, for which purpose the officers summoned by signal on board the Admiral or commander of any division whereof they make a part, are to attend with the orderly book of the ships to which they belong, to transcribe from that of the Admiral or other commanding officer's ship such orders and directions as are to be given out.

The orderly book to be kept on the quarter-deck, subject to the inspection of every person belonging to the ship.

2nd.

To form the ships' companies into divisions and subdivisions.

The petty officers and seamen of the ships' companies are to be formed into two or three divisions, according to the complement and classes of the ship, each division to be under the inspection of a lieutenant and subdivided into squads, with a midshipman appointed to each, who are respectively to be responsible for the good order and discipline of the men entrusted to their care.

In forming these divisions and subdivisions regard is to be had to make them as convenient as may be to the men's stations in the quarter and watch bills and to their berths; and each officer is to keep an exact list of the names of the men in their divisions and squads, noting thereon their several stations, and number of their hammocks; and like references are to be made on the watch and quarter bills to their divisions of squads for the more readily calling them to their duty, or being able to account for their absence. In port, they are to call the men over by the said lists, morning and evening, at such hours as the captain of the ship shall appoint, and finding any absent or faulty, report it to the commanding officer on board at the time. And, to enable them to perform this part of their duty with regularity, notice is always to be given them when any man under their care has leave of absence or otherwise, and for what time, that they may attend to the time of his return.

3rd.

Appointments in tours of duty of the marines in port and at sea.

The Marines or soldiers are to be put into divisions under their proper officers, as in the preceding article; at sea their relieves and tours of duty (except where placed as sentinels) are to be the same as seamen's, but in port, when the more necessary services in the ship and their number will admit of it, they are to be divided into three guards and to mount for twenty-four hours, or a shorter time, as the captain of the ship sees fit.

They are always to mount the guard in their uniforms, and after sunset the sentinels are to give word 'All's well' every ten minutes or quarter of an hour, beginning with the one on the starboard side of the poop, repeating it forward on that side, and round back on the larboard.

In case of not being answered, the sentinel who repeated the word last to alarm the guard.

The sentinels are to challenge all boats coming to or passing near the ship in the night; and not to permit any to come on board; nor any persons to enter or go from the ship after sunset and before sunrise without leave first obtained from the officer of the watch. They are not to suffer any noise to be made on their posts other than what is necessary in the business of the ship, and in case of any misdemeanour or neglect of duty, they are to be regularly relieved before any punishment be inflicted on them upon that account.

The Marines are not to be forced to go aloft, nor on the other hand are to be restrained from rendering themselves expert in a seaman's duty, at proper opportunities agreeable to the standing instructions.

4th.

To put the ship's company at third watch.

It is recommended to the captains to form their ships' companies into three watches at sea, whenever their number, health, ability, and diligence will admit of that indulgence, especially the petty officers, that they may execute their duty with greater punctuality and exactness whilst it is their turn to be upon the watch.

In order to facilitate this arrangement the admiral will have attention to give timely notice whenever he is about to tack or to make any other alteration that may require more assistance.

5th.

For the preservation of cleanliness and health.

Cleanliness and wholesome air between decks being of the greatest consequence to health, every convenient means of preserving and obtaining these important requisites are to be used, the upper decks to be washed daily, the lower decks twice or oftener, and the orlop at least once every week, the weather and other necessary services admitting thereof.

The beams and planks over the sick berths are to be occasionally washed with vinegar; the ships also to be fumigated once a month (or oftener in damp weather) by burning tar with a logger-head or firing small quantities of gun powder, if the sick are in a state to admit their being moved up from between decks, as it will be necessary the ports and hatches should be closed during these operations.

The windsails are to be kept down the hatchways in the day time and the ventilators worked uninterruptedly night and day.

The hammocks to be got up in fair weather and stowed in the nettings, or constantly lashed up when not occupied, and no greater number of chests or other incumbrances allowed between decks to interrupt the free circulation of air, than what are absolutely necessary for the requisite accommodation of the ship's company.

The times for washing the lower and orlop decks, fumigating the ship, and every other means taken for the preservation of health are to be set down in the log book, or the reasons why they were omitted.

6th.

Account to be taken and kept of the men's clothing.

As a sufficient provision of dry, warm clothing to afford the men a change when needful will much contribute to the beneficial purposes before mentioned, it is highly necessary an accurate account should be had of the several articles each man is furnished with, as well as to prevent thefts and frauds. The lieutenants having command of divisions are always therefore to take a muster of the clothing of each man under the degree of a petty officer in their respective divisions as soon as may be after the ships put to sea, and cause an entry to be made thereof in a book provided for that purpose. Every casual alteration by loss, exchange, purchase, or donation is to be noticed therein, that it may be had recourse to for comparing the claimant's demand on any complaint of theft, to ascertain the fact. And the men for whose peculiar benefit this regulation is calculated should be exhorted to punctuality in giving notice of such alterations to their officers, for the mutual justification of all parties.

No person is to appropriate to his own use any

cloathes, what kind soever, negligently left about the decks, under pretence of not being able to find an owner for them; but he is to bring such cloathing to the officer of the watch, for his directions in the disposal of it. And if it is discovered to be in his possession for any other intent, it shall be deemed a theft, and the offender punished accordingly.

The midshipmen are to examine the cloathing of their respective squads weekly, to take care that the men keep themselves clean; that they do not lose or otherwise dispose of their necessary clothing; and that their hammocks are scrubbed and washed at proper intervals. For which purpose the ordering up a certain number every morning in succession will probably be necessary.

They are to make due reports on these heads to the commanding lieutenants of their divisions.

The lieutenants are to see the midshipmen carefully perform this part of their duty and acquaint their captains from time to time what necessary clothing each man wants, that orders may be given for supplying them, as far as it may be done consisting with the general instructions concerning slops.

On the first muster of the clothing, the lieutenants are to direct such part thereof, as may be requisite for the men at sea, to be stowed in their hammocks, that there may be no occasion to keep between decks a greater number of chests than are absolutely necessary.

. . . .

Given on board H.M. ship the Eagle at Sandy Hook the 12th day of July, 1776,

To Capt. Wm. Chaloner Burnaby,
Comr. of H.M. sloop the Merlin,

By command of the Vice-Admiral,
JOSH. DAVIES.

INSTRUCTIONS RESPECTING THE ORDER OF BATTLE AND CONDUCT OF THE FLEET PREPARATIVE TO, AND IN ACTION WITH, THE ENEMY.

[Instructions for the conduct of the ships of war explanatory of and relative to the signals contained in the Signal Book herewith delivered. Extract, MS. Graves Collection.]

ARTICLE 1.

Ships how to take their stations in the line.

When the signal is made for the fleet to form in order of battle, each captain and commander is to get most speedily into his station, and keep the prescribed distance from his seconds ahead and astern upon the course steered, and under a proportion of sail suited to that carried by the admiral.

But when the signal is made for tacking, or on any similar occasion, care is to be taken to open in succession to a sufficient distance for performing the intended evolution. And the ships are to close back to their former distance respectively as soon as it has been executed.

2.

Ships to leeward to gain the Admiral's wake.

If it happens that any part of the fleet is so far to leeward of the Admiral, when he makes the signal for forming in order of battle, that he thinks it necessary to edge away to give such ships an opportunity to get sooner into their stations; he will bear up with the white flag abroad. The commanders of the ships to leeward are thereupon to shape their course for getting into his wake most speedily, and taking their stations in the line of battle accordingly.

3.

Signal for the line when not to regard ships detached.

Ships happening to have been previously detached on any service, separate from the body of the fleet, when the signal for forming in order of battle is made, are not meant to be comprehended in the intention of it, until they shall first have been called back to the fleet by the proper signal.

4.

Ships not able to keep their stations in the line, how to proceed.

The ships which, from the inequality of their rates of sailing, cannot readily keep their stations in the line are not to obstruct the compliance with the intent of the signal in others, nor to hazard throwing the fleet into disorder by persisting too long in their endeavours to preserve their stations under such circumstances; but they are to fall astern, and form in succession in the rear of the line.

The captains of such ships will not be thereby left in a situation less at liberty to distinguish themselves, as they will have an opportunity to render essential service by placing their ships to advantage when arrived up with the enemy already engaged with the other part of the fleet.

The ships next in succession in the order of battle are to occupy in turn, on this and every other similar occasion, the vacant spaces that would be otherwise left in the line; so that it may be always kept perfect at the appointed intervals of distance.

5.

The course to be always taken from the leading ship in a line ahead.

When the fleet is sailing in line of battle ahead the course is to be taken from the ship leading the van upon that occasion; the others in succession being to steer with their seconds ahead respectively, whilst they continue to be regulated by the example of the leading ship.

When to come to the wind in succession on either tack from sailing large.

And when the fleet is sailing large, or before the wind, in order of battle, and the Admiral makes the signal for coming to the wind, on either tack: the ship stationed to lead the line on that tack, first, and the others in succession, as they arrive in the wake of that ship and their seconds ahead respectively, are to haul to the wind without loss of time accordingly.

And all signals for regulating the course and motions of the fleet by day or night, after the signal for forming in order of battle has been made, are to be understood with reference to the continuance of the fleet in such order, until the general signal to chase, or to form again in order of sailing, is put abroad.

6.

Lines of bearing, their signification, and wherein to be observed on change of course.

By the starboard or larboard line of bearing is meant that line or point of the compass upon which the fleet would be formed, and the ships bear from each other in line of battle ahead, steering with the full sail, or about *one point* from the wind, as it may at any time happen to be, on either tack.

Such relative bearing of the ships from each other is to be thenceforth preserved through every change of course made, as often as any alteration thereof together shall be by signal directed. And the same is to be understood of the bearing indicated, though the Admiral should shape his course from the wind originally, when the signal for forming in order of battle upon either line of bearing is made. The ships will thereby become ranged immediately in line of battle ahead, in readiness for coming to action with the enemy, whenever it shall be requisite to haul to the wind, after having edged away to join them with that intent.

When, on the contrary, the signals to alter the course in succession have been put abroad, the relative bearing of the ships from each other will then be consequently changed ; and any alteration of the course subsequently directed to be made by ships together will thereafter have reference to the relative bearing last established. The same distinction will take place so often as the alteration of course in succession, as aforesaid, shall in future recur.

7.

When the signal is made to alter course, together for preserving the same bearing, attention to be then had.

When any alteration of the course is directed to be made by the ships together, in view to preserve the same relative bearing as in the preceding article mentioned, it will be necessary that the outer or leading ship on either tack, pointing towards which the change of course is to be made, should first begin the movement; in order to give room for the others to comply with the signal in turn, as fast as may be.

And upon all occasions, when the ships are formed in order of battle on any point of bearing from each other, different from the course then steered, they are to be equally governed by the example of the outer or leading ship on the tack towards which the course shall most incline; the captains of which leading ships respectively are to make or shorten sail, alter the course, &c., as by signal directed.

But when the fleet is sailing before the wind, the bearing for keeping their stations in that position is to be taken from the ships appointed to lead the line upon the starboard tack.

8.

When by an alteration in the disposition of the enemy a suitable change is requisite in the relative bearing of the ships of the fleet.

If the Admiral should observe that the enemy has altered his course, and the disposition of his order of battle, one, two, three, or any greater number of points (in which case it will be necessary to make a suitable change in the bearing of the ships from each other in the British fleet, supposed to be before formed in such respects correspondently to the first position of the enemy), he will make the signal for altering the course in succession, either way, according to the nature of the occasion. The leading ship of the line is thereupon immediately to alter the course pointed out, and (the others taking their places astern of her in succession, as they arrive in the wake of that ship and their seconds ahead respectively) she is to lead the fleet in line of battle ahead on the course so denoted until further order.

9.

When an alteration of sail is intended to be made whilst the fleet is in order of battle.

When it is necessary to shorten or to make more sail, whilst the fleet is in order of battle, and the proper signal in either case has been made, the ship referred to at either extremity of the line will have more particular notice of the alteration intended, by the example of the frigate appointed to repeat signals, which frigate, if then in her station, will on that occasion (immediately after having repeated the signal) hoist, lower, haul up, or set the same sail, and keep such only abroad for the time as the captain discovers, by the Admiral's preparations, he intends to carry in future.

The ship referred to is thereupon to be put under a proportion of sail correspondent to the known rate of sailing of the Admiral's ship, when such intended alteration of sail, signified as aforesaid, shall have been made.

Hence the necessity to be observant of the proportion of sail necessary in each ship, suited to that carried from time to time by the Admiral.

Hence it will be necessary that the captains in the fleet should studiously endeavour to obtain, by repeated observation and experiment, a perfect knowledge of the proportion of sail required for suiting their rate of sailing respectively to that of the Admiral's ship, under the various changes of circumstance and weather incident to cruising service. They will thereby be enabled not only to determine the proportion of sail requisite to be carried at all times for preserving their stations in order of battle by day and night, but also for keeping company with the fleet on all other occasions.

10.

Ships ordered to quit the line, how to proceed.

When, the ships of the Fleet being more in number than the enemy, the Admiral sees proper to order any particular ships to withdraw from the line, they are to be placed in a proper situation, in readiness to be employed occasionally as circumstances may thereafter require—to windward of the fleet, if then having the weather gage of the enemy, or towards the van and ahead, if the contrary, to relieve or go to the assistance of any disabled ship, or otherwise act, as by signal directed.

The captains of ships stationed next astern of those so withdrawn are directly to close to the van, and fill up the vacant spaces thereby made in the line.

That commanders of divisions may be opposed to those in the enemy's line in similar situations.

And when, in presence of an enemy equal or superior in number of ships, it shall happen that the Admiral or commander of any other division of the fleet would not, in their first position, be directly opposed to the commanders in similar stations in the enemy's line, and seeing fit to change the same accordingly, shall make this signal (which will then be with such intent) the captains referred to are on the occasion to place themselves forthwith against the ships of the enemy that would otherwise, by such alteration, remain unopposed; from whatever part of the van or rear they may have been removed, or to which they may have occasion to repair, in their respective divisions, for that purpose.

11.

When the ships are to keep in more open or closer order in line of battle.

When the fleet is sailing in a line of battle ahead, or upon any other bearing, and the signal is made for the ships to keep in more open order, it will be generally meant that they should keep from one to one and a half cable's length asunder, according as the milder or rougher state of the weather may require; also that they should close to the distance of half a cable, or at most a cable's length, in similar circumstances, when the same flag is shown in the mizen topmast shrouds.

But in both cases the distance pointed out to the Admiral's seconds ahead and astern, by the continuance of the flag abroad, as intimated in the Signal Book, is to be signified from them respectively to the ships succeeding them on either part—from the former by the signal 10, page 32, and from the latter by the signal 11 of the same page.

These signals are to be continued either way onward throughout the line if necessary.

Notice is to be taken, in the same manner, of any continued deviation from the limited distance; and to commence between the several commanders of private ships respectively independent of the Admiral's previous example, when they observe their seconds ahead or astern to be at any time separated from them farther than the regulated distance kept by the ships next to the Admiral, or that which was last appointed.

Particular ships to open to let the Admiral resume his station in the line.

N.B.—When the Admiral, being before withdrawn from the line, means to resume his station therein, he will make the signal as above, to keep in more open order, with the particular signals of the two ships between which he means to place himself, whether it be in his former station or in any other part of the line, better suited for his future purpose.

12.

When any number of ships are detached, not having a flag officer present.

When any number of ships are occasionally detached from the fleet for the same purpose, in regard to which it might at times be requisite to employ a complete division, they are, during their separation from the body of the fleet, to comply with all such signals as shall be made at any time whilst the signal flag appropriated for that occasion remains abroad.

When a flag officer is ordered on the same service.

But all the ships so appointed, having the commander in the second or third post in the detachment, will be considered for the time, and included in the purpose of every signal made to them, as if belonging to his division only. And his signals and instructions, or those from the senior officer for the time being of the number so detached, are to be complied with in the same manner as if the ships concerned had been in such division originally placed.

13.

Not to fire upon the enemy before the signal is made and that the ships are properly placed.

Great care is to be taken at all times, when coming to action, not to fire upon the enemy either over or near any ships of the fleet, liable to be injured thereby; nor when in order of battle, until the proper signal is made, and that the ships are properly placed, in respect to situation and distance, although the signal may have been before put abroad.

If bearing down to the enemy when the signal is made to engage, the ships to haul up for that purpose without waiting for any more particular signal.

And if, when the signal for battle is made, the ships are then steering down for the enemy in any oblique direction from each other, they are to haul to the wind, or any other parallel with the enemy, to engage them as they arrive in a proper situation and distance, without waiting for any more particular signal or order for that purpose; regard being only had by the several commanders in these circumstances to the motions of the ship preceding them on the tack whereunto the course most inclines, and upon or towards which the enemy is formed for action; that they may have convenient space for hauling up clear of each other.

14.

Not to separate in pursuit of a small number of the enemy until their main force is broken and disabled.

No ship is to separate in time of action from the body of the fleet in pursuit of any small number of the enemy's ships beaten out of the line; nor until their main body be also disabled or broken, except in the instance of their chief commander, or other principal officer so circumstanced. But the captains who have disabled or forced their opponents out of the line are to use their best endeavours to assist any ship of the fleet appearing to be much pressed, or the ships nearest to them, to hasten the defeat of the enemy, unless otherwise by signal or particular instruction directed.

15.

When any ship in the fleet is so much disabled as to be in the utmost danger and hazard of being taken by the enemy or destroyed, and makes the signal expressive of such extremity, the captains of the nearest ships, most at liberty, with respect to the state of their opponents in the enemy's line, are strictly enjoined to give all possible aid and protection to such disabled ship, as they are best able. And the captain of any frigate (or fire ship) happening to be at that time in a situation convenient for the purpose, is equally required to use his utmost endeavours for the relief of such disabled ship, either by joining in the attack of the ship of the enemy opposed to the disabled ship, if he sees opportunity to place his ship to advantage; by favouring the attempt of the fire ship to lay the enemy on board; or by taking out any of the crew of the disabled ship if practical and necessary, as may be most expedient.

16.

No ship to quit her station in battle but of extreme necessity without leave for it obtained.

No captain, though much pressed by the enemy, is to quit his station in time of battle, if possible to be avoided, without permission first obtained from the commanding officer of his division, or other nearest flag officer, for that purpose; but when compelled thereto by extreme necessity, before any adequate assistance is furnished, or that he is ordered out of the line on that account, the nearest ships, and those on each part of the disabled ship's station, are timely to occupy the vacant space occasioned by her absence, before the enemy can take advantage thereof.

Captains deficient in time of action are to be removed from their ships.

And if any captain shall be wanting in the due performance of his duty in time of battle, the commander of the division, or other flag officer nearest to him, is immediately to remove such deficient captain from his post, and appoint another commander to take the charge and conduct of the ship on that occasion.

17.

When the fleet is directed to disperse.

When from the advantage obtained by the enemy over the fleet, or from bad weather, or otherwise, the Admiral hath by signal signified his intention to leave the captains and other commanders at liberty to proceed at their discretion, they are then permitted to act as they see best under such circumstances, for the good of the King's service and preservation of their ships, without regard to his example. But they are, nevertheless, to endeavour at all times to gain the appointed rendezvous, in preference, if it can be done with safety.

18.

When the fleet or any part of it is to form in two separate and parallel lines of battle ahead.

When it is thought requisite to form the whole fleet, or any specified squadron or division thereof, into two separate and parallel lines of battle ahead, the lines are to be kept two cables' length distant asunder, the channel or space within which the fleet may be then confined to navigate admitting thereof.

The ships of each line are to keep one cable's length distant from each other respectively. Those of the starboard division of the fleet are to keep on the starboard hand, in this case; and those of the larboard division to port; unless the signal for changing this relative position of the two divisions should be at the same time made.

The ships stationed to lead the line on either tack are to lead their respective divisions on this occasion, in case no special appointment of the ships in any other manner hath been before delivered out.

Reference of signals when to ships of either division separately, or to both.

The reference of all signals, whether for opening to a greater distance, closing near together, &c., when meant of the ships in either division separately, will be signified by a red or blue pennant shown over the flag, as in the addition to the article referred to in the Signal Book is expressed. But when the signals alluded to are addressed to the two divisions jointly the signal will be repeatedly made with that expressive of the intended purpose.

19.

Ships to be kept at all times prepared for immediate action, and in what manner to proceed in respect to the aid and protection of fire ships ordered on service.

The ships are to be kept at all times prepared in readiness for action : and in case of coming to an engagement with the enemy then having the weather gage, their boats are to be kept manned and armed, and prepared with hand and fire-chain grapnels and other requisites, on the off side from the enemy; for the purpose of assisting any ship of the fleet attempted by the fire ships of the enemy; or for supporting the fire ships of the fleet when they are to proceed on service.

The ships appointed to protect and cover these last, or which may be otherwise in a situation to countenance their operations, are to take on board their crews occasionally, and proceed before them down, as near as possible, to the ships of the enemy they are destined to attempt.

The captains of such ships are likewise to be particularly attentive to employ the boats they are provided with as well to cover the retreat of the fire ship's boat so as to prevent the endeavours to be expected from the boats of the enemy to intercept the fire ship, or in any other manner to frustrate the execution of the proposed undertaking.

20.

Flag officers at liberty to move into other ships when their own are disabled.

If the ship of any flag officer be disabled in battle, the flag officer may embark on board any private ship that he sees fit, for carrying on the service. But it is to be of his own squadron or division in preference, when equally suitable for his purpose.

21.

Flag officers to repeat all signals. The purports thereof to be afterwards complied with by their several divisions respectively.

The flag officers, or commanders of divisions are on all occasions to repeat generally, as well as with reference to their respective divisions, the signals from the Admiral; they may be thereby more speedily communicated correspondent to his intentions.

And the purpose of all signals for the conduct of particular divisions is then only meant to be carried into execution when the signal has been repeated, or made, by the commanders of such particular divisions respectively, in which circumstances they are to be always regarded and complied with by the ships or divisions referred to, in the same manner as if such signals had been made by the Admiral commanding in chief.

. . . .

Given on board H.M.S. the Eagle at Sandy Hook, the 30th of July, 1778.

ADDITIONAL INSTRUCTIONS

Respecting the Conduct of the fleet preparative to and in action with the enemy.

By Lord Howe.

[MS. copy. Graves Collection.]

Art. 1st.

Inconveniences that may attend a too strict adherence to a limitation of place and distance in the stated order of battle on some occasions.

The chief purpose of a regular disposition of the ships limited to place and distance in the stated order of battle being that they may remain as little as possible exposed on their approach to the fire of more than the particular ships corresponding in station in the enemy's line, or be subject to receive any injury from each other; and as a strict adherence thereto may on many occasions be found prejudicial to the service, by restraining the captains from taking advantage of the favourable incidents which may occur in the progress of a general action: it is the object of these instructions to facilitate the means of improving such opportunity by an authorised deviation from those restrictive appointments.

2nd.

The fleet to be extended the length of the enemy's van, and the same of their rear, though they consist of a greater number of ships.

It is meant the British van should be extended to the headmost ships of the enemy's van at all times preparative to general action in regular order of battle between the two fleets, though they consist of a greater number of ships. And it is equally desirable on that occasion that the same care should be taken in the rear to engage more particularly the sternmost ships of their rear, that no unoccupied ships may be left at either extremity of their line to facilitate any attempt to double upon some part of the British fleet—though it is judged that such use of their superiority proposed to be made by an unexperienced enemy will be proportionately guarded against as the ships of the fleet subject to be affected thereby shall be more closely engaged with their immediate opponents in the enemy's line.

Of the choice to be made of the ships to be disengaged with a superior enemy.

In respect to the limitation and rule for the government of the captains with whom the option must remain in either case with relation to the particular parts of the enemy's line wherein it may be advisable to leave such unoccupied ships, in the meantime it is recommended to the commanding ships of greater force to disregard or pass the weaker and worst sailing ships of the enemy and confine their first endeavours solely to disable the stronger and more active, as their accidental situations in the line may afford opportunity.

3rd.

When weathering the enemy and on different tacks.

In case of weathering the enemy preparative to a general action, being then approaching each other on different tacks, the fleet is to continue standing on as before until further directions.

And as soon as the Admiral has judged the van to be advanced far enough on, towards the rear of the enemy to allow a sufficient space for the ships to form and bring up properly against those opposed to them in the enemy's line respectively when they come to on the other tack, he may be expected to make the signal for the rear to tack first or the whole fleet to tack together, as he sees most convenient for forming upon the line of bearing best suited to the position of the enemy. And he will afterwards shape a course for bringing the ships into action with them accordingly. The several commanders will therefore be prepared for such evolution.

If a number of ships of the enemy's rear should tack, an equal number of the ships of the fleet to do the same.

But if any number of ships of the enemy's rear should tack, an equal number of the sternmost ships of the British line are to do the same in succession after that which then becomes the leading ship, and being formed thereby in line ahead parallel to those of the enemy tacking as aforesaid are to engage them in that situation, unless otherwise by signal directed.

4th.

When coming up with the enemy and having the wind of them on the same tack.

When coming up with the enemy on the same tack, having the wind of them, and they are observed to be lying to, or waiting under easy sail by the wind in line of battle ahead, but at such a distance to leeward that the fleet is not liable to be materially injured by their fire, the Admiral will then most probably choose to continue on upon the same course until the van of the fleet appears to be advanced within a sufficient distance of the extent of the enemy's van. He may be thereupon expected to make the signal for shaping a course to join the enemy and come to action with them on bringing up—each ship of the fleet opposed to that of the enemy corresponding in situations respectively as before expressed.

5th.

When coming up with the enemy as before and meaning to approach their rear previous to a general action. Sig. 4 *and* 5, *p.* 11.[1]

But if the Admiral should think proper under the same circumstances in respect to the enemy to attempt upon their rear previous to the pursuit of a general action, and makes the signal 4 or 5, page 11th in the Signal Book delivered, the leading ship of the van is to open to a convenient distance, and upon coming up with the enemy to give their sternmost ships her fire upon the quarter, then tack or veer and fall into the rear of the line, according to the purport of the respective signals.

This method of attack is to be continued in succession by the ships of the fleet, or any particular division, so appointed until further signals, care being always taken to leave room as requisite from each other in the execution of this service.

[1] *Signal* 4, *p.* 11, is 'for the ships in succession to fire upon the sternmost ships in the enemy's line, then tack and take their stations in the rear of the squadron or division specified until forbidden.' *Signal* 5, 'to engage the enemy in the same manner, then wear and fall into the rear, as before.'

6th.

When to desist from such partial attacks to bring on a general action.

When from any movement of the enemy it is thought improper longer to continue the manner of attack specified in the preceding article, and that the Admiral would have the next succeeding ships to take their stations for the purpose of bringing on a general action, he will most probably make the signal 3, page 11,[1] to invert the line in succession primarily instituted for the circumstance of coming up at a small distance to windward of the enemy upon the same tack; then the headmost ship of the British line is thereupon to be placed against the sternmost ship, not before disabled in the enemy's line. The ship her second astern is to pass without her to attack the next ship of the enemy, and the others to do the same in order throughout the enemy's line: the meaning of the last appointment being to guard in some cases against the injury the headmost ships would be exposed to in passing onward under the fire of the enemy's whole line to the attack of their leading ship in the van, as is generally understood to be required in such relative positions of the two fleets by the 19th article of the General Printed Fighting Instructions, the most necessary purposes of which the particular Signals and Instructions delivered for the government of the ships on the present occasion are meant to supply.

7th.

When more in number than the enemy in the line how the supernumerary ships are to proceed.

On meeting with a fleet of the enemy inferior in number of ships to that under the Admiral's

1 'To invert the line in succession from van to rear.'

command, or if by the early desertion of their posts in battle the British fleet should become superior to them in the line, the ships of the van or rear in either circumstances over and above the number of the enemy so drawn up are to quit their stations in the line without waiting for farther signals and instructions to that effect. The captains thereof are to endeavour to distress and annoy any of the nearest ships of the enemy in conjunction with the ships of the fleet particularly opposed to them; or otherwise to assist or relieve any disabled ships thereof, as they can be employed with most advantage.

8th.

When directed to steer and engage independently the ships respectively opposed to those of the fleet in the enemy's line. Page 23, *sig.* 8.[1]

And it may be necessary on some occasions to set the ships of the fleet at liberty to steer for those opposed to them respectively in the enemy's line independent of that necessary regard to the uniformity in distance, course, and movements to be at other times observed. When the signal 8, page 23,[1] is made for that purpose it will be incumbent on the captains of the fleet to keep those ships of the enemy to which they are then separately directed upon the same constant bearings, if possible, as they advance towards them.

Suitable care is however to be taken by them mutually not to cross upon or otherwise subject themselves to any hazard of falling on board each other in execution thereof.

1 'For the ships to steer for, independent of each other, and *engage* respectively the ships opposed to them in the enemy's line.'

For which end when they are so straightened or confined in their situations by the ships near them that they have not sufficient space to shape or vary their course correspondent to the alterations in the enemy's position made according to their usual practice on such occasions, they will best remedy that inconvenience by a proportionable increase or decrease of sail carried so as to be assured of effecting the intended junction as near together as may be with all convenient despatch.

Are permitted to take their stations to windward or to leeward of the enemy as they see fit.

They are permitted on bringing up against the enemy to take their stations on either part, to windward or to leeward of their opponents, as they see most suitable for boarding or closing with them at advantage to disable them more speedily.

They must nevertheless be mindful that they are not drawn away by any impression feigned or actually appearing to be made upon the enemy so far that they cannot have assistance from the fleet occasionally. Being in such circumstances to consider wherein they may render the most effectual service against the enemy and govern themselves occasionally.

To prepare for action when it may be necessary to anchor for attacking the enemy's battery or ships of war in port. Sig. 2, *p.* 25.

The purpose of this signal being to have timely preparation made in the ships or division referred to when it is proposed to attack any ships of the enemy protected by their batteries in port, or otherwise obliged to anchor in shore for their security, and when neither the time nor circumstance of the case do admit of giving earlier notice of the Admiral's intentions therein, it has therefore been thought expedient to specify, in explanation thereof, some of the most necessary provisions for the military services thence likely to ensue.

To have springs on the bowers and the sheet cable taken in abaft.

The captains of the ships so pointed out are to prepare for such service in due time by having springs upon their bowers and the end of the sheet cable taken into their stern ports for stopping short without winding when they are to sail to their anchoring stations against the works of the enemy with the wind aft.

Boats with hawsers and stream or coasting anchors in them.

Their different boats are to be hoisted out and hawsers coiled in their launches or long boats with their stream or coasting anchors, in readiness to aid or transport their own ships to their destined stations, or to assist other ships of the fleet on the same occasions.

Booms and spare masts secured.

The spare topmasts and yards (wind and weather permitting) will be best secured from injury in action by being lashed alongside under their lower deck ports, or towed astern in smooth water when no opportunity offers for leaving them in care of any of the other ships or vessels attending upon the fleet.

Men not to be unnecessarily exposed whilst sailing to the anchoring station.

It is recommended to them whilst advancing to their stations under fire of the enemy to keep their unoccupied men laid close down upon their decks on the off side from the enemy's ships or works to prevent disorder amongst them by untimely accidents, and that they may be less exposed until the ships are duly placed.

GIVEN, &c. &c. . . .

1st July 1777.

H.

KEMPENFELT'S FIRST INSTRUCTIONS, 1779–80

The documents which enable us to get a glimpse of how Kempenfelt went about to introduce his reforms when, in the spring of 1779, he became chief of the staff of Sir Charles Hardy in Channel are two in number.

Firstly, there is in the *Graves Collection* a MS. Order Book belonging to Rear-Admiral Thomas Graves, afterwards Lord Graves, who then had a flag under Hardy. It contains various orders signed by Kempenfelt between September 15, when the fleet retired to Torbay after the first stage of the defensive campaign, and November 4, when it was practically at an end. The tactical orders are printed below, and it will be seen that they relate to squadronal organisation of the fleet, to sailing formations for the readier formation of the line of battle, and to the order of retreat—all borrowed from the French. So far as is known this was the first attempt to get rid of the clumsy English sailing order, under which a rapid formation of line was impossible.

The second document is a MS. Signal Book in the United Service Institution which once belonged to Admiral Sir Thomas Graves, who served as a lieutenant under his uncle in the Channel in 1779, and went out with him to reinforce Arbuthnot on the North American Station early in 1780. It is entitled—*The General and Additional Sailing and Fighting Instructions, together with all those additions and alterations made by Admiral Sir Charles Hardy, Vice-Admiral Arbuthnot, and Rear-Admiral Thomas Graves, arranged and digested for the ready making of signals*, 1780. In this book he has noted against each 'Additional Signal' the nitial of the admiral who established it and the number of the article in the Instructions to which it referred. We are thus able, though the Instructions are lost, to establish their drift by the 'signification' of the corresponding signals.

All the most striking alterations are assigned to Admiral Sir Charles Hardy, and so far as they relate to tactics they are printed below. From the correspondence in the *Barham Papers* we know that all reforms then introduced into the fleet must have been Kempenfelt's, and the matter is put beyond doubt by the fact that reforms attributed officially to Sir Charles Hardy are obviously the germ of the system which Kempenfelt afterwards drew up.

The first point that comes out is that Kempenfelt was not satisfied with the Instructions as they stood. The old General Fighting Instructions he retained as in duty bound, but the Additional Instructions he appears to have remodelled by breaking them up into separate sections, each section having its own numbering. The grouping is difficult to reconstruct with any degree of certainty. All we can tell is that the arrangement was entirely different from the old-established Instructions which Rodney took out to the West Indies, or from those which Howe had been using in America, and that it appears to have been founded on that drawn up by Morogues in his *Tactique Navale*.

It is not however in this more logical arrangement that the significance of the new Instructions lies. The pith of Kempenfelt's work is to be found in three groups of articles which occur after the others. At page 27 was a group of twenty-four, most of them new. They relate to forming and handling the line and engaging the enemy, and are much concerned with the tactical idea of the closely formed line, on which Rodney was working. What followed in the next eighteen pages we cannot tell. The Signal Book has no reference to them, but they may well have contained detailed instructions for evolutions with diagrams, such as we know Kempenfelt introduced from Bigot de Morogues' book shortly afterwards.[1] On pp. 35–7 were thirteen articles relating to the use of triangular flags for distinguishing squadrons, now first introduced into the service, and to the use of them for controlling the relative movements and positions of squadrons in the line of battle. At p. 47 was a new miscellaneous group of nine articles relating to chasing, false colours, &c., and containing the striking innovation of a sailing formation in three lines. Lastly, at the extreme end, on pages 49 and 50, was an entirely new group of thirteen articles regulating the manner of attack, which throw a striking new light on the development of naval tactics. In them we find the second note of the revolution which led directly to the golden age of sailing warfare; but before considering them it will be necessary to recall the circumstances in view of which they were drawn up.

To grasp the full significance of these remarkable articles it should be remembered that they were prepared in view of a defensive campaign for holding the command of the Channel in dispute against a combination of the two chief Naval Powers of the Continent, one of which was threatening an invasion. They should be studied in close connexion with Kempenfelt's correspondence of this period in the *Barham Papers*, and above all with his classical

[1] See *post*, p. 170 *n.* 2.

exposition of a naval defensive. 'Much, I may say almost all, depends upon this fleet; 'tis an inferior against a superior fleet; therefore the greatest skill and address is requisite to counteract the designs of the enemy, to watch and seize the favourable opportunity for action and to catch the advantage of making an effort at some or other feeble part of the enemy's line: or if such opportunities don't offer, to hover near the enemy, keep him at bay, and prevent his attempting to execute anything but at risk and hazard, to command their attention and oblige them to think of nothing but being on their guard against your attack.' We have only to read the significations, together with the orders in Graves's Order Book, to see how thoroughly these tactical ideas permeate them.

On comparing the list of signals he introduced with those which Howe established in 1777 it is clear he must have had Howe's book before him; but the most interesting of them are certainly his own. For those which are not in Howe's book his obligation to the French authorities appears throughout, and especially in his reintroduction of the order of retreat, of doubling, of Torrington's method of engaging a superior fleet, which Hoste on Tourville's authority so highly approved, of a sailing order in three columns, and finally of the manœuvre of breaking the line in line-ahead.

This last is of course their most striking feature. Nothing indeed could more thoroughly upset current impressions of tactical history than to know that such a signal existed in the Channel Fleet two years before Rodney made or was persuaded to make the manœuvre. It is difficult to believe that Sir Thomas Graves was mistaken; he was obviously a most careful student, and he has marked quite clearly against the signal the letters 'S. C. H. add.,' his regular symbol for additions made under Sir Charles Hardy. Moreover, we have corroborating evidence in the fact that the signal was certainly in the final code which Kempenfelt drew up, and which he and Barrington used in the Channel during April 1782, and Bickerton took out to India in February—that is, before ever Rodney's action had been fought.

Assuming, therefore, that the signal was introduced as Sir Thomas Graves records, Rodney must have known of it when he went out to the West Indies at the end of December 1779. Of this we may be sure for this reason. Graves notes that the Printed Signal Book contained certain MS. alterations, and these alterations were clearly made after Hardy had been reinforced and had divided his fleet into five divisions instead of three. This change of organisation we know took place when he returned to Spithead for supplies on September 4, 1779, and during the period of reorganisation Rodney was at Spithead preparing his own squadron for sea. Consequently, as the signal for breaking the line is printed and not a MS. addition, he cannot have been unaware of the change, and yet he did not include it in his own amendments.

In any case he must have known of it when he went out the second time in 1782, for he took with him Sir Charles Douglas, who had been commanding the Duke 98 in the Channel during the whole period of Kempenfelt's ascendency. As a senior captain and the admiral's second astern, Douglas must have been perfectly familiar with Kempenfelt's ideas, and it was natural enough he should urge the Channel manœuvre upon Rodney when he saw a chance for it in the crisis of the action off the Saints. It also follows, if we can rely on Graves's Signal Book, that Rodney, so far from being the father of the manœuvre, must have deliberately refused to adopt it. In the same way we can account for the story that Rodney at first refused to listen to Douglas's suggestion, and we can well understand why he was so silent about the manœuvre in his official despatch.

The reversal of received history which the discovery of this signal entails is of course startling. But the evidence is beyond dispute. For the existence of the signal in April 1782 we have a Signal Book actually issued by Barrington to a ship in the Channel Fleet the first week of that month. For its existence as early as December 1779 it is true we have no more than an unofficial memorandum in a copy of a Signal Book. Such evidence would of course have but little weight did we not know who it was who made the copy. It was not the first comer. For Graves was actually Affleck's flag-captain when, in Rodney's last action, he on his own account led through another gap in the enemy's line; and Affleck himself had come straight from the Channel Fleet when he went out with Rodney in December 1779.

Shortly the case stands thus: that the signal was in the Channel Book of April 1782, and was not in Rodney's; that the two officers who were responsible for the manœuvre at the battle of the Saints were both Channel men, and that the man who records the existence of the signal in the Channel Book of 1779 was the flag-captain of one of them.

If now Kempenfelt's innovations be compared with Rodney's, it will be seen that Rodney took nothing from Kempenfelt except the signals for attacking van, centre or rear, which Howe had also used in 1777. While Kempenfelt provides for every known form of concentration, even introduces a new one by 'crossing the T,' Rodney pins his faith on one alone, viz. that of closing up his line and massing his heavy ships. This method as we know was never adopted into the Service. Yet at the culminating moment of sailing tactics Nelson used it, and Rodney's introduction of it may claim for him a place beside Kempenfelt in the front rank of tactical reformers as a man of original thought. The difference between the two men is mainly in their method of getting things done. While Kempenfelt kept his finger on the pulse of the Service, was in constant consultation with leading officers, and never moved farther or faster than he felt he could carry opinion with him, Rodney was ploughing a lonely furrow, shrinking perversely from co-operation in the general movement of naval thought, with the result that it passed him by, and his great victory was marred by inability to use to the full the advantage the Channel men had given him.

Another important innovation not adopted by Howe or Rodney was the sailing order in three lines.[1] Till then it was unknown in our Service, but afterwards it was taken up warmly by Howe, as giving a much greater rapidity in forming the line of battle with a large fleet. It appears to have been introduced by Kempenfelt, for it is found only in the group of miscellaneous orders inserted immediately before those relating to the manner of attack. It was certainly another obligation to the French. Not only does it occur in Hoste's treatise, but it was the basis of Morogues' and Villehuet's whole system of evolutions. Still none of these men saw what the order lacked to make it perfect. It remained for Howe to give the final touch which doubled its value and made it essentially English. Graves's Order Book also contains Hardy's order of battle as Kempenfelt arranged it, after he had been reinforced. It is printed below, as showing his revival of the old organisation in five squadrons for a large fleet of over forty sail.

[1] See *supra*, p. 76. An instruction for the new order was added after Pigot superseded Rodney. See Art. 34, p. 301.

ORDERS, ETC., GIVEN BY SIR CHARLES HARDY TO THE GRAND FLEET

[Graves's Order Book. Collection Graves MS.]

FORM OF SAILING for the first squadron when the fleet is separated into two squadrons :—

LONDON		PRINCE GEORGE	
Egmount	Hector	Vallient	Isis
Prident	Romney	America	Shrewsbury
Blenheim	Canada	Ramillies	St. Albans
Bedford	Queen	Centaur	Namur

VICTORY

Foudroyant	Cumberland
Princess Amelia	Courageux
Terrible	Triumph
Berwick	Duke

EDGAR

When sailing from close hauled to the wind two points abaft the beam, the Admiral's division on either tack will keep to windward.

And when sailing large or before the wind, the Admiral's division will keep on the starboard hand of the other two divisions.

The frigates to keep to windward and abreast of the Admiral of their division.

Fire ships to keep to windward of the fleet.

The cutters to keep near and upon the weather quarter of their Admirals.

To Thomas Graves, Esq., &c.

Dated, &c., at Spithead, 15 Sept. 1779.

CHAS. HARDY.

Form of Sailing for the second squadron when the fleet is separated into two squadrons :—

Royal George		Britannia	
Thunderer	Culloden	Union	Resolution
Monarch	Buffalo	Alexander	Invincible
Arrogant	Jupiter	Marlborough	Alfred
Bienfaisant	Defence	Intrepid	Formidable

When sailing from close hauled to the wind two points abaft the beam, the Vice-Admiral's division on either tack will keep to windward.

And when sailing large or before the wind, the Vice-Admiral's division will keep on the starboard hand of the other division.

To Thomas Graves, Esq., Rear-
Admiral of the Blue.

Dated, &c., at Spithead, 15 Sept. 1779.

Chas. Hardy.

Memo.

For the better distinction of the different divisions of the fleet when at sea, the commander-in-chief of the fleet would have the following order observed by the Admirals with respect to the place and colour of their flags :—

The commander of the second posts to bear a red flag at the fore topmast head.

Ditto in 3rd post, blue at the fore topmast head.

Ditto in 4th post, red at the mizen topmast head.

Ditto in 5th post, blue at the mizen topmast head.

When under sail the fleet are to keep in two different squadrons distinct from each other.

The first squadron to consist of the Admiral's, or centre division—Rear-Admiral Graves and Rear-Admiral Digby's.

The second squadron to consist of Vice-Admiral Darby's and Rear-Admiral Sir John Ross's divisions.

The second squadron to separate from the first the distance of two miles from the nearest ship, and sailing by the wind or the wind not far abaft the beam, to keep on either tack to windward.

But when sailing large or before the wind, to keep on the starboard side of the first division.

The ships of the second squadron are to take their motions from, and to be governed by, the signals from the second in command.

When the fleet are in two separate squadrons signals intended for the second squadron only will be pointed out by the signal denoting the second in command.

When the Admiral would have the three divisions of the first squadron form into separate lines of battle ahead and to windward of each other, and for the readier forming of the whole squadron into one line ahead he would not have them equally abreast, but each somewhat ahead of the squadron to leeward of them, in such manner that the sternmost ship of the fourth division to be abreast of the ship next ahead of the Admiral in the third division, and in like manner the sternmost ship of the first or Admiral's division to be abreast of the ship next ahead of the Admiral of the fourth division.

The signal for forming in this manner will be the flag red pierced with white at the mizen peak with an English jack under.

The three divisions composing the first squadron will then be ranged with respect to each other as in the annexed scheme.

N.B.—When the Admiral would have the divisions of the squadron sail in three lines abreast of each other, and the flags not to lead the divisions, but keep in their station in the lines he will under the red flag pierced white fix a pennant.

The ships to be distant from each other in these lines a cable and a half.

The lines to be a full half-mile asunder from each other.

The signal to denote the fifth division of the fleet will be a Dutch flag with a flag half red, half white under it where best seen.

SIGNALS for the fifth in command to come on board the Admiral, the Union flag with a yellow pennant over main topmast head.

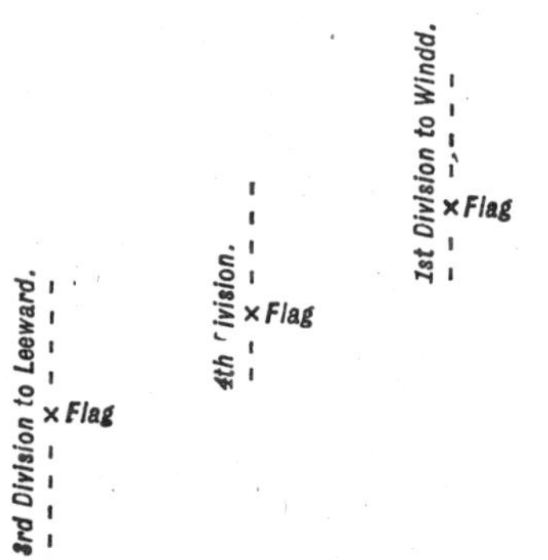

When the Admiral makes the signal for the line, and means it only for the three divisions of the first squadron, he will denote it by the signal pointing out the first squadron.

But when the signal for the line of battle is made simply by itself, the second squadron is then to close and take their station in the line.

To Thomas Graves, Esq.,
Rear-Admiral of the Blue.
Dated, &c., at Spithead, 16 Sept. 1779.

Night Signals.

For striking top-gallant masts and lower yards only two guns and one light at the ensign staff.

Chas. Hardy.

Of the Order of Retreat.

This order is made when the enemy is much superior, or after you have suffered much in an action. This disposition is chose rather than the order of sailing as you can more readily form the line of battle from it, and the Admiral has the fleet more under his eye.

In the order of retreat the fleet are ranged upon the sides of an obtuse angle of 135 degrees, formed of the two lines by the wind for the starboard and larboard tacks; the Admiral is to windward at the point of the angle and in the centre of his fleet.

The course or route of a retreat is commonly before the wind.

To Form the Order of Retreat.

The fleet being in order of battle and the Admiral would have them change to the order of retreat, as soon as the signal is made for that purpose, the hindmost ship in the line bears up four points, and all the ships ahead of the Admiral do the same as they come in her wake; by this means the commander-in-chief becomes the point of the angle and then shapes the course he intends to steer the ship on. Each wing are to pay great attention to keep exactly in the line by the wind in which they are ranged, whatever course the Admiral steers, and to be with respect to the ship opposite to them on the other wing in a line perpendicular to the wind. The principal utility of this form of sailing is to cover the disabled ships, frigates, fireships, &c., who are to be placed between the wings and ranged in lines parallel to them.

To Change the Order of Retreat to a Line of Battle.

The point G of the angle G to windward.

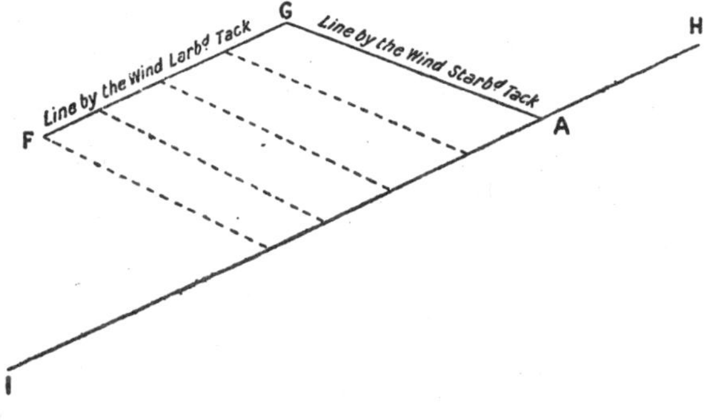

Suppose the order of retreat is to be changed to the line of battle ahead upon the larboard tack.

The ship at A hauls her wind to the larboard tack in the line I H, which is parallel to F G; the rest of the ships of the wing G A do the same as they come down into her wake; at the same time the ships of the wing F G go down in line parallel to G A till they reach the line I H, when they haul their wind together and form one line with the ships that were on the other wing. The whole fleet will then be formed in the line I H.[1]

[1] Here follow 'Regulations for the Treatment of the Sick in the fleet, particularly respecting Diet,' signed 'Richard Kempenfelt.' Then comes an order by him about anchoring in Torbay, Nov. 1, 1779. His last order in the book is Nov. 4.

LINE OF BATTLE

The Resolution to lead with the Starboard and the Bedford with the Larboard Tacks on Board

Frigates, &c.	Commanders	Rate	Ships	Commanders	Guns	Men	Division of
Ambuscade	Honble. Chas. Phipps	3	Resolution	Sir Chaloner Ogle, Bart.	74	600	VAN George Darby, Esq., Vice-Admiral of the Blue
Crescent	Chas. Hope	3	Invincible	Samuel Cornish	74	600	
Champion	Chas. Powell Hamilton	3	Alfred	William Bayne	74	600	
Hydra	Thos. Lloyd	2	Duke	Sir Chas. Douglas, Bart.	98	750	
Scarborough	R. Boyle Nicholas	1	Britannia	Vice-Adm. George Darby; Capt. Chas. M. Pole	100	872	
Triton, &c., to repeat Signals	Sk. Lutwidge	2	Union	John Dalrymple	90	750	
Bonetta, Sloop		3	Alexander	Rt. Honble. Lord Longford	74	600	
Infernal } Fire-ships		3	Marlborough	Taylor Penny	74	600	
Pluto } Fire-ships		3	Intrepid	Honble. Henry St. John	64	500	
		3	Culloden	George Balfour	74	600	FIFTH DIVISION Sir John Ross, Bart., Rear-Admiral of the Blue
		4	Buffalo	Hugh Bromadge	60	420	
		3	Arrogant	John Cleland	74	600	
		3	Defence	Thomas Cranston	74	600	
		1	Royal George	Rear-Admiral Sir John Ross; Capt. Jno. Colpoys	100	867	
		3	Thunderer	Honble. Robt. Boyle Walsingham	74	600	
		3	Monarch	Adam Duncan	74	600	
		4	Jupiter	Francis Reynolds	50	350	
Southampton	Wm. Garnier	3	Bienfaisant	John Macbride	64	500	

Milford, Lizard .		3	Cumberland	Joseph Peyton . .	74	600	
Phœnix, Stag .		3	Courageux	Rt. Hon. Lord Mulgrave	74	650	
Amazon, Quebec .		3	Triumph .	Philip Affleck . .	74	650	
Apollo, to repeat Signals	Phil. Pownall	2	Formidable	John Staunton . .	90	750	
Drake, Brig .	Wm. Brown	1	Victory .	Adml. Sir Chas. Hardy, Bt. Capt. Richd. Kempenfelt Capt. Henry Collins	100	894	**Centre** Sir Chas. Hardy, Kt., Admiral of the White and Commander-in-Chief
Cormorant, Sloop .	Rod. Home	3	Foudroyant	John Jervis . . .	80	700	
Firebrand } Fire-	Hon. G. Berkeley	3	P'ss Amelia	George Walters . .	80	650	
Incendiary } ships		3	Terrible .	Sir Chas. Bickerton, Bart.	74	600	
Kite } Cut- Griffin } ters Rattlesnake }	Henry Trollope	3	Berwick .	Honble. Keith Stewart .	74	600	
		3	Edgar .	John Elliot . . .	74	600	
		4	Isis . .	John Raynor . . .	50	350	
Richmond . .	Chas. Hudson	3	Shrewsbury	Mark Robinson . .	74	600	
Porcupine . .	Hon. H. Seymour Conway	3	St. Albans .	Richard Onslow . .	64	500	
Andromeda, to repeat Signals	Henry Boyne	2	Namur .	Chas. Fielding . .	90	750	**Fourth Division** Robt. Digby, Esq., Rear-Admiral of the Blue
True Briton, Cutter		2	Prince George	Rear-Admiral Robt. Digby Capt. Philip Patton	90	767	
		3	Valiant .	Samuel G. Goodall . .	74	650	
		3	America .	Saml. Thompson . .	64	500	
		3	Ramillies .	John Moutray . .	74	600	
		3	Centaur .	John N. P. Nott . .	74	600	
Brilliant . .	John Ford	3	Hector .	Sir John Hamilton, Bart.	74	600	
Medea . . .	Jas. Montagu	4	Romney .	George Johnstone . .	50	350	
Amphitrite . .	Thos. Gaborian	3	Canada .	Hugh Dalrymple . .	74	600	
Pegasus . .	Jno. Bazely	2	Queen .	Alexr. Innes . . .	90	750	
Camel, to repeat Signals	R. Rodney Bligh	2	London .	Rear-Admiral Graves Capt. David Graves	90	767	**Rear** Thomas Graves, Esq., Rear-Admiral of the Blue
Rambler } Cutters Flyingfish }	Jas. George	3	Egmont .	John Carter Allen . .	74	600	
Salamander } Fire-	Honble. Seyʳ Finch	3	Prudent .	Thos. Burnett . .	64	500	
Furnace } ships	Geo. Stoney	2	Blenheim .	Brodrick Hartwell . .	90	750	
Helena, Brig .	Sir John Borlase-Warren	3	Bedford .	Edmund Affleck . .	74	600	

PRINCIPAL TACTICAL SIGNALS ATTRIBUTED TO SIR CHARLES HARDY

[Graves's Signal Book MS. U.S.I.]

Instructions respecting the order of battle and conduct of the fleet preparative to or in action with the enemy (?)

1. To form order of sailing.

2. Ships to keep in close order in line of battle.

11. To form in close order of battle and astern of the admiral as most convenient.

12. To haul to the wind together when in line of battle.

13. The same on the larboard tack.

14. Ships of the fleet to open at greater distance from each other for performing an evolution.

15. To close again to the distance appointed before the evolution.

16. For the fire-ships to proceed to burn the enemy under cover of particular ships indicated.

17. Particular ships or divisions to attack any number of the enemy's ships of war seeming to be kept separate for any purpose from the body of the fleet.[1]

18. To engage the enemy in line of battle as the ships are able successively to arrive up with them.

[1] It is noteworthy in view of this signal that D'Orvilliers had organised two detachments whose function was to be, when the moment came, to proceed to St. Malo and Havre respectively to escort the two divisions of the army intended for the descent upon the Isle of Wight and Portsmouth; but the signal is actually taken from Howe's book of 1777.

19. To prepare for battle.

20. To discontinue the engagement.

21. For the leading ship in line and the rest in succession, still preserving the line, to alter their course to starboard or port. Number of points signified by guns.

24. More open order in line of battle or otherwise.

Miscellaneous additions.

1–4. Particular ships to chase north, south, east or west.

5. Prepare to hoist Spanish colours.

6. Prepare to hoist French colours.

7. Particular ship to go ahead and make the land.

8. To speak stranger standing into the fleet.

9. The fleet to form in three lines.

Instructions relating to the manner of attack.

1. A division of the fleet to attack the enemy's rear in succession by ranging up the length of some ship, then tacking or wearing, as they are to windward or leeward of the enemy, and form again in the rear of their division, continuing this manner of attack till they find it expedient to cease or are called off by signal.[1]

2. For certain particular ships to do the same, the signals for those ships will be made.

3. To discontinue the above action.

4. When fetching up to leeward of the enemy on the contrary tack to break through their line and attempt to cut off part of their rear.

[1] This form of concentration on the rear by 'defiling' was entirely new. It does not appear in the French books, and was probably Kempenfelt's own idea. Nothing like it had been known in our Instructions since the similar form of attack in Elizabethan times. *N.R.S.* xxix. (*Fighting Instructions*), pp. 42, 51.

5. When coming up narrow to windward of the enemy, for the headmost ship to engage the enemy's sternmost ship : the next to pass under cover of her to the second ship of the enemy's rear, and so on in succession till the rear ship reaches the van of the enemy.

6. For the van ship of the line to steer for and engage the enemy's van ship, when bearing down broad on them.

7. The van of the fleet to double on the enemy's van.

8. The van of the fleet to double on the enemy's rear.

9. The rear of the fleet to double on the enemy's rear.

10. The Admiral means to make his attack on the enemy's centre.

11. The Admiral means to make his attack on the enemy's van.

12. The Admiral means to make his attack on the enemy's rear.

13. If the fleet is inferior in number to the enemy, and the Admiral, to prevent being doubled upon in his van or rear, would have his van line the van of the enemy and his rear their rear, placing his own division against their centre, and by that means leaving the enemy's surplus ships out in the vacant spaces left between his van and centre and his van and rear.

KEMPENFELT'S SIGNALS AND EXPLANATORY INSTRUCTIONS, WITH HOWE'S MODIFICATIONS 1781–2

Introductory.

In the Society's previous volume there is a set of Instructions entitled 'Lord Howe, 1782,' which at the time of publication was the earliest known form of the Signal Book Explanatory Instructions. This view must now be modified by the discovery of three new documents which hitherto have escaped notice.

The first is a thin printed folio of Instructions in the library of the United Service Institution, similar to but shorter than those of 1782. It is entitled 'Instructions for the Conduct of the Ships of War Explanatory of and Relative to the Signals contained in the Signal Book,' but it is without name or date.

In the *Graves Collection* however is another copy with certain manuscript additions which has an issue clause at the end, as follows: 'Given under my hand on board H.M.S. Britannia, at Spithead, 11 Feb. 1781. G. Darby.' Darby was then commander-in-chief in the Channel. When Sir Charles Hardy died in 1780 he had been succeeded by Sir Francis Geary, and when Geary resigned the following August, Darby, the second in command, had taken his place.

Kempenfelt had remained on as first captain, and Graves has marked the book on the cover,

'Admiral Kempenfelt.' A manuscript copy of the Signal Book that was used with it is also in the collection—that is to say, the signal references correspond with the articles in the Instructions, and certain striped flags which in 1780 had been horizontal have been altered to vertical, a change which we know took place in February 1781.[1]

The Instructions are founded on those which Howe used in 1777—so far as they go. The first six sailing articles, except for a few verbal differences, are identical with the six that formed Howe's set; but to these Kempenfelt added as many more of considerable importance, relating mainly to fleet cruisers and sailing formations. Thus, as it proved, the characteristic British sailing formation, which so greatly accelerated the handling of the fleet for action, was permanently introduced into the Service. The new articles were certainly Kempenfelt's work, for the last of them is a manuscript addition, and all of them are a fundamental improvement on the corresponding French orders.

With regard to the Fighting Instructions it will be seen that they also are identical with Howe's of 1777, except for some slight changes in arrangement and wording.

In the United Service Institution is a third example of this document. It is a manuscript copy presented by Lieutenant Thomas Graves, R.N., in which the title of the printed book is followed by the words 'herewith delivered by Rear-Admiral Richard Kempenfelt.' The second document is the Signal Book belonging to it, now in the Editor's possession. It is in the same folio form, and is entitled 'Signal Book for the Ships of War.' This particular copy was first issued to Captain Keppel, of H.M.S. Fortitude, by Admiral

[1] *N.R.S.* xxxii. (*Barham Papers*), p. 337.

Barrington, who during April 1782 had the Channel Division of the Home Fleet, with Kempenfelt as his second in command. In May, Kempenfelt was in chief command and re-issued it to the same officer, erasing Barrington's name and substituting his own.[1]

So far, then, we know exactly what Instructions and Signals were in use, so long as Kempenfelt was the dominating mind in the Channel. In the spring of 1782 Howe was given the command, and we are able to tell with equal certainty that he continued Kempenfelt's edition of his own old Instructions, but with considerable additions. The evidence is a MS. copy (also in the United Service Institution) of the Instructions and Signal Book of 1782, assigned to Howe in the former volume. It was made by Admiral William Page, an officer who entered the Navy under the auspices of Sir Edward Hughes in 1778, and was present in his flagship at all his actions with Suffren. It is in this copy, which he dates erroneously 1780,[2] that Page tells us what he knew of the original. He says he made his transcript from a copy lent him by Captain Rainier, who was one of Hughes's captains. Page was thus in a position to know all about his document, and this is what he says of it: 'Differently though arranged, this is a true copy of the Signal Book used by Sir Richard Bickerton to the squadron he was entrusted with to India and the detachment he commanded home, and was generally said, and no one doubted, to be the compilation and much of the invention of the gallant and most able Admiral Richard Kempenfelt. Sir Edward Hughes also used it on his passage home to a single frigate. . . . N.B.—From hence all the signals used throughout the Navy are acknowledged to be selected and

[1] For further details see General Introduction, *ante*, p. 42.
[2] See *ante*, p. 50.

imitated, but acknowledged by Mr. Kempenfelt to be used by the French also.' Inside the cover Page has written this further note : 'This copy of the first improved code of signals in the British Navy was given me leave to make by Capt. Peter Rainier 1784, and was first used in the East Indies by Sir Richard Bickerton's squadron. Sir Edward Hughes did not get them till after the war ceased in July 1783. Admiral Kempenfelt compiled them for the British Navy 1781, but his untimely death retarded their use.'

Here then we have sufficiently convincing evidence not only that the longer set of Instructions was the one used by Howe in 1782, but that the shorter set, which it superseded, was actually issued, together with the Signal Book belonging to it, by Kempenfelt as Commander-in-Chief of a squadron. We can therefore fix it to one of two occasions. For some time after his promotion Kempenfelt continued as first captain or chief of the staff with Geary and Darby in the Channel Fleet. It was not till November 18, 1781, that he hoisted his flag, and on December 12 he sailed to achieve his famous exploit of cutting up a French convoy of storeships and transports for the West Indies in the face of De Guichen and his superior fleet. Although it is impossible to connect the few signals he is recorded to have made on that occasion with this particular set of Instructions, it is very probably the one he used. If not it must have been a few months later, as we have already seen, when at the end of April 1782 Howe, on resuming command in the Channel, immediately detached him to watch Brest, with special authority to establish such signals and instructions as he thought fit.[1]

It is now of course impossible, in spite of Admiral

[1] See *supra*, Introduction, p. 43.

Page's general testimony, to attribute either form of the Instructions entirely to Kempenfelt. Howe's hand is too plainly visible in the tangled style of the last additions, and the recovery of the *Graves Collection* enables us to trace much of the earlier form to Howe. What Page clearly meant is that the numerary system of signalling was the work of Kempenfelt and not the whole of the Instructions themselves.

In view of the close connexion between the two sets it has not been thought necessary to print both in full. But in order to permit of an easy comparison between them, and to enable readers to appreciate the importance of Howe's later additions, it has been decided to reprint the whole of the final set, indicating exactly how it was built up upon the first set. The parts which Howe added to Kempenfelt's set are given in square brackets, and where necessary the original form of altered passages is given in footnotes. The exact form which Kempenfelt established in 1781 can therefore be ascertained by reading the unbracketed passages with the footnotes.

KEMPENFELT AND HOWE, 1781–2[1]

[Page's Transcript in U.S.I. Library]

General instructions and directions for the conduct of the ships of war, when sailing or chasing by day.

Article I

Officers summoned on board the Admiral to be provided with an orderly book.

For the advantage of despatch and the more convenient distribution of orders, the officers summoned by signal are to attend on board the Admiral provided with an orderly book; wherein they are to minute down the receipt of all public letters and orders, then to be delivered; to enter all verbal directions given; and all written instructions to be copied from the day-book of the ship in which the Admiral is embarked; and to sign their names in evidence of the receipt of such orders and instructions when so required.[2]

Article II

Ships commanded by senior or junior officers, equally to bear up as may be most convenient.

In order to avoid inconvenience from the customary practice, founded on the regulations specified in

[1] Additions made to Kempenfelt's set and established by Howe are indicated with square brackets.

[2] This appears to have been the practice of the service. See Rodney's *Landing Instructions*, 1761–2, Art. I, p. 357.

the General Printed Sailing Instructions, with respect to the conduct of senior officers towards their juniors, the ships of war are to bear up for each other, shorten sail, &c., without regard to the seniority of the commanders, or other claim of distinction, in such manner as shall be found most convenient on either part, and may best guard against the hazard of falling on board each other. But when ships are upon different tacks, and must cross near each other, the ship on the starboard tack is to keep her wind, while that on the larboard is always to pass to leeward.

Attention is likewise to be had upon all occasions to give place to ships proceeding as directed by signal from the Admiral, or making the signal to speak with him.

Article III

Ships nearest to strange ships, passing near the fleet at anchor, to examine them.

The captains of ships lying, or stationed on, the part nearest to which any strange ships may happen to approach the fleet when at anchor, by day or night, are to examine such strange ships without waiting for more particular directions by signal, or otherwise, for that purpose.

And they are to make known, without loss of time, to the Admiral or the commander of their division, the particulars of any material information they may thereby obtain.

Article IV

The order in which ships in chase are successively to return to the fleet, upon signal for that purpose.

When more ships than one happen to be out in chase on the same quarter, or bearing from the

Admiral, and it is meant that any of them should return back to the fleet (which will be signified by the proper bearing-flag, shown at the fore topmast head) the ship furthest from the chase is first to return in compliance therewith.

If the signal be nevertheless continued abroad, after that ship has made sail to join the fleet, the next ship most distant from the chase is then to do the same, and so on, one after the other in succession, whilst the signal remains abroad.

But if the signal flag be taken in before all the chasing ships are upon their return to the fleet, the ships, one or more, that shall not then have made sail to join the fleet, are to continue the pursuit, until the signal is again made, requiring their return also to the fleet.

Article V

Of ships ordered to repeat signals between the Admiral and ships in chase.

Ships sent out in succession to repeat signals between the Admiral and ships in chase are to be kept at proper intervals asunder ; varying their stations occasionally according to the change of distance and number of ships ordered from the fleet upon that service.[1]

[1] The issue of 1781 had here, erased, the following article, numbered VI, as in the issue of 1777, which ended at this point : 'In case of separation in chase (which is to be avoided as much as possible without permission first obtained or upon extraordinary occasions) the ships are to be made known on their return in sight of the fleet by the respective daily signals instituted for that purpose, in preference to the distinguishing signal delivered when it can be done with equal convenience and effect.' It was erased before it was issued to Graves, Feb. 11, 1781. All the sailing articles that follow were Kempenfelt's additions.

Article VI *[1]

How to proceed when chasing to leeward—
When chasing to windward.

In chasing to leeward, the chaser is to try by degrees to find that course on which he can steer most down upon the chase, preserving her at the same time constantly upon one point of bearing from him, as that will be the shortest he can steer to come up with her.

In chasing to windward, the chaser should avoid long boards, as they may favour the escape of the chase if the wind should shift; for which reason it is judged best for him to tack as often he has the chase on the beam.

The above remarks however are only offered to the consideration of the chaser, who will act as from circumstances appear to him best.[2]

Article VII

When two or more ships are ordered to look out in the same direction.

If, in order to extend the view, two or more ships are ordered to look out in the same direction, the utmost care is to be had that the distance between them shall be such as to preserve the communication between the Admiral and that ship which is the most distant from him.

Article VIII *[1]

When the fleet is directed to anchor in three parallel lines, and on a particular bearing, the lines

[1] The meaning of these asterisks is not explained.

[2] Unlike the two previous chasing articles, which are from the regular Additional Sailing Instructions, Article VI is an innovation from the French, being taken from Bourdé de Villehuet, Part II, chap. viii. The last paragraph, however, is pure Kempenfelt, and characteristic of his antipathy to fixed tactical rules.

are to be abreast of each other at [1] two cables' length asunder, and the same distance is to be preserved between each ship.

Article IX

When out of sight of land, boats are sent on board the Admiral—Or when sent on board a strange ship, or on shore in a foreign port—Ships nearing each other in calm—No lights to appear but for signals—Not to lose company—Ships spoken with to take their bearings and distance from the land—Intelligence to be reported by the officer who receives it—A ship-of-the-line from each squadron to look out in rotation—To be attentive to signals—Movements to be made with expedition.

* When the fleet is out of sight of land, and a ship has occasion to send a boat on board the Admiral, the officer in such boat is to bring with him a copy of the day's work of the preceding noon.

When a boat is sent on board a strange ship, or on shore in a foreign port, a midshipman is always to go with the officer, and is constantly to remain in the boat to prevent impertinent or indiscreet answers from being given.

[In light winds, inclined to calm, the ships are to be attentive to keep at a proper distance from each other, and when calm to have their boats out in time upon nearing any ship.]

[* That no lights are suffered, but for signals, to appear from any ship in the night.]

[Great care is to be taken not to lose company, and this is particularly recommended to ships sent in chase, or to look out, who are always to stand towards the fleet before it is dark.]

1 Added in MS. in 1781 edition.

[* When a ship is spoke with that has lately parted from the land, her bearing and distance from such land at the time spoken with is to be taken down and communicated to the Admiral.]

[When intelligence has been received from any vessel that is judged necessary to communicate to the Admiral, the officer who received the intelligence is always to be sent with the report.]

[* By day, when the fleet is sailing by the wind, a ship of the line from the centre squadron is to keep two points on the Admiral's weather bow, one from the leeward squadron two points on his lee bow, and one from the weather squadron directly to windward, or two points before the Admiral's beam. They are to keep six miles distant from the Admiral, but in thick weather to close nearer.]

[* When sailing large, or before the wind, the ship from the centre squadron is to keep right-ahead of the Admiral, that from the starboard squadron two points out to starboard of the fleet, and that from the larboard squadron two points out to port.]

[* In the night each ship to keep ahead of her squadron about one mile distance.]

[They are to examine such ships as may pass near them.]

[* The ships are to take this duty in rotation (the three-decked ship excepted) beginning with the senior captain of the squadron. The relief to be in the evening an hour before sunset.]

[As a prompt observance of signals is often of the utmost consequence, it is required that the captains have a good look-out constantly kept towards the commander-in-chief's ship that his signals may be seen as soon as made, and that they always reply to them by the answering flag.]

[* And when signal is made for any manœuvre that requires a change of station, the ships are immediately to crowd sail, that the execution may be performed in the shortest time possible.]

Article X

Of the stations of the squadrons in the order of sailing—When the squadrons are formed in two lines; sig. 41, pa. 4—Squadrons forming from one into two lines—Ditto from two lines into one line—Distance of the lines in sailing order—Distance of the squadrons in sailing order—Squadrons not to change places when circumstances render it inconvenient—Ships to be attentive to keep their stations—And when each squadron is formed in one line; sig. 44, pa. 4.[1]

In the order of sailing the ships are to be stationed in such manner as may most favour the ready forming of the line of battle, in which the squadron of the second in command is to lead. For this reason the commander in the second post and his squadron is to be windward of the centre on both tacks, or on the starboard tack when sailing before the wind; the commander in the third post and his squadron, in like manner, to leeward, or on the larboard side. If this disposition is to be changed, the Admiral will signify the same by the proper signal for that purpose.

[1] This article is a radical innovation. It formally adopts the French 'Fifth order of Sailing'—*i.e.* in three or six columns as the normal order; but with two great improvements which are English. Paragraph 2 provides for forming from three columns, two 'grand divisions,' which became the regular organisation in the British service and gave great flexibility. Still more important for rapidity of forming order of battle is the paragraph marked A and the last. In the French order the three columns were exactly abreast. The simple expedient of ranging them in échelon was a great advance, and rapidly led to the final arrangement by which the columns bore for each other in the direction of the wind.

When the signal is made for each squadron to sail in two lines, the ships that are stationed ahead of the Admiral of a squadron, when the fleet is formed in line of battle, agreeable to the above regulation, constitute the weather, and those astern of him the leeward line of the squadron: and in both lines the ships are to follow each other according to that order.

[*When the squadrons are sailing in one line or column each, and signal is made for the columns to double, the van half braces-to, the rear half keeps large a point or more, and crowds sail up to leeward, till they have reached abreast of the weather half.]

[* When from sailing in two columns they are directed to form into one column each, the leeward lines brace-to, the weather ones make sail, edging something away to bring the others into their wake.]

[* When the squadrons are sailing in three lines abreast they are to keep at the distance of one mile from each other.]

[* And when they are sailing each in two lines, the lines are to be distant from each other five cables' length, one line to be 2½ cables on one side and the other line 2½ cables on the other side of the Admiral's wake, who leads the squadron.]

[* The squadrons also to be separated five cables' length, or a good half-mile from each other, thus:

* The weather line of the centre and the lee line of the van squadron to be that distance asunder, and

* The same distance to be observed between the lee line of the centre and the weather line of the rear squadron, so that the six lines in which the fleet are sailing will have a separation between each of five cables, which will prevent the squadrons from intermixing, and afford room for manœuvring without embarrassment.

* Although the squadron of the second in command, when in sailing order, is directed to keep to windward; or if going before the wind on the starboard side of the centre, yet, if from a shift of the wind, or change of course, he is put to leeward or on the larboard side of the centre, and the circumstance of wind or weather, or the situation of ships, then should render the squadrons changing places inconvenient, in such case it is not to take place until a more suitable opportunity presents; the second in command always to make the first movement for the change.

* Ships to pay great attention at all times to keep well closed-up, and in their stations, and particularly to be so at day-break, in order that the line may readily be formed if the enemy should appear near.]

* A. In the order appointed by sig. 44 page 4, the squadrons are to be ranged to windward, and partly ahead of each other; a disposition very favourable for the speedy forming of the line. The station of the squadron of the second in command is to windward and ahead; that of the commander-in-chief in the centre; and the squadron of the third in command to leeward, and in the rear.

The squadrons are to be half a mile distant from each other, and are to be situated so that the sternmost ship of the centre squadron shall be abreast of the ship next ahead of the Admiral in the rear, and the sternmost of the van or weather squadron abreast of the ship next ahead of the Admiral in the centre. In this, and in all other forms of sailing, the ships are to be distant from each other the length of [two cables, unless signal is made to close to one cable].[1] (*See diagram p.* 149.)

[1] The 1781 edition had 'a cable or a cable and a half, according to the state of the weather.' In the printed Admiralty copy the diagram is wrong, and there is a MS. note correcting it,

[1] The signal 45, page 4, is to be executed in the following manner :—

The first, or commander-in-chief's squadron, to be in the centre and to leeward.

The other two in their stations on the wings, half a mile to windward, or in the rear of the centre when going large, or before the wind, in such manner that

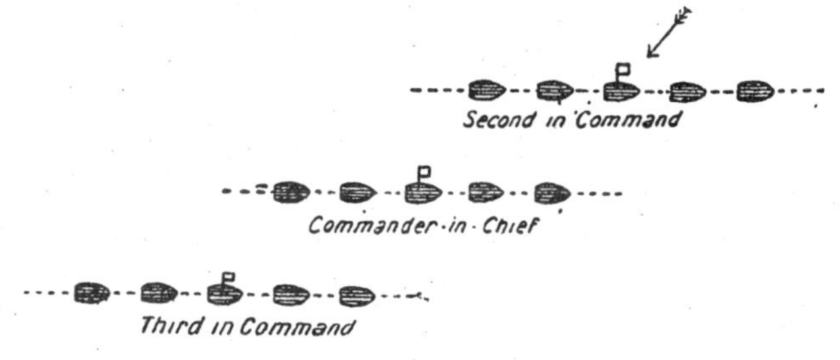

when (for instance) sailing by or before the wind, the sternmost ship of the van squadron covers the commander-in-chief's second ahead, and the headmost ship of the rear squadron his second astern.

And this position of the squadron is to be observed, whatever course the Admiral steers, the same ships always to cover his seconds.

as above. It shows five ships however instead of four in each squadron—flags in the centre.

In Kempenfelt's Signal Book the orders of sailing are as follows (Signals 102–5, p. 9) :—

1. Each squadron in two lines. Ships at 2 cables.

2. Each squadron in one line. Ships at 1 to $1\frac{1}{2}$ cables. The Admirals commanding the squadrons to lead.

3. The same with the Admirals in their stations as in line of battle.

4. The same with the squadrons ranged as in the last paragraph of the instruction.

[1] This and the following paragraphs to the end of the Sailing Instructions were added by Kempenfelt in MS. in 1781. The signal in his book is No. 395, p. 33.

Figure by the wind :[1]—

Figure before the wind :—

The purpose of this form of sailing is that going large, or before the wind particularly. The fleet is thereby kept compact, and in such order as expeditiously to form the line upon either tack when necessary.

[1] In the Admiralty copy the centre squadron is closed up like the others. Squadron flags are shown in the centre of each squadron. The French arrangement, as laid down by Morogues, was that the columns should be disposed at such a

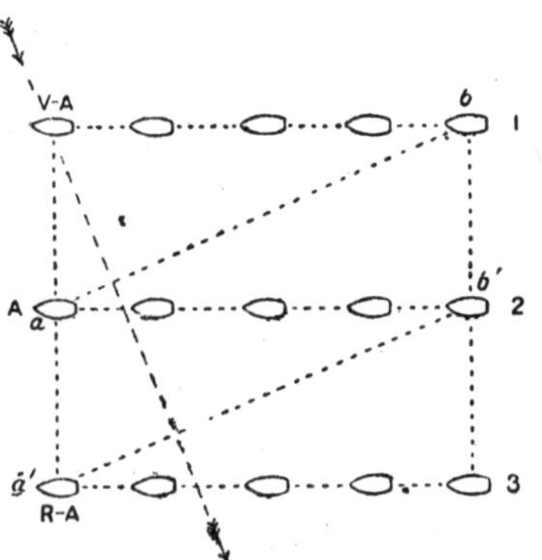

distance from each other, as that the last ship of the first and second columns (*b b′*) should bear from the leading ship of the second and third columns (*a a′*) in a direction perpendicular to the wind, the columns being disposed abreast from to windward—*i.e.* the lines *a b* and *a′ b′* are at right angles to the wind.

Instructions respecting the order of battle and conduct of the fleet, preparative to and in action with the enemy.

ARTICLE I

Ships, how to take their stations in the line.

When the signal is made for the fleet to form in order of battle, each captain or commander is to get most speedily into his station, and keep the prescribed distance from his seconds ahead and astern upon the course steered, and under a proportion of sail suited to that carried by the Admiral.

* But when the signal is made for tacking, or any similar occasion, care is to be taken to open, in succession, to a sufficient distance for performing the intended evolution. And the ships are to close back to their former distance respectively as soon as it has been executed.

II

* Flag of commander-in-chief the direction for the line.

[In line of battle, the flag of the Admiral commanding-in-chief is always to be considered as the point of direction to the whole fleet for forming and preserving the line.][1]

[1] This article may have been added to prevent a recurrence of the mistake which spoiled Rodney's attack in 1780. Like all the rest in square brackets it does not appear in the original form of Kempenfelt's Instructions.

III

Second squadron to lead in the line ahead, and to be on the starboard side of the centre in the line abreast, when these lines are formed from the order of sailing. When line is formed, the squadrons not to change places without signal—Ships of each squadron to be ranged in the line, in the same order as when in the form of sailing each squadron in one line.—Signal for the line not to regard ships detached.

[The squadron of the second in command is to lead when forming the line ahead, and to take the starboard side of the centre when forming the line abreast, unless signal is made to the contrary; these positions, however, are only restrained to the first forming of the lines from the order of sailing.]

[For when the fleet is formed upon a line, then in all subsequent evolutions the squadrons are not to change their places, but preserve the same situation in the line whatever position it may bring them into the centre, with respect to being in the van or rear on the starboard or larboard side, unless directed so to do by signal.]

[Suppose the fleet sailing in line ahead on the larboard tack, the second in command leading, and signal is made to form a line abreast to sail large, or before the wind, the second squadron, in that case, is to form on the larboard side of the centre.]

[Again, suppose in this last situation signal is made to haul to the wind, and form a line ahead on the starboard tack, in this case the squadron of the third in command is to lead, that of the second in command forming the rear.]

[And when from a line ahead, the squadron of the second in command leading, the Admiral would immediately form the line on the contrary tack, by tacking or veering together, the squadron of the third in command will then become the van.]

[These evolutions could not otherways be performed with regularity and expedition.]

[When forming the line, from the order of sailing, the ships of each squadron are to be ranged with respect to each other in the line, in the same manner as when in order of sailing each squadron in one line, and, as when the second in command is in the van, the headmost ship of his squadron (in sailing order) becomes the leading ship of the line, so likewise the headmost ship of the third squadron (in sailing order) becomes the leading ship of the line when the third in command takes the van, except when the signal is made to form the line reversed.]

Ships happening to have been previously detached on any service, separate from the body of the fleet, when the signal for forming in order of battle is made are not meant to be comprehended in the intention of it, until they shall first have been called back to the fleet by the proper signal.[1]

IV

The course to be always taken from the leading ship in line ahead.

When the fleet is sailing in line of battle ahead, the course is to be taken from the ship leading the van upon that occasion; the others in succession being to steer with their seconds ahead respectively, whilst they continue to be regulated by the example of the leading ship.[2]

[1] No. 2 in 1781. The article consisted of the last paragraph only. All the rest is an addition by Howe. Possibly he had in his mind the confusion caused by Powlet in Knowles's action off Havana, October 1, 1748, which this instruction would have prevented.

[2] In 1781 this article was continued by the last two paragraphs of Article V.

V[1]

Ships not able to keep their stations in the line, how to proceed—When to come to the wind in succession on either tack from sailing large.

The ships which from the inequality of their rates of sailing cannot readily keep their stations in the line, are not to obstruct the compliance with the intent of the signal in others; nor to hazard throwing the fleet into disorder by persisting too long in their endeavours to preserve their stations under such circumstances; but they are to fall astern and form in succession in the rear of the line.

The captains of such ships will not be thereby left in a situation less at liberty to distinguish themselves, as they will have an opportunity to render essential service by placing their ships to advantage when arrived up with the enemy already engaged with the other part of the fleet.

The ships next in succession in the order of battle, are to occupy in turn, on this and every other similar occasion, the vacant spaces that would be otherwise left in the line; so that it may be always kept perfect at the appointed intervals of distance.

And when the fleet is sailing large, or before the wind, in order of battle, and the Admiral makes the signal for coming to the wind on either tack, the ship stationed to lead the line on that tack, first, and the others in succession as they arrive in the wake of that ship and of their seconds ahead respectively, are to haul to the wind without loss of time, accordingly.[2]

And all the signals for regulating the course and motions of the fleet by day or night, after the

[1] In 1781 this article preceded No. 4 and formed article No. 3.

[2] In 1781 this and the next paragraph concluded Article IV.

signal for forming in order of battle has been made, are to be understood with reference to the continuance of the fleet in such order, until the general signal to chase, or to form again in order of sailing, is put abroad.

VI[1]

Relative bearings to be preserved—On altering course in succession, the point specified to be steered to be considered as line of bearing on other evolutions.

[When the fleet is formed on any line pointed out by the compass signal][2] the relative bearing of the ships from each other is to be preserved through every change of course made, as often as any alteration thereof together shall be by signal directed. *And the same is to be understood of the bearing indicated, though the Admiral should shape his course from the wind originally, when the signal for forming upon any line of bearing is made.*[3]

When, on the contrary, the signal to alter the course in succession has been put abroad, the relative bearing of the ships from each other will be then consequently changed; and any alteration of the course subsequently directed to be made by the

[1] No. 5 of 1781. No. 6 of 1781 was No. 7 of 1782, and so on till Article XII.

[2] The 1781 edition reads: 'By the starboard line of bearing is meant that line or point of the compass upon which the fleet would be formed, and the ships bear from each other, in line of battle ahead, steering with a full sail, or about one point from the wind, as it may at any time happen to be, on either tack. The relative bearing, &c.'

[3] In the Admiralty copy the passage in italics has been erased. The 1781 edition adds: 'The ships will thereby become ranged immediately in line of battle ahead, in readiness for coming to action with the enemy, whenever it shall be requisite to haul to the wind after having edged away to join them with that intent.'

ships *together* will thereafter have reference to the relative bearing last established.

The same distinction will take place, so often as the alteration of course in *succession*, as aforesaid, shall in future recur.

VII

When by an alteration in the disposition of the enemy a suitable change is requisite in the relative bearings of the ships of the fleet.

If the Admiral should observe that the enemy has altered his course, and the disposition of his order of battle, one, two, three, or any greater number of points (in which case it will be necessary to make a suitable change in the bearing of the ships from each other in the British fleet, supposed to be formed in such respects correspondently to the first position of the enemy), he will make the signal for altering course in succession, according to the nature of the occasion. The leading ship of the line is thereupon immediately to alter to the course pointed out; and (the others taking their places astern of her, in succession, as they arrive in the wake of that ship and of their seconds ahead respectively) she is to lead the fleet in line of battle ahead on the course so denoted, until further order.

VIII

When an alteration of sail is intended to be made whilst the fleet is in order of battle—Hence the necessity for each captain to acquire a knowledge of the comparative rate of sailing between his own and the Admiral's ship.

When it is necessary to shorten sail or make more sail whilst the fleet is in order of battle, and the proper signal in either case has been made, the fleet is to be regulated by the example of the frigate appointed to repeat signals; which frigate is to set or take in the sail the Admiral is observed to do.

The ship referred to is thereupon to suit her sail to the known comparative rate of sailing between her and the Admiral's ship.

Hence it is necessary that the captains of the fleet be very attentive to acquire a perfect knowledge of the comparative rate of sailing between their own and the Admiral's ship, so as under whatever sail the Admiral may be, they may know what proportion to carry, to go at an equal rate with him.

IX

How to proceed when ordered to quit the line.

When, the ships of the fleet being more in number than the enemy, the Admiral sees proper to order any particular ships to withdraw from the line, they are to be placed in a proper situation, in readiness to be employed occasionally as circumstances may thereafter require; to windward of the fleet, if then having the weather-gage of the enemy, or towards the van and ahead if the contrary; to relieve, or to go to the assistance of any disabled ship or otherwise act as by signal directed.

The captains of ships stationed next astern of those so withdrawn are directly to close to the van, and fill up the vacant spaces thereby made in the line.

When in presence of an enemy the Admiral or commander of any division of the fleet finds it necessary to change his station in the line, in order to oppose himself against the Admiral or commander in a similar part of the enemy's line, he will make the signal for that purpose; and the ships referred to on this occasion are to place themselves forthwith against the ships of the enemy, that would otherwise by such alteration remain unopposed.

X

When the ships are to keep in more open or closer order in line of battle—Particular ships to open to let the Admiral resume his station in the line.

* When the fleet is sailing in a line of battle a-head, or upon any other bearing, and the signal is made for the ships to keep in more open order, it will be generally meant that they should keep from one to [two][1] cables' length asunder, according as the mild or rougher state of the weather may require; also that they should close to the distance of half a cable, or at least a cable's length, in similar circumstances, when the signal for that purpose is put abroad.

But in both cases the distance pointed out to the Admiral's second ahead and astern, by the continuance of the flag abroad, as intimated in the Signal Book, is to be signified from them respectively to the ships succeeding them on either part, by signals.[2]

These signals are to be continued either way, onward, throughout the line if necessary.

Notice is to be taken, in the same manner, of any continued deviation from the limited distance, and to commence between the several commanders of private ships respectively, independent of the Admiral's previous example, when they observe their seconds ahead or astern to be at any time

[1] The 1781 edition has, 'from one to one-and-a-half cable's length.'

[2] In the 1781 edition these signals are given as '29, 30, 31, and 32, in page 39.' These are references to the Kempenfelt book in the Editor's possession. They are respectively signals for the second ahead or the second astern to open or to close,

separated from them further than the regulated distance kept by the ships next to the Admiral, or that which was last appointed.

When the Admiral, being before withdrawn from the line, means to resume his station therein he will make the signal for the particular ships between which he means to place himself to open to a greater distance, whether it be in his former station, or in any other part of the line better suited for his future purpose.

XI

When any number of ships is detached, not having a flag officer present—When a flag officer is ordered on the same service.

When any number of ships is occasionally detached from the fleet for the same purpose, they are, during their separation from the body of the fleet, to comply with all such signals as shall be made at any time whilst the signal flag appropriated for that occasion remains abroad.

But the signals made to all ships so appointed having the commander of a squadron or a division with them, will be under the flag descriptive of such commander's squadron or division, whose signals and instructions they are to obey.

XII

Not to fire upon the enemy before the signal is made, and that the ships are properly placed—Bearing down to the enemy when the signal is made to engage, the ship to haul up for that purpose without waiting for any more particular signal—Engaging the enemy's fleet upon the contrary tack.

Great care is to be taken at all times when coming to action not to fire upon the enemy either over or near any ships of the fleet liable to be injured thereby; nor, when in order of battle, until the proper signal is made, and that the ships are properly placed, in respect to situation and distance, although the signal may have been before put abroad.

And if, when the signal for battle is made, the ships are then steering down for the enemy in an oblique direction from each other, they are to haul to the wind, or to any other parallel with the enemy, to engage them as they arrive, in a proper situation and distance, without waiting for any more particular order or signal for that purpose; regard being only had by the several commanders in these circumstances to the motions of the ships preceding them on the tack whereunto the course more inclines, and upon and towards which the enemy is formed for action, that they may have convenient space for hauling up clear of each other.

[When our fleet is upon the contrary tack to that of the enemy, and standing towards them, and the Admiral makes the signal to engage, the van ship is then to lead close along their line, with a moderate sail and engage; the rest of the fleet doing the same, passing to windward or to leeward of the enemy, as the Admiral may direct.] [1]

XIII

[When weathering the enemy upon the contrary tack and signal is made to engage their van, the

[1] It should be noted that Howe's addition to the article contains no provision for breaking the line, as in the corresponding Article 35 added to Rodney's set of 1782 (*supra*, p. 302), although the Signal Book did provide a signal (see No. 235, *post*, p. 173). The only explanation seems to be that Howe disapproved of this form of the manœuvre, and, in common with all the older school, did not believe in trying to cut an unbroken line in line-ahead.

leading ship is then to bear down to the van ship of the enemy and engage, passing along their line to windward to the sternmost ship of their van squadron; then to haul off close to the wind, the rest of the fleet doing the same in succession.[1]]

XIV [2]

Not to separate in pursuit of a small number of the enemy until their main force is broken or disabled.

No ship is to separate in time of action from the body of the fleet, in pursuit of any small number of the enemy's ships beaten out of the line; nor until their main body be also broken or disabled. But the captains, who have disabled or forced their opponents out of the line, are to use their best endeavours to assist any ship of the fleet appearing to be much pressed, or the ships nearest to them, to hasten the defeat of the enemy, unless otherwise by signal or particular instruction directed.

XV

Ships making the signal in distress, in what manner to be assisted.

When any ship in the fleet is so much disabled as to be in the utmost danger and hazard of being taken by the enemy, or destroyed, and makes the signal expressive of such extremity; the captains of the nearest ships, most at liberty, with respect to the state of their opponents in the enemy's line, are

[1] For Nelson's improvement on this form of attack by applying Howe's manœuvre of breaking the line in all parts see his Memorandum of 1803, *Fighting Instructions*, *N.R.S.* xxix. p. 314.

[2] From here the numeration of the 1781 edition runs 12, 13, &c.

strictly enjoined to give all possible aid and protection to such disabled ship as they are best able. and the captain of any frigate (or fire-ship) happening at that time to be in a situation convenient for that purpose is equally required to use his utmost endeavour for the relief of such disabled ship, by joining in the attack of the ship of the enemy opposed to the disabled ship, if he sees opportunity to place his ship to advantage, by favouring the attempt of the fire-ship to lay the enemy on board; or by taking out any of the crew of the disabled ship, if practicable and necessary, as may be most expedient.

XVI

No ship to quit her station in battle but of extreme necessity without leave first obtained—Captains deficient in time of action are to be removed from their ships.

No captain, though much pressed by the enemy, is to quit his station in time of battle, if possible to be avoided, without permission first obtained from the commanding officer of his division, or other nearest flag-officer, for that purpose; but when compelled thereto by extreme necessity, before any adequate assistance is furnished, or that he is ordered out of the line on that account, the nearest ships, and those on each part of the disabled ship's station, are timely to occupy the vacant space occasioned by her absence before the enemy can take advantage thereof.

And if any captain shall be wanting in the due performance of his duty in time of battle, the commander of the division, or other flag-officer nearest to him, is immediately to remove such deficient captain from his post, and appoint another commander to take the charge and conduct of the ship on that occasion.

XVII

When the fleet is directed to disperse.

When from the advantage obtained by the enemy over the fleet, or from bad weather, or otherwise, the Admiral hath by signal signified his intention to leave the captains and other commanders at liberty to proceed at their discretion, they are then permitted to act as they see best under such circumstances for the good of the king's service and the preservation of their ships without regard to his example. But they are, nevertheless, to endeavour, at all times, to gain the appointed rendezvous in preference, if it can be done with safety.

XVIII

Ships to be kept at all times prepared for immediate action, and in what manner to proceed in respect to the aid and protection of fire-ships ordered on service.

The ships are to be kept at all times prepared in readiness for action. And in case of coming to an engagement with the enemy, their boats are to be kept manned and armed, and prepared with hand and fire chain grapnels, and other requisites, on the off-side from the enemy, for the purpose of assisting any ship of the fleet attempted by the fire-ships of the enemy; or for supporting the fire-ships of the fleet when they are to proceed on service.

The ships appointed to protect and cover these last, or which may be otherwise in a situation to countenance their operations, are to take on board their crews occasionally, and proceed before them down, as near as possible, to the ships of the enemy they are destined to attempt.

The captains of such ships are likewise to be particularly attentive to employ the boats they are provided with, as well to cover the retreat of the fire-ship's boat, as to prevent the endeavours to be expected from the boats of the enemy to intercept the fire-ship, or in any other manner to frustrate the execution of the proposed undertaking.

XIX

Flag-officers at liberty to move into other ships when their own are disabled.

If the ship of any flag-officer be disabled in battle, the flag-officer may embark on board any private ship that he sees fit for carrying on the service. But it is to be of his own squadron or division in preference when equally suitable for his purpose.

XX*

Flag-officers to repeat all signals—The purports thereof to be complied with by their respective divisions respectively.

[The flag-officers, or commanders of divisions, are on all occasions to repeat generally, as well as with reference to their respective divisions, the signals from the Admiral that they may thereby be more speedily communicated correspondent to his intentions.]

[And the purpose of all signals for the conduct of particular divisions is then only meant to be carried into execution when the signal has been repeated, or made, by the commanders of such particular divisions respectively; in which circumstances they are to be always regarded and complied with by the ships or divisions referred to in the same manner as if such signals had been made by the Admiral commanding-in-chief.]

XXI*

How to be carried into execution.

When ships have been detached to attack the enemy's rear, the headmost ship of such detachment, and the rest in succession, after having ranged up their line as far as is judged proper, is then to fall astern; and the ship that next follows, passing between her and the enemy, is to tack or wear as engaged to windward or leeward, and form in the rear of the detachment.

XXII*

In tacking in succession, how to proceed—To maintain the prescribed distance between the ships and a regular order throughout the line.

When the fleet is to tack in succession, the ship immediately following the one going in stays should observe to bear-up a little to give her room; and the moment for putting in stays is that when a ship discovers the weather quarter of her second ahead and which has just tacked before her.

On this and every other occasion, when the fleet is in order of battle, it should be the attention of each ship strictly to regulate her motions by those of the one preceding her; a due regard to such conduct being the only means of maintaining the prescribed distance between the ships and of preserving a regular order throughout the line.

XXIII

How fire-ships are to proceed when the fleet is ordered to prepare for battle—To place themselves abreast of the ships of the line and keep a good look-out on the Admiral—To keep ahead, and to windward, of the ship that is to escort them—And to keep their yards braced up—When the captains are to quit them.

As soon as the signal is made to prepare for battle, the fire-ships are to get their boarding grapnels fixed; and when in presence of an enemy, and that they perceive the fleet is likely to come to action, they are to prime, although the signal for that purpose should not have been made, being likewise to signify when they are ready to proceed on service by putting abroad the appointed signal.

They are to place themselves abreast of the ships of the line, and not in the openings between them, the better to be sheltered from the enemy's fire, keeping a watchful eye upon the Admiral, so as to be prepared to put themselves in motion the moment the signal is made, which they are to answer as soon as observed.

*A fire-ship, ordered to proceed on service, is to keep a little ahead and to windward of the ship that is to escort her, to be the more ready to bear down on the vessel she is to board, if possible, in the fore-shrouds. By proceeding in this manner she will not be in the way of preventing the ship appointed to escort her from firing upon the enemy, and will run less risk of being disabled herself; and the ship so appointed, and the two other nearest ships, are to assist her with their boats, manned and armed.

* She is to keep her yards braced up, that when she goes down to board and has approached

the ship she is to attempt, she may have nothing to do but to spring her luff.

Captains of fire-ships are not to quit them till they have grappled the enemy and have set fire to the train.

XXIV

The duty of frigates with respect to fire-ships.

Frigates have it in particular charge to frustrate the attempts of the enemy's fire-ships and to favour those of our own. When a fire-ship of the enemy therefore attempts to board a ship of the line, they are to endeavour to cut off the boats that attend her, and even to board her if necessary.

XXV

Boats to attempt to tow off a fire-ship.

The boats of a ship attempted by an enemy's fire-ship with those of her seconds ahead and astern are to use their utmost efforts to tow her off, the ships at the same time firing to sink her.

XXVI

In action all the ships in the fleet are to wear red ensigns.[1]

1 This was done by Hughes against Suffren in 1782, and by Howe on June 1, 1794, presumably to ensure a clear distinction from the white ensign of the French. For Rodney's practice, see *post*, p. 299 *n*. Jervis and Nelson subsequently adopted the white ensign as distinct from the French tricolor.

Instructions for the government of the ships of war during a fog.

N.B.—It is to be observed that the signal guns will be all fired to windward, or on the same side, during the continuance of the fog.

I

The Admiral will not act in consequence of any signal till after it has been fully repeated.

The Admiral, in execution of his intentions to tack, wear, &c., subsequent to the appointed signals made expressive of those purposes, will not begin to change his situation [correspondent therewith, until after the respective signals shall have been fully repeated, except upon any extraordinary emergency ; meaning thereby to allow a sufficient time for the ships near him to be prepared for and proceed as requisite on the same occasion].[1]

II

On a sudden shift of wind, or intended change of course in consequence thereof.

In case of a sudden shift of wind, or wind springing up after a calm, and not being then favourable for continuing the course as before steered, or that the Admiral thinks proper to steer a different course

[1] The 1781 edition has : 'Until ten minutes after the respective signals shall have been made and fully repeated.' The involved phraseology of the substituted passage is strongly redolent of Howe's style.

on such occasions, he will make the signals for lying-to or the signals for sailing by the wind on either tack that will best correspond with his further intentions. And if the wind by such alteration becomes favourable for sailing large on the course he intends to steer, he will soon after signify, by the proper signal, the number of points he means to steer from the wind, on either tack, accordingly.

III

If before sailing by the wind to keep to the wind till further signal.

If the fleet was sailing by the wind, the ships are to alter course as the wind alters, and always keep to the wind on the same tack (if no consequent danger is to be thence apprehended) until some signal for altering the course by tacking, or bearing-up is made.

IV*

A frigate from each squadron to keep ahead.

When a fog comes on, the ships which may be ahead of the fleet are to close in nearer for the better hearing of signals; but if no ships should be then ahead, the senior captain of the frigates in each squadron is to proceed ahead, and keep at a moderate distance from the fleet during its continuance.

V*

What sail will be carried.

In a fog the Admiral will continue the same course; and if the wind should come ahead, he will keep close to it with a full sail, not going more than three knots per hour. If the wind slackens he will set all his sails, except his studding-sails.

VI*

Signals to be repeated by flag-ships only.

To prevent the firing of a great number of guns, which may occasion confusion and mistake, the Admiral's signals are to be repeated by the flag-officers only in succession and according to seniority. An interval of five minutes is to be observed between each repetition.[1]

VII

Under what sail the fleet will bring-to.

When the fleet brings-to, if under the top-sails, the main top-sail will be to the mast; if under the courses, it will be with the mainsail and the fore-yard braced up.

VIII

When to anchor.

When in the Channel, or on a coast, the signal is made for anchoring, the ships are to anchor immediately after the signal has been repeated by the several Admirals.

IX*

Boats sent from ships in thick or foggy weather are to be provided with a compass and a speaking-trumpet.

'Order of the commander-in-chief.'[2]

[1] In the 1781 edition the interval between each repetition is put at 'two minutes'; the following paragraph also is added:

'In quick firing an interval of four seconds, and in slow firing an interval of twelve seconds is to be observed between each gun. Between quick and slow firing there is to be an interval of half-a-minute.'

[2] In the Admiralty copy there follows here, 'Sailing and Fighting Instructions by Night,' and the volume ends with 'Directions for performing some necessary evolutions,' comprising twenty-five articles with diagrams. In the 1781 edition there were twenty-four, the twenty-fourth being added in MS. just before the issue

BATTLE SIGNALS.

[Channel Fleet Signal Book, 1782.[1] Extracts]

Signals directing the manner of attack.
Pa. 19, *Art.* 21.

218

To attack the enemy's rear in succession by ranging up with and firing upon the sternmost of their ships; then to tack or veer, as being to the windward, or to the leeward of the enemy, and form again in the rear,* [*Page's transcript adds:* unless any particular squadron or division is specified to form upon, by hoisting the divisional flag or pennant after the signal has been answered].

219

* To discontinue the evolution directed by the preceding signal.

220

To engage the enemy to windward.

221

To engage the enemy to leeward.

clause, which is dated February 11, 1781. Article XV is 'to form order of battle when sailing in the form of an obtuse angle,' *i.e.* the order of retreat. Article XVI is as follows: 'In this order the fleet is arranged upon the two lines by the wind [cf. the French *les deux lignes du plus près*], forming an obtuse angle of 135°, the ship of the commander-in-chief making the point of the angle to windward.' This is Bigot de Morogues' *Ordre de Retraite.* See his *Tactique Navale*, part i. chap. xii. § 101.

[1] Original in Admiralty Library. Admiral Page's transcript is in the United Service Institution.

222[1]

For the van to double on the enemy's van.

223[1]

For the van to double on the enemy's rear.

224[1]

For the rear to double on the enemy's rear.

225

For particular ships to attack any number of the enemy's ships of war seeming to be kept separate from the body of their fleet.[2]

226

To attack the enemy's convoy of transports or trade.

227

Particular ships to attack the enemy's frigates and fire-ships.

228

To engage the enemy's centre.

229

To engage the enemy's van.

230

To engage the enemy's rear.

231

For the van ship of the line to steer for and engage the enemy's van ship.

[1] These three articles are marked in pencil 'additional.'

[2] See *supra*, p. 132 *n*.

232

When inferior in number to the enemy, and to prevent being doubled upon in the van or rear, for the van squadron to engage the headmost ship of the enemy's line, the rear their sternmost, and the centre that of the enemy whose surplus ships will then be left out in the vacant spaces between our squadrons.[1]

233

* In working to gain the wind of the enemy, for the headmost and sternmost ships to signify when they can weather them, by sig. 8, pa. 56, or if to windward of the enemy, and on the contrary tack, for the sternmost ship to signify when she is far enough astern of their rear to be able to lead down out of their line of fire.

234

When coming up astern, and to windward of the enemy, to engage by inverting the line ; that is for the ship leading the van to engage the sternmost ship of the enemy's line, the next ship to pass under cover of her, and engage the second ship of the enemy's rear, and the rest to proceed on in succession, until the ship that was the sternmost in the line shall have reached the van ship of the enemy.

235

When fetching up with the enemy to leeward, and on the contrary tack, to break through their line and endeavour to cut off part of their van or rear.[2]

[1] See *supra*, p. 77. This form of attack was first used by De Ruyter at the battle of the Texel in 1673; see note to *Lord Dartmouth's Drawings*, *N.R.S.* xxxiv. It was approved by Hoste, and Morogues, but not by Bourdé de Villehuet. (See *Manœuvrier*, Part IV. ch. v. art. 5)

[2] See *supra*, p. 160, *n.*

236

For the ships to steer for, independent of each other, and engage respectively the ships opposed to them in the enemy's line.

237

To board the enemy as arriving up with them.

238

To pursue and attack a ship of the enemy that is disabled.

239

To reinforce the van.

240

To reinforce the centre.

241

To reinforce the rear.

242

To go to the assistance of a ship or ships engaged.

243

* For the van ship to put upon the same tack as the enemy, and engage the rear to windward, the rest to do the same as they arrive in his wake.

244

* For the van ship to put upon the same tack as the enemy, and engage his rear to leeward, the rest of the ships to do the same as they arrive in his wake.

245

* For the van ship to steer so as to pass close to the enemy's sternmost ship.

246

* For the van ship to steer so as to pass close ahead of the enemy's leading ship.

247

* For the van ship to keep the wind no nearer than is requisite, to prevent the enemy's passing to windward of our fleet, and to be at the same time within engaging distance, in case the fleet should come to action on contrary tacks.

248

(*Blank.*)

249

For *fire-ships to prime.*

N.B.—Fire-ships are to signify their being primed and ready to proceed on service by hoisting a red ensign at the main topmast head.

250

Pa. *Art.* 18.

For fire-ships to proceed on service under cover of the ships of war, whose signals are made herewith.

251

Action.

To engage the enemy.

252

To come to a closer engagement.

253

For particular ships to come to a closer engagement.

254

To discontinue the engagement.

Explanatory Observations[1]

I

The signals will generally be made without guns when it may be done with the same effect, unless it happens that two or more guns are necessary to constitute a part of the signal, or that it does not appear to have been timely observed; and all signal guns will be fired on the same side; to windward only, in a fog.

II

The signals are to be complied with by all the ships of the fleet, generally; unless when accompanied with one or more particular signals, distinguishing the ships, squadron, or division referred to, and to which it is then meant only to relate. Nevertheless when the column of signification points out any limitation of the signal, those instances are to be excepted from this construction.

III

When the commander-in-chief tacks, veers, lays-to, makes or shortens sail, &c., without making the signal expressive of such intention, the ships of the fleet are to do the same or not as may best conduce to the purpose of preserving or regaining their appointed stations respectively.

[1] These also occur at the beginning of the Kempenfelt book. There, however, they begin with four articles, giving minute directions for hoisting signals so as to prevent mistakes. Only the fourth is retained here, and that is numbered VII.

IV

It is to be observed, that when the signal has been made for engaging the enemy, for forming in order of battle, or for any other purpose on which occasions it may have been usual to have kept the signal flag abroad; such signal is to be deemed equally in force until annulled or contradicted by some subsequent signal for a different purpose, although the flag significant thereof has been taken in, as generally intended, immediately after the signal has been observed duly to have been complied with.[1]

V

All the signals contained in the General Printed Signal Book[2] which are likely to be needful being provided for in this signal book, the signals as appointed in the General Printed Signal Book will only be made when in company with other ships not of the fleet under the Admiral's command, and unprovided with these particular signals.

VI

When a general signal is meant to respect particular ships only, and when the distance or position

[1] The Kempenfelt book here inserts the following article: 'Several signals will be found to have the same signification. They are so appointed that the signal may be shown from the part of the ship most commodious for view from the ship wherewith it is addressed.' In the final Signal Book this article became unnecessary because it was a numerary code, and the numbers could be hoisted anywhere.

[2] This of course refers to the two Books of Instructions. The various sections of the *General Sailing and Fighting Instructions* were headed 'Signals by day,' 'Signals by night,' &c. The Additional Instructions were entitled *Signals and Instructions in addition to, &c.* Hence the two together were currently called 'The Signal Book.' No official printed Signal Book existed at this time apart from the Instructions.

of the Admiral's ship is unfavourable for the view of the particular distinguishing pennants; to prevent mistakes, and to denote the limitation of such general signal to the ships referred to, a blue pennant with yellow fly will be hoisted where most easily seen.

VII

[The signal-flags expressed to be shown at the topmast head and shrouds are nevertheless to be hoisted on the flag staves at the top-gallant-mast head and at the top-gallant-shrouds, when those masts are aloft; when they are down, the flags are to be hoisted at the topmast heads and shrouds, and at the heads and shrouds of the lower masts, if the topmasts should be shot and carried away.] [1]

[1] MS. addition.

THE REGULAR ADDITIONAL INSTRUCTIONS 1778

AS ESTABLISHED AT THE OPENING OF THE WAR OF AMERICAN INDEPENDENCE, TOGETHER WITH RODNEY'S FIRST ALTERATIONS, 1779–80

Introductory

Of this long lost set of Instructions, one of the most important in the history of tactics, six copies are now known to exist. Two are among the 'Rodney Papers' recently presented to the Public Record Office by Mr. Harley Rodney, the Admiral's descendant. One of these, which was never issued and is specially bound, appears to have been Rodney's own copy. The other is also marked 'Admiral' but has on the title-page the name of Captain Walter Young, his flag-captain. Three others are in the *Graves Collection.* Of these one was never issued and has the text intact without any MS. alterations. Another, which has Lieutenant Graves's name on the title, is marked as issued from the Princess Royal (Byron's flagship) at Gros Islet Bay, St. Lucia, on March 3, 1779. It is of peculiar interest, from the criticisms which Graves scrawled on it in pencil as he read it through. They are given as notes to the text below, as well as the MS. alterations it contains. Another was issued 'to Captain Graves, of H.M. Sloop Savage,' by Rodney from H.M. Ship, Sandwich, also at Gros Islet Bay, on March 29, 1780—that is, two days after he had arrived out to take over the command from Parker. This also has a number of MS. alterations, which differ slightly from those in Byron's copy. The sixth copy has recently been acquired by the British Museum.[1] It was issued by Rodney to Captain John Douglas, of the Terrible, on December 18, 1779, while the fleet was waiting in Causand Bay for a wind to sail for the West Indies. Two entries in Rodney's Journal explain the usual procedure in regard to delivering these instructions. Shortly after sailing from St. Helen's, and being well out in the Channel, he records under December 15, 'Made signal for all lieutenants and delivered the signal-books, line of battle, private signals, rendezvous, &c., to the respective ships,'[2] and again on the 20th in Causand Bay, 'At 9 A.M. made signal for recalling signal-books in order to rectify an omission in them and to prevent any ill consequences that might otherwise arise therefrom.'[3]

Each consists of a complete printed set of additional instructions entitled 'Signals and Instructions in Addition to the General Printed Sailing and Fighting Instructions.' They contain all the usual sections: 'Sailing Instructions and Signals by Day,' 44 articles, including chasing and cruiser instructions; 'Sailing Instructions and Signals by Night,' 10 articles; 'Sailing Instructions and Signals in a Fog,' 8 articles; 'Fighting Instructions and Signals by Day,' 38 articles; 'Fighting Instructions and

1 Until lately it was in the possession of Mr. George Pritchard, of Mount Pleasant, Poole. Attention was first called to its existence by Mr. William Grey, a descendant of Lord Rodney's, in his memoir of the Admiral (*Naval Heroes*, Murray, 1901), and while it was still believed to be unique Mr. Pritchard most generously placed it at the disposal of the Society for publication.

2 Officers' calls were made under the old Standing General Instructions, which were never altered.

3 In the *Rodney Papers*, Public Record Office.

Signals by Night,' consisting of 2 articles only. It also contained a tabular abstract of signals with references to the various instructions to enable their meaning to be ascertained rapidly. This arrangement is nowhere found in the earlier sets, and there can be little doubt that the printed text, as it stood before Byron's and Rodney's MS. alterations, was a new form approved by the Admiralty at the beginning of the war, though, as we shall see, a different set was in use on the North American station as early as April 1779. In any case the signals they contain exactly correspond to those made by Keppel in his action with Orvilliers off Ushant on July 7, 1778, and in the *Graves Collection* is a MS. signal book which refers to them as the 'Sailing and Fighting Instructions 1778.'[1] It is possible they are even earlier and that they were originally issued to the fleet mobilised in 1770 on the occasion of our dispute with Spain over the Falkland Islands, when Hawke was still all-powerful at the Admiralty. Whether this was so or not there is no doubt the printed part represents the last word of Hawke's school and the final outcome of the Seven Years' War.

It will be remembered that the last set of the Anson-Hawke period that had come down to us were those used in 1759, printed in the former volume, and known as 'Boscawen's set.'[2] On these the present set are a great advance and everywhere display the influence of Hawke.

[1] It is inscribed on the cover 'Thomas Graves, Magnificent.' The Magnificent was in Shuldham's squadron, Dec. 1778.

[2] This is the first 'Additional' set known with separate Fighting Instructions. Till this time Admirals were issuing 'The Sailing and Fighting Instructions, with the Printed Additional Signals and further Additional Signals.' (See *post*, Appendix A.) In 1760 Boscawen issued 'Additional Printed Sailing and Fighting Instructions' (*post*, p. 185).

To begin with, just as Russell or his predecessor Torrington recast the ill-arranged 'General Fighting Instructions' of the Duke of York into logical form, so the older 'Additional Instructions' have been treated here. Up till 1760 at least they had been a set of articles strung together haphazard as they had been officially adopted in turn from the 'Squadronal Orders' of various Admirals. Now all this is changed for logical sequence. They began like the old permanent 'General Instructions' with a series of articles for forming the line in various ways. After two articles for forming line ahead and abreast we have seven articles dealing with lines of bearing, or as they are here called for the first time 'Bow and Quarter Lines.' This formation, which is believed to have been first practised by Lord Anson in 1747, was established by Hawke as a 'squadronal order' in the Mediterranean in 1756. For some reason they do not appear in the Boscawen set, but they were certainly issued by Hawke (together with his modification of the normal form of attack by each ship steering for her opposite number) to his fleet before Brest on May 28, 1759.[1] There is therefore much reason to believe that additional instructions later than the very imperfect set of Boscawen were issued before the end of the war, or at least when Hawke recovered his influence and became First Lord, and that they were the model for those which Rodney used. Still it must be noted that the continual changes that were made in the 'Bow and Quarter Line' instructions would tend to show that

[1] See Hawke to Hood, *Bridport Papers*, *Add. MSS.* 35193, f. 82. For Hawke's additions see *N.R.S.* xxix. *Fighting Instructions*, pp. 216-8. Possibly the new formation had been elaborated by Anson when he was at sea in 1758. Writing to Lord Hardwicke on July 22 he says he has been exercising the Channel Fleet in tactics 'which are in a great part new.'—*Add. MSS.* 35376, and cf. *England in the Seven Years' War*, i. 274.

even during the war of American Independence it was imperfectly understood.

The next prominent change which appears in the present set is the adoption of Hawke's modification of the normal attack just mentioned, which also was omitted from the Boscawen set.

The third modification of the Boscawen set is even more interesting and more characteristic of Hawke. The form of attack most closely associated with his name is the headlong swoop upon an unwilling or inferior enemy. The germ of the idea is seen in the 9th and 10th articles of Boscawen's set, which provide for bringing a flying enemy to action by attack in general chase—the leading five or seven ships to form line as they chase and commence action with the rear of the enemy, the rest to support as they come up. On this plan the victories of Hawke and Boscawen in 1759 were won. But for the author of the present Instructions even this was not direct or drastic enough. Besides the above two articles we find one of a still more vehement character. Article 18 provides for an attack by chasing without previously forming line at all. By Article 18 the leading ship is to engage the rearmost of the enemy, and the rest as they come up are to form line in reverse order ahead of her, alongside the enemy's line. Both forms of attack it will be seen provide for a rapid and stunning concentration on the enemy's rear, with a possibility of the latecomers containing his van if it tacks to come down to the rescue.

With these significant indications it is difficult not to believe that the Instructions we are considering, if not the actual work of Hawke, were at least founded on a lost set which was issued towards the end of or shortly after the Seven Years' War. Indeed we know from Boscawen's *Journal* for

1760 in the Public Record Office that from April to June he was issuing from his headquarters in Quiberon Bay to captains as they joined him a set of 'General and Additional Printed Sailing and Fighting Instructions and Private Signals (or Day and Night Signals)' which may well have been a modification of those he used the previous year.

The other point of importance about these copies of the Instructions of 1778 is the MS. alterations and additions made by Rodney and others. How far Rodney's changes were made before the action of April 17, 1780, we cannot always tell with any certainty. With regard, however, to his additional Articles 43–58 there is reason to believe they must have been made after the battle. Articles 57 and 58, of those he added to the Sailing Instructions (p. 213) regarding signals not understood and an annulling flag, seem clearly intended to prevent such a misunderstanding of signals as spoiled Rodney's attack on that occasion. But as explained below (p. 213 note) there is evidence that these two articles were issued before any of the others, since they were originally numbered 1 and 2. Had No. 58 at least existed at the time the action was fought, Carkett and the rest of the captains could hardly have pleaded that Rodney's signal 'to attack the rear' did not continue in force. It would clearly have remained operative till expressly annulled.

The general significance of all these new articles in the history of tactics, as well as the extent to which they are borrowed from Kempenfelt, has already been dealt with in the General Introduction. It remains to consider the new light they throw on the action of April 17, 1780, and the question of who was to blame for Captain Carkett's having spoiled the attack by misunderstanding Rodney's intention and the signal that conveyed it to the fleet.

The signal in question runs, by Article 33, 'When the commander-in-chief means to make an attack upon the enemy's rear, he will hoist a flag half blue and yellow, &c.' To this he might have added some such words as, 'Whereupon the whole fleet shall attack the rear of the enemy, notwithstanding the 19th Article of the printed Fighting Instructions'—that is, the old cast-iron article which enjoined van to van and rear to rear. For this there was good precedent, but who could tell it was necessary? Yet so it was; for what happened was this. After making the new signal, 'the commander-in-chief means to make an attack on the enemy's rear,' Rodney signalled to close the line to one cable, and in this formation attempted to deliver his attack, which De Guichen cleverly avoided. Rodney thereupon hauled his wind into line ahead again at two cables' length, and continued to manœuvre till he had got his whole line opposite the enemy's rear and rear centre. That was his moment, and, after he had called on ships astern to close to the centre, the 'Union' went up at the main top-gallant-mast head. Under Article XXI it meant, for a squadron sailing in a line of battle ahead to windward of the enemy, as this one was:—

> The commander would have the course altered in order to lead down to them. . . . Whereupon every ship in the squadron is to steer for the ship of the enemy, which from the disposition of the two squadrons it must be her lot to engage, notwithstanding the signal for the line ahead will be kept flying; making or shortening sail in such proportion as to preserve the distance assigned by the signal for the line.

Now, by Article XII, the distance had to be kept from the commander-in-chief in the centre.

It would therefore seem plain enough that the whole fleet was to bear down upon the enemy, each ship engaging the adversary to which her correct distance from the centre brought her opposite. Yet Carkett, who, as captain of the first ship in the line, was leading the fleet and had to commence the movement, chose to hold on and make for the enemy's van. In spite of signals the whole British van followed him, and the triumphant concentration against De Guichen's rear, which Rodney had so brilliantly brought about, was ruined. Carkett afterwards pleaded that he considered the signal to attack the rear had been annulled by the subsequent signals. But even if Rodney had never signified his intention to attack the rear at all, still it was the duty of the van not to break away from the centre, but, keeping its distance, to attack whatever it found in front of it.

Clearly this was what Rodney expected and we can now see that the signals he made did actually express the idea that was in his mind. It is equally clear that they did not convey it to the fleet. And here it seems difficult to say he did not fall short of perfect leadership. A leader in real touch with his captains would have understood that tactical preoccupations—traditional in the Service—cannot be eradicated simply by new signals. He would have doubted whether his captains would regard the time-honoured attack, van to van, as overridden by the rule to take distance from the centre. On the whole, seeing that tactical training then hardly existed, it is impossible to lay severe blame upon Carkett. And if any fault lay with Rodney it was one of character. The defect was his persistence in ploughing his lonely furrow. He could not see that unless he worked with his fellows his ideas must be sterile. He could not see that for practical result he must carry the mind of his fleet with him, as Kempenfelt saw he must carry the mind of the Service. So far and no further it was possible to advance, and Rodney holding always aloof from his captains and brother flag-officers had to learn the lesson in the bitterness of failure.[1]

The method pursued in printing these Instructions is to give them as they originally stood. The MS. alterations are indicated in footnotes and Rodney's additions are given at the end as they stand in the copies he issued. The italics occur in the original, but what they signify apart from the rest of the text is nowhere explained. Usually, as will be seen, it is the signals that are in italics, but sometimes it is other parts of the articles, and sometimes even whole articles. The subject-matter of the latter leaves little doubt that they were recent additions.

The most important of them are as follows: In the Sailing Instructions, Article 6, a new order of sailing with the ships on either bow-and-quarter line from the Admiral; and Articles 14, 20–3, 25–7, 30–2, which are designed to give the Admiral increased control over ships chasing or scouting. In the Fighting Instructions, Articles 20 and parts of 1 and 8, which all relate to performing evolutions; Article 26, enjoining superfluous ships to rake the enemy, which appears in addition to the old article as to superfluous ships falling out of the line; and Article 28, which directs a boat to be kept manned and armed in action on the off-side from the enemy.

The alteration in the numbering of the articles noted in the text occurs only in the British Museum copy, but it is of some interest. Instead of keeping to the old arrangement of a separate numeration of each section of the articles, the whole have been renumbered consecutively, making 73

[1] Cf. a fuller review of the case by Sir John K. Laughton in *N.R.S.* xxxii. (*Barham Papers*, i.) *Introduction.*

articles in all. The new arrangement would look as though it had been made with a view to working a numerary system of signals on Kempenfelt's plan. Probably it was made after Rodney had left the fleet. At any rate his own copy makes it certain he did not adopt the new numeration.

From the discovery of the *Graves Collection* we now know that this form of the Instructions continued in force on the Leeward Island station till Rodney came out again in 1782. The collection contains a copy issued by Sir Samuel Hood to Captain Thomas Graves, of the Bedford (Affleck's flagship), on January 12, 1782. Hood was then at Barbadoes, and two days later, having heard De Grasse had gone to St. Kitts with a large body of troops, he sailed for his memorable campaign against him. On January 24 Hood was at Nevis, intending to deliver a bold attack on his superior enemy as he lay at anchor in Basseterre Road. Accordingly on January 23 we find the following instruction and signals added :—

1. In attacking the enemy's ships to leeward at anchor, the ship to exchange her fire with the first and second ship of the enemy, stop at the third, and having given her fire to the third ship, to veer short round and fall into the rear, each ship following in succession.

2. To discontinue the same.

3. To anchor in line ahead with springs.

We thus know exactly how Hood intended to make his attack had De Grasse awaited it. But he avoided it at the cost of losing his anchorage to Hood, and the book contains a neat water-colour sketch of De Grasse's ineffectual attempt to dislodge his tricky opponent.

The last addition of this time is dated February 14, and is a signal for getting under way from Basseterre Road in reverse order.

SIGNALS AND INSTRUCTIONS

In Addition to the General Printed Sailing and Fighting Instructions

[**Folio, printed. Rodney Papers, P.R.O.**]

Sailing Instructions and Signals by Day

I

For all officers, &c., to repair on board their respective ships.

When the commander-in-chief shall hoist *a blue flag pierced with white at the main top-gallant-mast head and fire a gun*, all officers and other persons belonging to the squadron are to repair on board their respective ships, and no boat is to be suffered to go on shore afterwards, on any account whatsoever, without his leave.

II

For the state and condition of the ships.

When the commander-in-chief would have an account of the state and condition of all the ships in the squadron sent on board him, he will make the signal for all lieutenants and hoist *a flag half blue and half white at the mizen-peak: if of particular ships only*, the signal for a lieutenant from those ships will be the same flag at the mizen-peak. [At all times when the signal is made for lieutenants they are to come provided with an order book to take down in writing the orders for which the signal was made, and sign their names, and put down the name of the ship they belong to. [1]]

III

The masters of the ships-of-war.

When the commander-in-chief would have the masters of all the ships-of-war in the squadron to come on board him, he will put abroad *an English ensign in the main-shrouds* (instead of the mizen-shrouds, as appointed by the second article of the General Printed Instructions for calling officers on board the Admiral) *and fire a gun*; if only the masters of particular ships, he will display an ensign in the main-shrouds and make such ships signals.

IV

For the pilots of the squadron.

When the commander-in-chief would have all the pilots of the squadron come on board him, he will hoist *a flag chequered blue and yellow at the mizen topmast head*: if only the pilots of particular ships, *the same flag with a red pennant over it*, and the signal for speaking with the captains of such ships; and a lieutenant is to come on board with each pilot.

V

To unmoor.

Instead of making the signals appointed by the second and third articles of the General Printed Instructions for unmooring and weighing in the day-time: The commander-in-chief when he would have the squadron unmoor *will loose the top-sails*, and fire a gun; and when he would have them

[1] The passage in brackets is a MS. addition of Rodney's.

weigh *he will fire a gun and haul home the top-sail sheets.*

To weigh.

[If the commander-in-chief would have any particular ship or ships to weigh and come close to him, he will put out the captains' signal and a Spanish jack at the mizen top-gallant-mast head. But if to cut or slip, a red pennant under it.[1]]

VI

Order of sailing.

In case no other form of sailing shall be prescribed (which convoys, &c., may sometimes render necessary) every ship is to keep in such station on the quarter of the commander-in-chief as may enable her to form the line-of-battle with the greatest despatch, viz. the seconds nearest to him, the leaders on the wings, and the intermediate ships agreeable to the written order: and if the signal should be made to tack, the ships that shall happen to be to windward at that time are to remain so after they shall be about on the other tack.

[To form the order of sailing a white flag pierced red at the mizen peak.[1]]

VII

When a ship is out of her station.

If the commander-in-chief should observe any particular ship to be out of her station, he will make the signal for speaking with her captain, and hoist *a flag half red and half white at the main top-gallant-mast head* [under his own flag [1]].

[1] MS. addition.

VIII

To hog ship.

When the commander-in-chief purposes lying-to to hog, he will hoist an *English jack at the ensign-staff*, which is to be repeated by all the ships that want to do the same, and to be kept flying till they have finished.

IX

To set up the rigging.

When the commander-in-chief purposes lying-to to set up the rigging, he will hoist an *English jack at the ensign-staff with a common pennant over it*, which is to be repeated by all the ships that want to do the same, and to be kept flying till they have finished. *And if at any time a particular ship should have occasion to set up her rigging, it is to be made known to the commander-in-chief by the signal aforesaid, and in case he would have her lie by for that purpose though he himself stand on, he will answer with the same signal: whereupon she is to use all possible despatch in completing the same, and then to make all the sail she can to rejoin him.*

X

To prevent Divine Service being interrupted.

In order that the performance of Divine Service may meet with as little interruption as possible, the ships are to hoist a common pennant[1] *at the mizen peak before they begin the same, and to keep it flying till they have finished.*

[1] The 'common pennant' was one with a St. George's Cross and a Dutch fly. It is still the signal for 'church.' It seems to have dated from the old Anglo-Dutch alliance, and may have been regarded as appropriate for Divine Service as being the symbol of the Protestant coalition.

XI

To make more sail.

When the commander-in-chief would have any particular ship make more sail, he will put abroad the pennant for speaking with her captain, and hoist a flag half blue and half white at the main top-gallant-mast head [under his own flag. If to shorten sail a red pennant under[1]].

XII

To come within hail of the commander-in-chief.

When the commander-in-chief would have any ship come under his stern within hail, he will make the signal for speaking with her captain and hoist *a flag chequered red and blue at the mizen-peak.*[2]

XIII

To speak with a strange ship passing near the squadron.

If at any time a strange ship should pass near the squadron, and the commander-in-chief would have a particular ship speak with her, he will make such ship's signal and hoist *a white flag with a red cross at the ensign-staff.*[3]

XIV

Upon seeing a strange sail.

Any ship in the squadron discovering a strange sail is to make known the same by hoisting

[1] MS. addition. In some copies this article is not in italics.

[2] For this signal Rodney substituted 'a flag quartered red and white and at the ensign-staff nearest mizen-peak.' Cf. p. 217 *n.*

[3] Rodney substituted 'the chasing flag for the particular quarter of the compass at the ensign-staff.'

If in the	N.E. a French jack N.W. a Dutch jack	At the mizen-peak.
If in the	S.E. a French jack S.W. a Dutch jack	At the ensign-staff.

Which, *upon being answered from the commander-in-chief by a French jack at the ensign-staff*, is to be lowered and answered again as many times as there are ships discovered. [If the ship suspects them to be enemies she is to make it known by hoisting a Dutch jack at the main top-gallant-mast head, and firing two guns one after another.[1]]

XV

To chase.

And if the commander-in-chief would have any particular ships chase[2] he will make the signals accordingly as directed in the General Printed Instructions [with this addition : if to chase east a flag quartered red and blue in the mizen-shrouds, if to the west a flag quartered red and white at ditto. If to the north a white flag with a red cross at ditto. If to the south a flag half red half white, mizen-shrouds. To call in ships from chase, the flags for the different quarters at the fore top-gallant-mast head[3]]. But if he would have the whole squadron chase, he will hoist a *yellow pennant at the mizen-peak and the chasing flag (expressive of the quarter) in the mizen-shrouds.*

XVI

To tack in chasing upon a wind.

If in chasing upon a wind the commander-in-chief would have a particular ship tack, he will make

[1] MS. addition. [2] 'Chased' in original.
[3] The passage in brackets is inserted in MS.

the signal for speaking with her captain, and if she be ahead of him hoist *a Dutch flag at the fore top-gallant-mast head; but if astern, the same flag at the mizen-topmast head.*

XVII

Ships in chase to alter their course.

If at any time the commander-in-chief would have the ships in chase alter their course, he will make such ships signals and hoist *a flag striped blue and white at the main top-gallant-mast head*, which when they answer by hoisting a common pennant at the same place, *will be lowered and hoisted as many times as he would have their course altered points to windward; if to leeward, a gun will be fired; and if chasing right before the wind, without a gun is to be understood to starboard, and with a gun to port.* In case no particular ship's signals shall be made when the flag aforementioned shall be hoisted, it is intended that all the ships in chase shall alter their course agreeable to the signal.

XVIII

To bring down the chase to the commander-in-chief.

When the commander-in-chief would have the ship or ships that chase bring down the chase to him, he will hoist *a blue flag pierced with white halfway up the fore top-gallant-mast.*

XIX

To keep between the squadron and ships in chase, to repeat signals.

When any ships shall be in chase, and the commander-in-chief would have another ship between them and the squadron to repeat signals and guide them back, he will make such ships signal for chasing on that quarter and hoist *a flag chequered red and white*[1] *at* the mizen topmast head, and if there should afterwards be occasion for a second or more to lie within the former he will make the same signal for those ships, successively, which he would have perform that service; who are to be particularly careful to repeat all signals the chasing ships shall make.

XX

Ships stationed between those in chase and the squadron to make known to them the signal to give over chase.

When the commander-in-chief shall see occasion to recall ships from chase, and make the proper signal accordingly, it is to be made known by the ships stationed between them and the squadron, by hoisting a Dutch ensign at the fore top-gallant-mast head, and firing one gun or more, as may be necessary.

XXI

When ships come up with the chase and the signal is made for recalling them.

If when the commander-in-chief shall make the signal to recall ships from chase, their captains should judge they come up with the chase so as to be able to speak with it, they are to hoist a red English ensign at the mizen-peak,[2] and fire a gun; *but if the signal should be repeated by firing one or two guns, they are then, notwithstanding, to leave off chase, and return to the squadron.*

[1] Rodney substituted 'half red, half blue.' See note p. 217.
[2] Rodney substituted 'Main top-gallant-mast head.'

XXII

On discovering the chase to be an enemy.

Any ship discovering her chase to be an enemy is to give notice of the same by hoisting a Dutch ensign at the mizen-peak and firing two guns; *and if she believes she shall be able to get up with it, without losing company with the squadron, she shall then hoist* the Dutch ensign at the mizen topmast head, and fire two guns.

XXIII

If the ships in chase discover a force superior to themselves—The ships between them and the commander-in-chief to go to their assistance.

If any ship in chase discover a force superior to themselves, they are to hoist a white flag at the main top-gallant-mast head, and fire one or more guns, as may be necessary, *which the commander-in-chief will answer by hoisting a blue flag pierced with white at the fore top-gallant-mast head, and the ships between him and them are thereupon to make what sail they can to their assistance*, having first repeated the signal, which will be answered from the commander-in-chief as before.

XXIV

When more ships than one shall be in chase, and the commander-in-chief would recall some of them.

When at any time more ships than one shall happen to be in chase on the same quarter of the compass, and the commander-in-chief would call some or all of them into the squadron, he will make the signal by hoisting *the chasing flag for that quarter at the fore top-gallant-mast head;* whereupon the ship that shall be the furthest from the chase shall immediately return, and if the signal should be kept out after she makes sail towards the squadron, the next to her in chase is to do the same, and so are all the rest in regular succession; but if the signal should be hauled down before all the ships leave off chase, then those that are nearest the chase are to keep on, till it shall be thought proper to make the signal again for calling them to the squadron.

XXV

Upon discovering a number of the enemy's ships under convoy.

If one or more of the squadron in chase shall discover a number of the enemy's ships under convoy (that the commander-in-chief may be cognisant with their strength in order to despatch after their trade) the ships that are nearest the enemy are carefully to observe what number of line of battle ships the enemy consists of, and to make the same known by hoisting a Spanish flag at the main top-gallant-mast head, which, upon being answered from the commander-in-chief by the same signal, is to be lowered and hoisted as many times as they imagine there are ships of the line, and he will do the same after them that they may know whether he judge of the signal properly; and if he should not, they are to repeat it in ten minutes after. And if by that signal it should appear that the enemy are much inferior to his Majesty's squadron, the ships are to repeat the signal for some or all of them to chase.

XXVI

If in pursuit of more of the enemy's ships than one, and the headmost ship should bring to any of them, and pass on without securing them.

If at any time the squadron should be in pursuit of more of the enemy's ships than one, and the head-

most ship should bring to any of them without boarding and securing them (in order to her better pursuing the rest) she is to acquaint the squadron by hoisting a white flag at the mizen topmast head and firing guns till the next ship shall answer by firing one gun, *and that ship is afterwards to make the same signal in case she passes on.*

XXVII

To go right ahead of the commander-in-chief, to look out at such a distance as plainly to discover signals—To keep the same distance right astern upon seeing strange ships whilst on the look-out —To chase until[1] recalled—ships at a great distance from the commander-in-chief to make known in the same manner the number of ships they discover.

When the commander-in-chief would have a particular ship go right ahead of him to look out, and keep at such a distance as plainly to discern signals, he will hoist *a flag half red and half white at the mizen topmast head*, and make the signal for speaking with her captain ; and if to keep the same distance right astern, *a blue pennant will be hoisted at the same time over the flag. Whereupon such ship is to make sail accordingly, and upon seeing any strange ships to hoist*

If in the	N.E. an English jack N.W. the broadest pennant she has	At the fore top-gallant-mast head.
If in the	S.E. an English jack S.W. the broadest pennant she has	At the fore top-gallant-mast head.

which, *being answered from the commander-in-chief by a blue pennant at the fore top-gallant-mast head,*

[1] Original has 'under.'

is to be lowered and hoisted again as many times as there are ships discovered, *and after the commander-in-chief has again answered by lowering and hoisting the blue pennant the same number of times she is immediately to chase unless the signal should be made for recalling her. The ships of the squadron are also to make known in the same manner the number of strange ships they discover at any other time when they happen to be at such a distance that they judge the commander-in-chief will not be able to distinguish the signals appointed by the fourteenth article for that purpose, and to chase unless recalled.*

XXVIII

To keep two points on the starboard bow of the commander-in-chief to look out at such a distance as clearly to discern signals—To keep two points on his larboard bow at the like distance—To look out at the same distance to windward, or to leeward, or on any quarter of the compass.

When the commander-in-chief would have a particular ship go ahead to look out and keep two points on his starboard bow at such a distance as clearly to discern signals, he will make the signal for speaking with her captain and hoist *a flag striped yellow and white at the mizen topmast head:* but if to keep two points on his larboard bow at the like distance *the same flag will be hoisted in the mizen-shrouds*, and if he would have any ship look out to windward or to leeward, or on any quarter of the compass, at the like distance, *her signal will be made for chasing that way and an English jack hoisted at the same time in the mizen top-mast shrouds.*

XXIX

To spread in a line abreast at half a mile's [1] distance—To spread in a line ahead at the same distance—To keep two miles asunder.

When at any time in cruising the commander-in-chief would have the squadron spread in a line abreast, each ship keeping at the distance of half a mile [1] from the other, he will hoist a flag striped red and white, at the mizen-peak, and fire a gun; and if he would have them spread in a line ahead, and keep at the like distance, he will hoist *a flag chequered* [2] *red and white at the same place and fire a gun:* Whereupon every ship is to make sail into the station assigned to her by the order of battle (observing the method prescribed by the first and second articles of the following Fighting Instructions); *and if a yellow pennant should be hoisted under the above-mentioned flags*, the ships are then to keep at the distance of a [3] mile asunder.

XXX

The signal for seeing a sail to be kept flying till taken notice of by the next ships and to be repeated by them—An equal number of ships to those discovered to chase.

Any ship (whilst formed as mentioned in the foregoing article) making the signal for seeing a sail is to keep it flying till the ships next her shall take notice of it, and repeat it, then she who first made the signal is to lower and hoist it again as many times as there are ships discovered, which is to be repeated by every ship between her and the commander-in-chief till he shall

[1] Rodney substituted 'one mile.'

[2] Rodney struck out 'chequered' and substituted '*blue*, red, and white.'

[3] Rodney substituted 'two.'

take notice of it by hoisting a blue flag pierced with white at the fore top-gallant-mast head; *after which an equal number of the nearest ships to those discovered are to chase and endeavour to speak with them, and if they gain any intelligence relating to the enemy, to acquaint the commander-in-chief with it immediately.*

XXXI

To close the commander-in-chief every evening—Exception.

Every evening the ships are to close the commander-in-chief, so as to run no hazard of separation; and if he would have them close him sooner, he will make the signal for calling in all cruisers, which is to be repeated (with or without a gun, as may be necessary) by the ships at a distance, in case those without them do not immediately take notice of it. But if any ship should be in chase, an equal number of the headmost and nearest to the chase are to pursue provided they discover it to be an enemy and have a likelihood of coming up with it, and all the rest are to close the commander-in-chief as before directed.

XXXII[1]

Ships chasing out of sight—To make themselves known upon discovering the squadron again.

If any ships of the squadron at any time chase out of sight (which they are to be very careful not to do unless they have reason to believe the chase is an enemy and have a good prospect of getting up with it), they are to set the commander-in-chief just before they lose sight of him, and after leaving off chase to look out for him, at or near the place where he then

[1] This article is cancelled in Graves's copy, but restored by the following note: 'This 32nd Article to continue in force.'

was, before they proceed to the appointed rendezvous, and to make themselves known at joining again by hoisting [blank], *which the commander-in-chief will answer by hoisting* [blank].[1]

XXXIII

If any transports or merchant ships under convoy, for the ships of war to draw from among them—For the convoy to lie by—For the convoy to make sail.

If the squadron should have a number of transports or merchant ships under convoy, and the commander-in-chief should think it necessary to form the line of battle, either to attack or oppose a squadron of the enemy's ships, or to exercise his own, and would have the ships of war draw from among the convoy that they may be the readier to form or pursue, he will hoist *a flag chequered red and blue*[2] *at the mizen topmast head:* and if, after that, he would have the convoy lie by, although himself with the ships of war make sail, he will hoist *an English ensign at the fore top-gallant-mast head*, but if he would have the convoy continue their course and make sail, although himself with the ships of war alter the position of sailing or lie by, he will hoist an *English ensign at the mizen topmast head:* and if, when he shall make any of these signals, he would have any of the ships of war stay by the convoy, he will make such ships signals and hoist *a flag striped blue and white at the mizen topmast head;* the senior officer of which ships is, for the better direction of the convoy, immediately to display his jack, ensign and pennant, and to keep them flying till he shall observe all the convoy take notice of him.

[1] The private recognition signals are not filled in.

[2] Rodney substitutes 'half blue, half yellow.' See note, p. 217.

XXXIV

To go and close any straggling ships of the convoy.

If at any time the commander-in-chief would have a particular ship go and close any straggling ships of the convoy, he will make her signal for chasing on that quarter, and hoist a yellow pennant at the mizen top-gallant mast head.[1]

XXXV

To stay by any disabled ships or prizes.

If in time of cruising there should be any disabled ships or prizes in company, and, upon making sail, the commander-in-chief would have a particular ship stay by them, he will make such ship's signal and hoist *a yellow flag in the mizen-shrouds* [over the signal for the quarter of the compass the disabled ship is in],[2] and if he should afterwards find it necessary for her to leave them and follow him, he will hoist *a Dutch flag at the mizen-peak.*

XXXVI

To take any disabled king's ship, attendant vessel, transport, tender, or prize in tow.

If at any time the commander-in-chief would have a particular ship make sail upon either quarter of the compass to take any attendant vessel, transport, tender, or prize in tow, he will make such ship's signal and hoist *the chasing flag for that quarter at the ensign staff.*[3]

[1] Rodney altered the place where to 'mizen-shrouds under the flag.' It is so also in Byron's copy.

[2] Inserted in MS. It should read 'ships are in.'

[3] Rodney substitutes 'a flag quartered white, red, and blue at the mizen-peak.'

XXXVII

To keep ahead in the night and carry a light.

When the commander-in-chief would have a particular ship go right ahead of him in the night and keep out a mile's distance, carrying a light at her ensign staff, he will at sunset make that ship's signal and hoist *a blue flag pierced with white at the mizen topmast head.*

XXXVIII

To make the land.

When the commander-in-chief would have any ship of the squadron make sail to windward, or to leeward, or upon either quarter of the compass, to make the land, he will *make her signal to chase that way, and at the same time hoist the standard at the fore top-gallant-mast head.*[1] Whereupon such ship is to make the best of her way accordingly, and, when she shall have made the land, to return to the squadron with her ensign spread at her fore or main top-gallant-mast head, which is to be kept flying till answered from the commander-in-chief by a *blue pennant at the fore top-gallant-mast head.*

XXXIX

On sounding and finding ground.

If, when sailing or lying by, any particular ship should sound and find ground, she is to hoist an English jack at her main top-gallant-mast head, which being answered from the commander-in-chief by hoisting his ensign, is to be lowered and hoisted once for every ten fathoms, and in case of odd fathoms to be hoisted only half-staff up.[2]

[1] Rodney substitutes 'hoist the signal for the quarter of the compass in the main top-gallant shrouds.'

[2] In Byron's and some other copies this article is in italics.

XL

Upon discovery of danger.

The twelfth article of the Day Signals appointed by the General Printed Instructions, to be made upon discovery of danger, requiring too much time in the execution, the following signal is to be made in its stead, viz.:

Any ship discovering danger is to tack or bear-up from it, hoist her ensign half-staff up and fire a gun; but if she should strike and stick fast, she is to continue firing guns till all the ships in the squadron have observed her, by endeavouring to avoid the danger.

XLI

Going into port.

When going into port the ships are to follow [*the commander-in-chief, according to seniority, in order to prevent any accident by running foul of each other*[1]]. But if the commander-in-chief should observe any ships can fetch in, though he cannot, and would have them do so, he will make their signals and hoist *a blue flag with a red cross at the mizen topmast head, and fire a gun.*

XLII

To prepare to anchor.

When the commander-in-chief would have the squadron prepare to anchor, he will *fire a gun and hoist a flag striped red, white, and blue at the mizen-peak* (instead of hoisting it at the ensign staff as

[1] For the words in brackets Rodney substitutes 'each other agreeable to the form of sailing, and anchor in that form if the road will admit of it.'

appointed by the twentieth article of the Day Signals in the General Printed Instructions).

[But if he would have them anchor with the stern anchor he will hoist a red pennant under the above flag at the mizen-peak.[1]]

XLIII[2]

For the boats of the squadron to tow a particular ship.

If at any time there should be occasion for the assistance of the boats of the squadron to tow any particular ship, the commander-in-chief will make the signal appointed by the General Printed Instructions for such boats manned and armed, and *a blue flag pierced with white at the ensign-staff*, whereupon they are without repairing on board him to proceed immediately to the assistance of the ship whose signal will be shown at the same time.

XLIV[2]

For the boats of the squadron (when chasing) to leave off chasing.

If at any time the boats of the squadron should be in chase, and the commander-in-chief would have them leave off chase and return to their respective ships, he will hoist *a flag half red and half white at the fore top-gallant-mast head and fire a gun.*

XLV[3]

If at any time the commander-in-chief would have a particular ship make more sail, he will put

[1] MS. addition, probably by Rodney. It is not in Byron's copy.

[2] This and the next three articles were cancelled by Rodney. He substituted for them those on pp. 209–10. Article XLIV is the last of Byron's set.

[3] This Rodney cancelled and substituted at the end of the General Fighting Instructions the similar Article 11 of the Additional Sailing Instructions.

out the signal for speaking with the captain, and hoist a flag striped blue and white at the main top-gallant-mast head, under the flag.

XLVI[1]

When sailing upon a wind, those ships who are to windward are at all times in tacking to take care to preserve that station; but should a shift of wind take place in the day or night, which may occasion their being to leeward-most, they are to continue in that situation until a favourable opportunity offer for regaining their station.

XLVII[2]

If the commander-in-chief at any time would have all the rendezvouses returned he will hoist a white flag pierced with red, under his flag at the main top-gallant-mast head.

If for all the Signal Books the same flag with a blue pennant under it.

RODNEYS ADDITIONAL ARTICLES.[3]

43

If at any time there should be occasion for the assistance of the boats of the squadron to tow any particular ship, the commander-in-chief will make the signal appointed by the General Printed Instructions for such boats mann'd and arm'd and

[1] Cancelled by Rodney. Article 48 below took its place.

[2] Cancelled by Rodney. Article 50 below took its place.

[3] Articles 43 to 56 are what Rodney substituted for those he cancelled, or else are new ones. In Captain Young's copy and that in the British Museum they are in MS. In Rodney's own copy a roughly printed leaf of smaller paper has been fastened in.

hoist a blue flag pierced with white at the ensign staff, when they are without referring on board him to proceed immediately to the ship whose signal will be shown at the same time.

44

When the Admiral would have all the pinnaces and barges in the fleet come on board him mann'd and arm'd, he will hoist a red pennant on the flag staff at the fore top-gallant-mast head and fire one gun; and if he would have them chase any ship, vessel or boat in view without repairing on board him, he will hoist the chasing flag for the quarter of the compass the ship or vessel is in, in the mizen-shrouds and fire 2 guns; each boat to have their grapnels, fire grapnels and ropes in them.[1]

45

When the Admiral would have all the long-boats, launches, and flat boats in the fleet come on board him mann'd and arm'd, he will hoist a red pennant on the flag staff at the mizen topmast head, and fire a gun; and if he would have them chase any ship, vessel, or boat in view, he will hoist the chasing flag as aforesaid and fire two guns; such long boat, launch and flat boat, to have their grapnels, fire grapnels, &c. as aforesaid.

46

When the Admiral would have all the boats in the fleet come on board him mann'd and arm'd,

[1] '*Grapnel*, or *grapling*, a sort of small anchor for boats, having a ring at one end and four palmed claws at the other. *Fire-grapnel*, resembling the former, but its flukes are furnished with strong fish-hook barbs on their points.'—Smyth, *Sailors' Word Book*.

he will hoist a red pennant on the flag staff at the fore top-gallant-mast head, and another at the mizen topmast head, and fire one gun; and if he would have them chase he will hoist the chasing flags as aforesaid, and fire 2 guns; the boats to be supplied with grapnels, &c. &c. as aforesaid.

47

If at any time the boats of the squadron should be in chase, and the commander-in-chief would have them leave off chase and return to their respective ships, he will hoist a flag half red half white at the fore top-gallant-mast head, and the pennants at the mast heads likewise, that at the fore under the recalling flag, and fire 2 guns.

48

When sailing upon a wind those ships who are to windward are at all times in tacking to take care and preserve that station; but should a shift of wind take place in the day or night which may occasion their being the leewardmost they are to continue in that situation until a favourable opportunity offers for regaining their station.

49

When the commander-in-chief would have all the ships sheathed with copper chase on any point or quarter of the compass he will put out a flag for the point or quarter and hoist a red flag pierced with white at the main top-gallant-mast head under his own flag and fire a gun.

50

If the commander-in-chief would at any time have all the rendezvous returned, he will hoist a white flag pierced with red under his own at the main top-gallant-mast head. If for all the signal books, the same flag and a blue pennant under it.

51

All ships are to answer the Admiral's signals by a Dutch flag reversed at the main top-gallant-mast head.[1]

52

All signals made by private ships (exclusive of those for seeing strange sails) will be answered by the Admiral's putting out a flag half white half blue at the fore or mizen top-mast-head.

53

When the commander-in-chief intends to make any general signal, previous to its being made he will hoist a preparative one which will be a white flag with a blue cross from corner to corner at the fore top-gallant-mast head with or without a gun.[2]

54 [3]

The ship upon the starboard tack is always to keep to the wind. The ship upon the larboard tack is to bear up both day and night, to prevent accidents; and on tacking in the night the ships astern and to leeward are to tack first and bring to till their Admirals become their leaders.

55

When a flag quartered red and white is hoisted at the mizen topmast head it is to signify that

[1] This is the first appearance known of a general 'answering' flag.

[2] The device of a preparative flag has just been introduced by Kempenfelt in the Channel Fleet.

[3] This and the next article were added later than the rest. In Graves's copy Art. 54 appears as a separate memo; Art. 55 does not occur at all in any but Rodney's new copies.

the purpose of the signal made therewith has to be carried into execution after the close of the day, when attention is to be had for the night signal to that effect.

56

If at any time the Admiral should make the signal for the line of battle ahead, and would have the Admiral who commands in the second post lead with his division he will hoist a flag half white half red at the fore top-gallant-mast head, and if he would have the Admiral who commands in the third post and his division do the same, he will hoist a flag half white half red at the mizen topmast head, when they are to form accordingly.

57 [1]

Should the ships of the squadron at any time not clearly discern or understand the meaning of any signal made from the ship my flag is in they are to make the same known to me by hoisting the Dutch jack at the main top-gallant-mast head, which being done the signal that was made will be repeated.

58 [1]

When I would annul any signal that I have made to any ship or ships of the squadron I will hoist a flag half blue half yellow at the main top-gallant-mast head under my own flag.

[1] These two articles must have been the first Rodney issued. They were originally issued by themselves on a printed slip, and numbered 1 and 2. This probably accounts for their being missing in the British Museum copy. In Young's copy the slip has been stuck in as above, and the articles renumbered. In the admiral's copy they are printed with the rest of the new articles. Kempenfelt introduced similar signals in the Channel.

Fighting Instructions and Signals by Day.

I. 48[1]

To draw into a line of battle one ship ahead of another, and keep two cables' length asunder—To keep only a cable's length asunder—When in a line ahead the course to be taken from the leading ship.

When the signal shall be made for the squadron to draw into a line of battle, one ship ahead of another, by hoisting *an Union flag at the mizen-peak and firing a gun*, the ships are to make all the sail they can into their respective stations, and keep at the distance of two cables' length asunder, [those which shall happen to be to windward, at the time of making the signal, forming the van of the line, and those to leeward the rear];[2] but if the commander-in-chief would have them keep only a cable's length asunder, he will hoist *a blue flag with a red cross under the Union flag at the mizen-peak and fire a gun:* and it is to be observed that *whenever the squadron shall be in a line ahead, the course is to be taken from the leading ship, the others in succession being always to be guided therein by their seconds ahead.*[3]

[1] The Arabic figures are the numeration of the British Museum copy, referred to in the Introduction (see *supra*, p. 188). It was certainly not established by Rodney, for it will be seen that the Fighting Instructions were renumbered before he had added his last nine articles to the Sailing Instructions.

[2] The bracketed passage was erased by Byron and restored by Rodney in MS.

[3] The passage in italics was cancelled by Byron and written in again by Rodney.

II. 49

To draw into a line abreast.

When the commander-in-chief would have the squadron draw into a line of battle, one ship abreast of another, and keep at the distances directed in the foregoing article, [the ships that shall happen to be on the starboard quarter at the time of making the signal, forming the starboard wing of the line, and those on the larboard quarter the larboard wing]:[1] he will hoist *a blue pennant under the flags therein mentioned at the mizen peak and fire a gun.*

III.[2]

When on a wind, to form a line on each other's bow and quarter.

If the commander-in-chief would have the squadron, when on a wind, draw into a line on each other's bow and quarter, and keep at the distance directed in the first article, [those ships which shall happen to be to leeward, at the time of making the signal, forming the van of the line, and those to windward the rear, and all the ships from the van to the rear bearing from each other on the point of the compass whereon they will be on the other tack (always taking it from the centre)]: he will hoist *a red pennant under the flags mentioned in the said article at the mizen-peak and fire a gun.* And if he should afterwards tack in order to bring the squadron into a line ahead, the ship that becomes the headmost is to continue leading.

[1] Cancelled by Byron and restored by Rodney.

[2] Cancelled by Rodney, and therefore not renumbered. Graves notes on Byron's copy: 'How is this to be executed? And are the ships to be on the lee or weather quarters of their leaders?' The bracket passage was erased by Byron.

IV.

To draw into a line of battle and bear on particular points of the compass from each other.

When the commander-in-chief would have the squadron draw into a line of battle and regulate themselves by bearing on some particular point of the compass from each other, without having any regard to their being abreast or ahead of each other, but always steering the same course as the commander-in-chief: he will *make the signal expressed against the points of the compass in the following table:* and if he would have them keep at the distance of two cables' length asunder, fire one gun; but if he would have them keep only a cable's length asunder, *he will fire two guns.*[1]

If to bear from each other	Signals
North and South . . .	A flag striped blue and white at the mizen-peak.
N. by E. and S. by W. . .	A red pennant under the said flag.
NNE. and SSW. . . .	A white pennant under the said flag.
NE. by N. and SW. by S. .	A blue pennant under the said flag.
NE. and SW. . . .	A blue flag pierced with white at the mizen-peak.
NE. by E. and SW. by W. .	A red pennant under the said flag.
ENE. and WSW. . . .	A white pennant under the said flag.
E. by N. and W. by S. . .	A blue pennant under the said flag.
East and West . . .	A red flag with a white cross on the mizen-peak.
E. by S. and W. by N. . .	A red pennant under the said flag.
ESE. and WNW. . . .	A white pennant under the said flag.
SE. by E. and NW. by W. .	A blue pennant under the said flag.
SE. and NW. . . .	A yellow flag at the mizen-peak.
SE. by S. and NW. by N. .	A red pennant under the said flag.
SSE. and NNW. . . .	A white pennant under the said flag.
S. by E. and N. by W. . .	A blue pennant under the said flag.

[1] Graves notes: 'The bow and quarter line and the line ahead should also be formed on the different points of the compass.'

V. 51

When in a line of battle, for all the ships to alter their course and preserve the same bearings and distances from each other as before—To starboard—To port—The number of points.

When sailing in a line of battle (either ahead, abreast, or in any other position) and the commander-in-chief would have all the ships alter their course at one and the same time, still preserving their bearings and distance from each other, as before always taking it from the centre, if to starboard, he will hoist *a blue flag with a red cross at the main top-gallant-mast head and fire* a *gun;* if to port, a flag *chequered red and white* [1] at the same place and fire a gun; and after the signal has been repeated, he will fire one gun for every point of the compass he would have the course altered: whereupon every ship in the line is immediately to alter her course accordingly, without waiting for the number of guns being repeated.

VI. 52

When in a line of battle ahead, for the leading ship to alter her course, and the rest of the ships to get into her wake, preserving the line ahead.

When sailing in a line of battle ahead, and the commander-in-chief would have the ship that leads alter her course and the rest of the ships get into her wake, still preserving the line ahead: he will hoist a *white pennant under the flags mentioned in the foregoing article at the main top-gallant-mast*

[1] Rodney substituted a flag 'half blue, half red.' His flag-captain regarded all chequered flags as objectionable, being difficult to distinguish at a distance.—See *N.R.S.* xxxii. (*Barham Papers*, i.), 69, 72. Kempenfelt at once adopted the suggestion. *Ibid.* 337.

head and fire a gun; and after the signal has been repeated, he will *fire one gun for every point of the compass he would have the course altered;* whereupon the leading ship is immediately to alter her course accordingly, without waiting for the number of guns being repeated, and the rest of the ships in the line are to get into her wake as fast as possible.

VII. 53

If the signal should be made for the headmost ship to tack whilst in a line of battle the ship that then leads is to continue leading on the other tack.

If the signal should be made for the headmost ship to tack first, whilst in a line of battle, the ship that then leads is to continue leading on the other tack after she shall be about, and the rest of the ships in the line are to follow her in the same order they did on the former tack.

VIII. 54

If the signal should be made for the whole squadron to tack together, whilst in a line ahead, for the ships to preserve the same bearings from each other as before.

If when sailing in a line of battle ahead, the commander-in-chief should make *the signal for the whole squadron to tack together and at the same time hoist a red pennant under the signal for the line ahead*, every ship when about is carefully to preserve the same bearing as before the signal was made. *For instance if they were drawn up in a line N.E. and S.W. all their main-masts when about are to bear on those points of the compass from each other, taking it from the centre, and making or shortening sail so as to preserve their stations with the distance prescribed by the signal; but in case the wind should shift, their main-masts are to bear from each other on the points of the compass whereon they will lie on the other tack (always allowing twelve points) so that whenever they put about again they may be in a direct line ahead.*

IX.[1]

When in a line ahead, to form a bow and quarter line the headmost ship making first and continuing to lead.

When the squadron shall be in a line of battle ahead, and the commander-in-chief would have them form a line on each other's bow and quarter, the headmost ship tacking first and continuing to lead, and the rest of the ships forming in succession as they are about, he will make the signal for the headmost ships to tack first, and at the same time noist a red pennant under the signal for the line ahead.

X.[2]

When in a line ahead, to wear and form a bow and quarter line on the other tack.

When the squadron shall be in a line of battle ahead, and the commander-in-chief would have them wear and form a bow and quarter line on the other tack, he will *hoist a flag chequered blue and yellow at the main top-gallant-mast head. The leading ship is then to wear first,* and steer four points from the course whereon she will lie on the other

[1] Cancelled by Rodney. Graves notes in Byron's copy: 'How is this instruction to be executed? or does he mean that the ships should be on the *lee* or *weather* quarter of their leaders?'

[2] Cancelled by Rodney. Graves notes: 'Here they form on the weather quarter of their leaders and the manner of the execution directed.'

tack, until all the ships have wore in succession, and formed a direct line after her; and *whenever the chequered flag shall be hauled down, and a red pennant hoisted under the signal for the line ahead* (*at which time a gun will be fired*) the ships are to come to the wind together and the bow and quarter line will be formed.

XI.[1]

To form the line of battle ahead by the second ship's passing the headmost, and so on till the sternmost becomes the leader.

When the squadron shall be in a bow and quarter line (or in any other position that will admit of it) and the commander-in-chief would have the line ahead formed by the second ship passing the headmost, and so on in regular succession till the sternmost becomes the leader, and the headmost brings up the rear, he will *hoist a yellow pennant under the signal for the line ahead and fire a gun;* and as soon as the line is formed the pennant shall be taken in.

XII. 55

When in the line of battle, to keep the same distance asunder those ships do that are next the commander-in-chief—For the ships ahead or on the starboard beam, to close to the centre.

In sailing in a line of battle, every ship is to keep at the same distance those ships do that are next the commander-in-chief, always taking it from the centre: and if at any time the com-

[1] Cancelled by Rodney. Graves notes: 'It appears by all these signals that the ships are to form on the weather quarter of their leaders, which is very proper if an enemy is coming up with them to leeward, but if the enemy is coming up with them to windward they should be formed on the lee quarter of their leader.'

mander-in-chief shall think the ship next ahead of him, or next on his starboard beam, is at too great a distance, he will make the same known to her by putting abroad *a common pennant at the jib-boom-end*, which will be kept flying till she is closed to the proper distance; *and if that ship shall find the next ahead of her, or the next on her starboard beam, is at a greater distance from her than she is from the ship of the commander-in-chief*, she is to make the same signal *and keep it flying till the other shall be closed to the proper distance; and so on to the van, or the outermost ship of the starboard wing of the line.*[1]

XIII. 56

For the ships astern or on the larboard beam to close to the centre.

But when the commander-in-chief shall think the ship next astern of him, or next on his larboard beam, is at too great a distance, he will make it known to her by putting abroad *a common pennant at the cross-jack*[2] *yard arm*, which will be kept flying till she is closed to the proposed distance; *and if that ship shall find the next astern of her, or the next on her larboard beam, is at a greater distance from her than she is from the ship of the commander-in-chief, she is to make the same signal, and keep it flying till the other shall be closed to the proper distance, and so on to the rear, or the outermost ship of the larboard wing of the line.*

1 Graves notes: 'N.B.—All bow and quarter lines should be formed on the weather or lee quarter as the enemy is approaching to leeward or to windward, by which means the ship ahead will always enfilade the ship that engages her second astern, which is a great advantage of the bow and quarter line, and makes it stronger than any other.'

2 Rodney substituted 'mizen top-sail.'

XIV. 57

For any particular ship to close her second.

And if at any time the captain of any particular ship in the line shall think the ship without him at a greater distance than the ships which are next the centre, he is to make the same known to her by the signal appointed for that purpose in either of the two aforegoing articles; *whereupon such ship is immediately to close to the proper distance.*

XV. 58

If the squadron should be in two divisions, for them to form in separate lines of battle.

If the squadron should happen to be in two divisions, and the commander-in-chief would have them form themselves into separate lines of battle, one ship ahead of another at the distance of a cable's length asunder, and each division to be abreast of the other, when formed, at the distance of two cables' length asunder, he will hoist a flag chequered blue and yellow at the mizen peak and fire a gun.

XVI. 59

Bringing to in line of battle.

If the commander-in-chief should make the signal appointed by the fifteenth article of the General Printed Fighting Instructions for bringing to in a line of battle, the ships are to bring to with the main top-sail to the mast, instead of bracing their headsails to the mast, as is there prescribed.

XVII. 60

To change stations in the line.

If at any time the commander-in-chief shall think it necessary to alter the disposition of the ships in the line of battle, and would have any two of them change stations with each other, he will make the signal for speaking with the captains of such ships, and hoist *a flag, chequered*[1] *red and blue at the main top-gallant-mast head.*

XVIII. 61

The whole squadron being in chase, to engage the enemy in succession as they may happen to get up.

If the commander-in-chief should chase with the whole squadron, and would have those ships that are nearest attack the enemy, the headmost opposing their sternmost, the next passing on under cover of her fire, and engaging the second from the enemy's rear, and so on in succession as they may happen to get up, without respect to seniority or the prescribed order of battle, he will hoist *a Dutch flag at the main top-gallant-mast head and fire a gun*, keeping at the same time the signal for chase flying. [If to engage to windward the above flag as specified. If to leeward a blue pennant under the same flag. When each ship as they get up are to engage their opponents and on no pretence to quit them until they are so disabled that they cannot get away, or submit.[2]]

XIX. 62

The whole squadron being in chase for somc of the headmost ships to draw into a line of battle ahead—And the rest to strengthen that line as they get up.

If at any time when the whole squadron shall be in chase the commander-in-chief would have a

[1] Rodney substituted 'quartered.'

[2] The passage in brackets is a MS. addition by Rodney. The new signal was successfully used for his attack on Langara, off

certain number of ships that are nearest the enemy draw into a line of battle ahead, in order to engage the ships in their rear, endeavouring at the same time to get up with the van, he will hoist *a red flag with a white cross at the main top-gallant-mast head and fire :*

Three guns	if he	five ships	draw into a line ahead of each other.
One gun	would have	seven ships	

Whereupon those ships are immediately to form the line without any regard to seniority or the general form delivered, but according to their distances from the enemy, viz. the headmost and nearest ship to the enemy is to lead, and the sternmost to bring up the rear, that no time may be lost in the pursuit, and the rest of the ships are to form and strengthen that line as they get up, without paying any respect to the prescribed order of battle.

XX. 63

When turning to windward on the enemy, the headmost and sternmost ships to make known when they can weather them.

If the squadron should be turning to windward on the enemy in a line of battle, the headmost ship is to make known when she can weather them by hoisting a common pennant at the mizen topmast head, *which is to be repeated by every ship between her and the commander-in-chief until he make the same signal, and if he should think proper to stand on till the sternmost ship can weather them, she is to make the same known by hoisting* a common pennant at the fore top-gallant-mast head, which is to be repeated as before. *The sternmost ship is likewise to do so,*

Cape St. Vincent, January 16, 1780. See Young to Middleton, *N.R.S.* xxxii. (*Barham Papers*, i.), 65.

whenever the squadron shall be to windward of the enemy, and her commander shall think himself far enough astern of their rear to lead down out of their line of fire.

XXI. 64

When in a line of battle ahead to windward of the enemy to lead down to them, and every ship to steer for her opponent.

If the squadron should be sailing in a line of battle ahead to windward of the enemy, and the commander-in-chief would have the course altered in order to lead down to them, he will *hoist an Union flag at the main top-gallant-mast head and fire a gun.* Whereupon every ship in the squadron is to steer for the ship of the enemy, which, from the disposition of the two squadrons, it must be her lot to engage notwithstanding the signal for the line ahead will be kept flying; making or shortening sail in such proportion as to preserve the distance assigned by the signal for the line, in order that the whole squadron may, as near as possible, come to action at the same time.

XXII. 65

The headmost ship to attack the enemy's rear, and so on in succession till the sternmost become the leader and opposed to the enemy's van.

If the squadron should be in a bow and quarter line [1] to windward of the enemy (or in any other position that will admit of it) and the commander-in-chief would have the headmost ship lead down out of their line of fire, and attack their rear, he will hoist *a Dutch flag at the main top-gallant-mast head and fire a gun.* The second from the leader is then to pass on under the

[1] Rodney struck out 'in a bow and quarter line.'

cover of her fire, and attack the second ship from the enemy's rear, and so on until the sternmost ship becomes the leader, and opposed to the enemy's van [If to engage to windward the above flag as mentioned. If to leeward a blue pennant under it. *N.B.*—You are referred to the latter part of the 18th article respecting your opponents when up with them.[1]]

XXIII. 66

To come to a closer engagement.

If at any time whilst engaged with the enemy, the commander-in-chief shall judge it necessary to come to a closer engagement, he will *hoist a flag half blue and half white under the signal for engaging at the fore top-gallant-mast head and fire a gun*,[2] whereupon every ship is to engage the enemy as close as possible.

XXIV. 67

Upon meeting with an enemy of inferior force, for some of the smallest ships to quit the Line.

In case of meeting with an enemy inferior to His Majesty's squadron, if the commander-in-chief would have any of the smaller ships quit the line, that those of the greatest force may be opposed to the enemy, he will put abroad the signal for speaking with the captains of such ships as he would have quit the line, and hoist a flag striped yellow and white at the main top-gallant-mast head: whereupon the next ships are immediately to close up the line and those that have quitted it are to hold themselves in readiness to assist any ship that may be disabled, or hard pressed, or to take her station, if she should be obliged to go out of the line, in

[1] The passage in brackets is a MS. addition by Rodney.
[2] Rodney struck out 'and fire a gun.'

which case the strongest ship that is withdrawn from the line is strictly enjoined to supply her place, and fill up the vacancy. [If he engages to windward of the enemy the ships are to draw out of the line and lay-to to windward, if to leeward of the enemy they are to draw out ahead or to the rear.[1]]

XXV. 68

Upon meeting with an enemy with merchant ships under convoy, for some of the ships to fall upon the convoy.

And in case of meeting with a squadron of the enemy's ships of war, with merchant ships under their convoy; if the commander-in-chief (though the signal for the line of battle should be out) would have any of the frigates that are out of the line, or any of the ships in the line, fall upon the convoy, whilst the others are engaged, he will hoist a *flag striped yellow and white at the main top-gallant-mast head, with a white pennant under it*, and make the signal for speaking with the captains of such ships as he would have perform that service.

XXVI[2]

Upon meeting with an enemy of inferior force, and ships of the squadron as shall be over and above the number of them are to quit the line (though no signal be made for that purpose) and rake the enemy's van and rear.

But in case of meeting with a squadron of the enemy's ships inferior in number to his Majesty's

[1] The passage in brackets is a MS. addition by Rodney.

[2] This newly established article was cancelled by Rodney, in view presumably of his intention to concentrate by closing the line. See *supra*, p. 13. Howe restored it; see *post*, p. 323. For Art. 24 of the General Instructions, see *post*, p. 276.

squadron, and the commander-in-chief should not make either of the signals mentioned in the two afore-going articles, those ships over and above the number of the enemy that happen to fall in either ahead of their van or astern of their rear are hereby directed, whilst the rest of the ships are engaged, to quit the line (notwithstanding the first part of the twenty-fourth article of the General Printed Fighting Instructions to the contrary) and endeavour to distress the enemy by raking the ships of their van and rear, having a regard at the same time to the latter part of the twenty-fourth article of these instructions, in case any of his Majesty's ships should be disabled or obliged to go out of the line.

XXVII. 69

For the fire-ships to prime.

When the commander-in-chief would have the fire-ships prime, he will hoist a *pennant chequered blue and yellow*[1] *at the main top-gallant-mast head and fire a gun;* but if the squadron should at any time be in chase of the enemy's fleet, the fire-ships are to prime as fast as possible, whether the signal be made or not.

XXVIII. 70

The ships to be held in constant readiness for action, and in case of engaging, a boat to be kept manned and armed, &c., on the off-side of the enemy.

Every ship in the squadron is to be held in constant readiness for action; and, in case of coming to an engagement, a boat is to be kept manned and armed with hand and fire-chain grapnels, &c., on the off-side, to be ready to assist as well any ship

[1] Rodney substituted a 'flag half yellow, half blue.'

that may be attempted by the fire-ships of the enemy, as our own fire-ships, should they be ordered on service.[1]

RODNEY'S ADDITIONAL ARTICLES[2]

XXIX. [71]

If the commander-in-chief would have all the three-decked and heavy ships draw out of their places in the line of battle, and form in the van of the fleet, he will hoist a white flag pierced with red at the fore top-gallant-mast head; but if he would have those ships draw out of the line and form in the rear of the fleet, he will put out the above flag and a red pennant under it; in both the above cases the ships who preceded and followed those ships, who have quitted the line to form in the van or rear, are immediately to close the line and fill up their places.

72

If the commander-in-chief would have the ships to close in order in line of battle or otherwise, he will hoist a flag half red half blue at the main top-gallant-mast head under his own flag, but if he would have the ships to open in line of battle or otherwise to give room for manœuvring he will hoist a red pennant under the above flag.

[1] Here in Byron's copy of 1779 Graves has this remarkable note: 'Is it not wonderful that there are no signals for breaking the enemy's line which may be advantageously done by the fleet to windward bearing down on the rear of the enemy, or when on different tacks to cut off the rear of the enemy to leeward.'

[2] All in MS. In Graves's copy they were numbered 29–33, but he has altered the numbers in pencil to 24–27—that is, he omitted from his enumeration the articles Rodney had cancelled. These additions, therefore, must have been made before the others were cancelled.

73

When the commander-in-chief means to make an attack upon the enemy's centre he will hoist a flag half blue half yellow at the main top-gallant-mast head.

74

Ditto on his van.	Ditto flag with a red pennant over it.
Ditto on his rear.	Ditto with a white pennant under it.

If the commander-in-chief would at any time have all the rendezvouses returned he will hoist a white flag pierced with red under his own flag at the main top-gallant-mast head.

If for all the Signal Books, the same flag with a blue pennant under it.[1]

[1] The last two paragraphs are cancelled, and transferred to the end of the Sailing Instructions, article 50. *Supra*, p. 211. They do not occur in Graves's copy.

FIGHTING INSTRUCTIONS AND SIGNALS BY NIGHT.[1]

I

If the commander-in-chief would have the squadron draw into a line of battle ahead he will show two lights in the main topmast shrouds one above the other, with or without a gun as there may be occasion.

II

When the squadron shall be in line of battle ahead, and the commander-in-chief would have them tack and preserve the same order of battle after they shall be about, he will in addition to the usual signal for tacking show two lights one under the other at the bowsprit end, whereupon the headmost ship is to tack first and continue to lead, the rest of the ships tacking in her wake, and forming a direct line after her.

III

In case of engaging the enemy in the night, the better to know our own ships and prevent their

[1] From Rodney's copy in the Record Office it appears that in the original form of the Instructions the first two articles only existed. The rest are Rodney's additions. The page containing them was followed by a full Index to the Signals. These pages have been cut out of the British Museum copy, and the new articles substituted. In Rodney's copy they are on a printed leaf; in Young's and Graves's they are in MS. Byron's has only the first two articles printed, but he has a third in MS as follows: 'For the better knowing each other, coming up with or engaging the enemy, every ship shall carry three lights in a triangle at the mizen peak.'

firing into each other, every ship in action is to hoist three lights in a triangle at the mizen peak, and two at the bowsprit end, one over the other—the Admiral will hoist the same signals exclusive of the usual lights.

IV

For the better ascertaining what course the enemy may steer in the night, the headmost ship in chase (while she keeps sight of the enemy) shall carry one light in her middle poop lanthorn and one at her main topmast head.

V

In case of engaging the king's ships of the enemy, the ships are to form the line of battle ahead in the best manner they can, taking it from the headmost ship without paying attention to the form of the line of battle; and to pass on in succession, the headmost opposing their sternmost, the next passing on under cover of her fire and engaging the second ship of the enemy's rear, and so on, as they may happen to get up, and on no pretence whatever to pass by the ship they ought to engage, but to stay by her until she submits or is so disabled that she cannot get away.

VI

In case of meeting a squadron of king's ships of the enemy and they should disperse and take different courses on purpose to get away, the ships as they get up are to engage the first ship they meet with and not to quit her (except distressed) on any account whatever until she strikes or is so disabled that she cannot get away.

VII

When in battle should any ship of the squadron be disabled or in distress, the captain of the said ship is to show four lights one over the other where they may be most easily seen and fire two guns ; when the ships nearest to the ship who made the signal are to give her immediate assistance with boats, &c. &c.

VIII

If the commander-in-chief when in battle should think it necessary to bear up and sail large or before the wind, he will hoist two lights one under the other at the mizen peak, and two lights one under the other on the ensign-staff and fire one gun. If to keep the wind and sail on the starboard tack he will put abroad four lights in a square where they will be most easily seen and fire one gun. If to do the same to port, four lights in a lozenge where most easily seen and fire one gun ; and when the Admiral fires a gun after the signal guns have been fired the ships are to alter their course accordingly.

IX

If the commander-in-chief should bring to and lie by on the starboard tack, he will show triangular lights inverted there where most easily seen and fire two guns. If to bring to on the larboard tack, three lights one over the other where most easily seen and fire two guns.

X

If the Admiral would have all the transports and vessels under convoy disperse and shift for themselves, he will hoist two lights one under the other at the fore and main topmast heads, and fire two guns quick, and two minutes after two guns more quick.

Given under my hand on board His Majesty's Ship Sandwich at Spithead, 18 Dec-r 1779.

G. B. RODNEY. (Signed.)

To Capt. Douglas,[1]
of His Majesty's Ship the Terrible.
By command of the Admiral.

WILL PAGETT. (signed.)

[1] So in the British Museum copy. Captain John Douglas commanded the Terrible in the action of April 17, but appears soon after to have been invalided, for he was succeeded by Captain James Ferguson, who had highly distinguished himself in the battle while in command of the Venus frigate.—Beatson, v. 63. Rodney specially testified to Douglas's fine behaviour in the action.—Mundy, *Life of Rodney*, i. 342. Graves's copy is inscribed 'To Capt. Graves, of H.M. Sloop Savage, Gros Islet Bay, 29 March, 1780.' She was commanded from April 1778, the time of her completion at 'Nova Scotia Yard,' Harwich, by John Graves till March 14, 1779. Thos. Graves succeeded to the command next day. She joined Byron on the Leeward Islands Station from Halifax on Feb. 13, 1778, and was with him till July 1780, when she returned to Halifax to refit.—*Log of the Savage*, P.R.O.

NORTH AMERICAN STATION, 1779-82.

ARBUTHNOT, GRAVES, AND DIGBY.

Of the Instructions used on the North American station nothing was known till the discovery of the *Graves Collection.* It proved to contain two copies of those issued by Arbuthnot—one to Captain Graves, of the Bedford, Commodore Affleck's flag-ship, and the other to Captain Swiney, Arbuthnot's flag-captain. The latter is sewn up with a copy of the old General Instructions, and is endorsed as being the form from which all signal and instruction books were to be written up. These instructions were subsequently modified by the set of additional signals which follow them in the text below. Both sets are in signal book form, but in the text below, in order to save space, only the additional signals are printed as they stand in the original. In the case of the 'Fighting Instructions,' the articles alone are printed from the signification column, the signal columns being omitted.

The circumstances under which they, as well as the subsequent modifications by Graves and Digby, were issued and used have been fully dealt with in the General Introduction.

The additional signals, &c., which Graves instituted both after his action and on the eve of sailing with Clinton's army to save Lord Cornwallis, are carefully noted and dated in a MS. Signal Book made by Captain Graves for his own use. It also contains a number of signals for communicating with the Army Officers and for conducting landing operations.

ARBUTHNOT'S ADDITIONAL INSTRUCTIONS, 1779.

[PRINTED FOLIO. GRAVES COLLECTION. R.U.S.I.]

Fighting instructions by day.

ARTICLE I

When the signal is made for the fleet to draw into a line of battle, one ship ahead of another, by hoisting a Union flag at the mizen peak, and firing one gun, every ship is to make all the sail she can into her station, and keep at the distance of half a cable's length asunder.

But if I would have them keep a cable's length asunder, I will hoist a blue flag with a red cross under the Union flag at the mizen peak, and fire one gun.

And if I would have them keep two cables' lengths asunder, I will hoist a flag half blue and half white under the Union flag at the mizen peak, and fire one gun.

But when I would have the fleet draw into a line of battle, one ship abreast of another, and keep at the distances as above directed, I will hoist a blue pennant under the said flags at the mizen-peak.[1]

[1] This is the old Articles I. and II. condensed into one. The old Article III., relating to bow and quarter line, is omitted. It was cancelled in Rodney's set of 1780. See note on Articles III. and IV., next page.

II

When I would have the fleet draw into a line of battle, and regulate themselves by bearing on some particular point of the compass from each other, without having any regard to their being abreast or ahead of another, yet steering the same course as I do, I will make the signal expressed against the points of the compass in the following table, and if I would have them keep at the distance of two cables' lengths asunder, I will fire one gun; but if I would have them keep only one cable's length asunder, I will fire two guns.[1] (*Here follows the usual compass table.*)

III

When a line of battle is formed on any particular point of the compass, and I would have the fleet work to windward, still preserving that line; I will, whenever I judge it necessary to tack, make the signal for the whole fleet to tack together, by hoisting a Union flag on the flag-staves, at the fore and mizen topmast heads, and firing one gun; and when the signal has been fully repeated, I soon after will fire another gun; whereupon every ship in the line is instantly to put her helm a-lee, that no accident may happen from any one ship putting in stays sooner or later than another.[2]

IV

If instead of tacking, I would have the fleet wear, and come to sail on the other tack, still preserving the line of battle; I will hoist the Union flag, with a pennant chequered blue and yellow

[1] This is the old Article IV.

[2] Articles III. and IV. are new, and take the place of the old Article III.

under it, at the flag-staves at the fore and mizen topmast heads and fire two guns; and when the signal has been fully repeated, I soon after will fire one gun, then every ship in the line is instantly to put her helm a-weather, wear and come to sail on the other tack, without delay.[1]

V

If when sailing in a line of battle I shall think it proper to alter the course I will make my intention known by the following signals, viz.—if I would alter the course to starboard, I will hoist a flag chequered blue and red at the fore topmast head, and fire one gun.

If I would alter the course to port, I will hoist a flag striped blue and white, at the same place, and fire one gun, and after the signal has been repeated by the other flag-ships, I will fire one gun for every point of the compass I alter my course; then every ship in the line is to alter her course immediately, without waiting for the number of guns being repeated.[1]

VI

If the fleet at any time should happen to be in two divisions, and I would have them form themselves into separate lines of battle, one ship ahead of another, at the distance of a cable's length asunder, and each division to be abreast of the other, when formed, at the distance of two cables' lengths asunder, I will hoist a flag chequered blue and yellow at the mizen-peak and fire one gun.[2]

[1] The same as the old Article V.
[2] A new Article ;=No. XI. of Rodney's 1782.

VII

When at any time I would have the ship that leads on a particular tack, to continue to lead on the other tack, after she is about, I will hoist a red pennant under the signal for tacking, which signal the other ships are carefully to observe, and follow her in the same order they did on the former tack.[1]

VIII

In sailing in a line of battle, every ship is to keep at the same distance those ships do that are next me, always taking it from the centre; and if at any time I should think the ship ahead of me is at too great a distance, I will make it known to her by putting abroad a common pennant at the jib-boom-end, and keep it flying till she is in her proper station; and if she finds the ship ahead of her is at a greater distance from her than she is from me, she shall make the same signal, and keep it flying till she thinks that ship is at a proper distance, and so on to the van of the line.[2]

IX

When I think the ship astern of me is at too great a distance, I will make it known to her by putting abroad a common pennant at the cross-jack-yard-arm, and keep it flying till she is in her proper station; and if she finds the ship astern of her is at a greater distance from her than she is from me, she shall make the same signal, and keep it flying till she thinks that ship at a proper distance, and so on to the rear of the line.[3]

[1] A new Article;=No. VI. of Rodney's 1782. Here the old set had six Articles for handling the line, all of which Arbuthnot omits. The last three of them were also cancelled by Rodney in 1780.

[2] This is old Article XII. and No. VIII. of Rodney 1782.

[3] This is old Article XIII. and No. IX. in Rodney 1782.

X

And if at any time the captain of any particular ship of the line thinks the ship without him at a greater distance than those ships are that are next the centre, he shall make the above signals, when that ship is immediately to close and get into her proper station.[1]

XI

If I should observe any particular ship to be out of her station in the line of battle, I will make the signal for speaking with the captain, and hoist a pennant striped red and white at the main topmast head.[2]

XII

If at any time I shall think it necessary to alter the disposition of the ships in the line of battle, and would have any two ships change stations with each other, I will make the signal for speaking with the captains of such ships, and hoist a flag chequered red and blue at the mizen topmast head.[3]

XIII

If at any time when the whole fleet is in chase, I would have a certain number of ships that are nearest the enemy draw into a line of battle ahead, in order to engage the ships in their rear, endeavouring at the same time to get up with their van, I will hoist a white flag with a red cross

[1] Old Art. XIV. and No. X. of Rodney 1782.

[2] A new Article, not used by Rodney. After this Arbuthnot omits old Art. XV., 'Separate lines of battle,' and old XVI., 'Bringing-to in line of battle.'

[3] Old Art. XVII. and No. XIII. in Rodney 1782. The old Art. XVIII., 'Attack in general chase,' is omitted. It was retained by Rodney 1782.

at the fore topmast head, and fire the number of guns as follows: When I would have

Five ships	draw into a line ahead of each other I will fire	one gun
Seven ships		two guns ;

then those ships are immediately to form the line, without any regard to seniority, or the general form delivered, but according to their distances from the enemy, viz. the headmost and nearest ship to the enemy is to lead, and the sternmost is to bring up the rear, that no time may be lost in the pursuit: and the rest of the ships are to form and strengthen that line as they come up, without regard to the general form of the order of battle.[1]

XIV

If at any time while engaged with the enemy I shall judge it necessary to come to a closer engagement, I will hoist a flag chequered blue and yellow, under the signal for engaging, at the fore topmast head; then every ship is to engage the enemy as close as possible; and if I would have any particular ship do so, I will make the same signal, and the signal for speaking with the captain.[2]

XV

If at any time when the fleet is formed in the order of battle, I would have the van of the fleet make more sail, I will hoist a pennant striped red and white at the fore topmast head.[3]

[1] Old Art. XIX. and No. XV. of Rodney 1782. After this the old set had three Articles, XX.–XXII., containing the formal old battle tactics. Arbuthnot omits them. Rodney retained them in 1782.

[2] Old Art. XXIII. and No. XIX. of Rodney 1782.

[3] A new Article, not adopted by Rodney.

XVI

If at any time I should meet with the fleet of the enemy inferior in number to that of his Majesty under my command, those ships over and above the number of the enemy, that happen to fall in either ahead of their van or astern of their rear, are hereby directed, whilst the rest of the ships are engaged, to quit the line without waiting for the signal, and endeavour to distress the enemy, by raking the ships of the van and rear, notwithstanding the first part of the 24th article of the printed fighting instructions to the contrary.[1]

XVII

In case of meeting with a fleet of the enemy that may be less in number than his Majesty's under my command, if I would have any of the smallest ships quit the line, that those of the greatest force may be opposed to the enemy, I will put abroad the signal for speaking with the captain or captains of such ship or ships as I would have quit the line, and hoist a flag chequered red and white at the main topmast head; then the next ships are immediately to close up the line, and those that have quitted the line are to hold themselves in readiness to assist any ship that may be disabled or hard pressed, or to take her station, if she shall be compelled to go out of the line; in which case the strongest ship that is withdrawn from the line is strictly enjoined to supply her place and fill up the vacancy.[2]

XVIII

In case of meeting with a fleet, or any number of ships of the enemy, that have merchant ships

[1] This is a new Article, not adopted by Rodney.
[2] Old Art. XXV. and No. XXI. of Rodney 1782.

under their convoy, if I would have any of the frigates that are out of the line, or any of the ships of the line (though the signal for the line of battle is out), fall upon the convoy, whilst the others are engaged, I will put abroad the signal for speaking with the captain or captains of such ship or ships, and hoist a flag chequered red and white at the main topmast head, with a common pennant under it.[1]

XIX

When I would have the fire-ships prime I will hoist a pennant striped red and white at the mizen topmast head and fire one gun; but if at any time I am in chase of the enemy's fleet, the fire-ships are to prime as fast as possible, whether the signal is made or not.[2]

XX

You are to hold his Majesty's ship under your command in constant readiness for action; and in case of coming to an engagement with the enemy, if they have the wind of us, you are to keep your barge manned and armed with hand and fire-chain grapples, &c., on the off side, to be ready to assist, as well any ship that may be attempted by fire-ships of the enemy, as our own fire-ships when they shall be ordered upon service.[2]

[1] Old Art. XXV. and No. XXI. of Rodney 1782.

[2] Old Articles XXVII. and XXVIII., and Nos. XXII. and XXIII. of Rodney 1782. It should be noted that none of Rodney's supplementary Articles appear in Arbuthnot's set.

ADDITIONAL BATTLE SIGNALS. JUNE 1780.

By MARIOT ARBUTHNOT, Esquire, Vice-Admiral of the Blue and Commander-in-Chief, &c. &c.

YOU are hereby required and directed to observe the following signals, in addition to the line of battle signals.

I

If the commander-in-chief would have the squadron on a wind, draw into a line of battle on each other's bow and quarter, and keep half a cable's length asunder, those ships which should happen to be to leeward at the time of making the signal, forming the van of the line, and those to windward the rear, bearing from each other on the point of the compass, whereon they will be on the other tack, always taking it from the centre, he will hoist a red pennant under the union at the mizen-peak, and fire a gun; and if he should afterwards tack in order to bring the squadron into a line ahead, the ship that becomes the headmost is to continue leading.[1]

II

When the squadron shall be in a line of battle ahead, and the commander-in-chief would have them form a line on each other's bow and quarter, he will hoist a Union jack at his fore topmast head,

[1] This is the old Art. III. restored.

and a red pennant under the signal for the line ahead, when they are all to tack together, and the bow and quarter line will be formed.[1]

III

When the squadron shall be in a line of battle ahead, and the commander would have them wear, and form a line on each other's bow and quarter, on the other tack, he will hoist a flag chequered blue and yellow at the main top-gallant-mast head; the leading ship is then to wear first, and steer four points from the course whereon she will lie, on the other tack, until all the ships have wore in succession, and formed a direct line after her; and when the chequered flag shall be hauled down, and a red pennant hoisted under the signal for the line ahead, at which time a gun will be fired, the ships are to come to the wind together, and the bow and quarter line will be formed.[2]

Given under my hand, on board His Majesty's Ship the EUROPE, off Staten Island, June the 17th 1780.

(Sgd.) MT. ARBUTHNOT.

To the respective Captains and Commanders of the North American Squadron.

By command of the Admiral,

(Signed) WILL. GREEN.

[1] Takes the place of old Art. IX.
[2] Takes the place of old Art. X.

ADDITIONAL INSTRUCTION FOR EXTENDING THE LINE FOR SEARCH.[1]

By MARIOT ARBUTHNOT, Esquire, Vice-Admiral of the Blue and Commander-in-Chief, &c. &c. &c.

When I would have the fleet spread to look out, I will make the signal for the line of bearings as per additional instructions, and at the same time hoist a flag half red half white at the mizen topmast head.

Then the ships are to spread about two leagues asunder in that line; if I would have them spread about one league asunder, I will hoist a blue pennant over the flag at the mizen topmast head.

All the frigates except the repeating ship or such whose signals I may throw out at the same time with the signal for the line are to form in the line in the same manner as the line of battle ships, the senior frigate going ahead of the leading ship in the line and the next senior astern of the sternmost, the third senior ahead, and the fourth astern and so on till all are placed, seniority to be considered according to the seniority of the ships' signals.

Signals are to be made for single sails seen by hoisting the N.E. and N.W. flags at the main topgallant-mast head and the S.E. and S.W. flags at the main topmast head close above the cap.

[1] When these instructions were issued Arbuthnot was engaged in watching the French squadron in Newport from positions about New York and Rhode Island.

The signal for more than eight sail is to be made by a flag of some kind at each mast head, the top-gallant sheets being let fly if set, guns fired and the ship's head laid towards them as near as possible till answered by a St. George's ensign at my main top-gallt.-mast head.

The ship first seeing the strangers is to stand towards them and the rest to stand for her, till it appears they may be nearly equal in force to me; in that case you are immediately to join me and take care not to be cut off.

When I would have the line broke and common sailing form resumed, I will hoist a red flag at my main top-gallt.-mast head, and the ships are to repeat it with their ensign at the main top-gallant-mast head and join me immediately.

If it comes on foggy unexpectedly and I would have the line broke and the form of sailing resumed as near as the weather will admit, I will fire five guns one minute asunder, then one every half-hour or occasionally, as the weather may prove, shortening a little sail, that the ships astern may come up: all the ships are to repeat the first five minute guns and afterwards attend to my half-hour guns, the commanding officers only repeating them.

Signals made to signify that ships are too far distant from each other in this line will be made with an Union flag instead of a pennant. The ships are never to keep farther distant than hull down from each other; when the signal for the line appears fully understood it will be hauled down.

All ships are to repeat signals till they are communicated to me.

When the signal for seeing a sail is answered, the ship which made it is to chase, and if two are seen the next ahead of her is to chase also, but the greatest care must be taken not to lose sight of the fleet on any account whatsoever without orders and to return to the fleet before sunset.

When one or two ships chase from the line, the rest are to close by the headmost bringing to and the sternmost making sail up to them, or those are to close the line who have a leading wind for so doing. Private ships are to acknowledge all signals made in this line by their ensign at the main top-gallant-mast head.

I will acknowledge them by hoisting the yellow flag at the main top-gallant-mast head except where otherways expressed.

The ships in the extremes of the line are to keep their lead going.

Given on board His Majesty's Ship EUROPE this 19th August 1780.

(Signed) MT. ARBUTHNOT.

To Captain Affleck, Commander of His Majesty's Ship the BEDFORD

By command of the Admiral,

(Signed) WILL. GREEN.

ADDITIONAL SIGNALS FOR THE NORTH AMERICAN STATION. 1781

[**Printed folio. Graves Collection.**]

By MARIOT ARBUTHNOT, Esq., Vice-Admiral of the White and Commander-in-Chief, &c. &c. &c.

In addition to the General and Additional Signals and Instructions which you have already received from me,

You are hereby required and directed to follow and observe the following, and for so doing this shall be your order.

Signification	Flags	Place where Hoisted
ARTICLE I That ship to take a vessel in tow in that quarter	Chasing flags for the quarter of the compass and a yellow pendant under it	Mizen - shrouds and ship's signal
II That ship to take charge of the guard 24 hours, and speak all vessels coming into the harbour or road, reporting occurrences to the commanding officer at the end of their guard	White flag	Mizen topmast head and ship's signal
III To weigh when I may not think proper to loose the topsails, or want a particular ship to weigh	Half blue, half white	Ensign-staff

Signification	Flags	Place where Hoisted
IV To cover boats sounding	Ditto with a common pennant under it	Ditto
V To reconnoitre the enemy	Yellow and white striped flag	Ditto
VI To discontinue the engagement	Blue and yellow checquered pennant	Fore topmast head & ship's signal
VII If I should think proper at any time to lead the squadron in a line myself I will hoist a flag, half blue, half white, at the main top-gallant-mast head : In that case the ships are to fall into my wake in the same form as prescribed in the line of battle, the leading ship on that tack next to me, and the rest in succession	Half blue, half white	Main top-gallant-mast head
VIII If, upon discovering the enemy's line, I should think proper to alter mine, so that the force on both sides may be as equally opposed as possible, I will make it known by hoisting a St. George's ensign at the main top-gallant-mast head, after which I will hoist the ship's pennant which I would have to lead; when that ship has answered I will make the next ship's signal that is to follow her, and shall continue to hoist each ship's signal until the line is entirely disposed of agreeable to the above idea, and if I should think fit at any time during an engagement or otherwise to alter the line, it will always be done by the above method	St. George's Ensign, preparative	Main top-gallant-mast head

Signification	Flags	Place where Hoisted
IX When I would have the van of my fleet engage the rear of the enemy without passing them, each ship engaging the first ship that she comes up with, & passing those already engaged, the van ship of my fleet bringing to action the rear ship of the enemy, and so in succession, I will hoist a flag, blue pierced white, at the main top-gallant-mast head	Blue pierced white	Main top-gallant-mast-head
X If at any time I would have the leading ship in the line alter the course to starboard, I will hoist a flag half red, half white at the main topmast head	Half red, half white	Main topmast head
If to port, I will hoist the same flag at the fore topmast head, then the leading ship to answer by hoisting the broadest pennant she has at her mizen topmast head (which the repeating ships are also to repeat), & then I will lower and hoist the signal once for every point I would have her alter her course	Ditto	Fore topmast head
XI If I should think proper to remove at any time into the repeating ship, notwithstanding my flag continues flying in the flag-ship, I will previous to such removal hoist a red flag at the main top-gallant-mast head	Red flag	Main top-gallant-mast head

N.B.—It is directed that in action a portion of every ship's fire be reserved for and directed against the masts and rigging of the enemy, and that all the ships in action wear red colours.

When the commanding officers make any signals, the ships which they concern are to acknowledge their being observed and understood by hoisting a Spanish or Union jack, where it can be best seen by the ship which made the signal, and when general signals are made, the answering signal is to be kept up no longer than five minutes, but otherwise, till the signal is hauled down.

The repeating frigate is to repeat the signals made by private ships to the Admiral, with the ship's pennant that makes them.

Signification	Flags	Place where Hoisted
XII Annul. To annul the purpose of the signal previously made by the Admiral or herewith put abroad, and to signify that it is to be no longer regarded	Flag striped red and white	Mizen-peak
XIII Action. The fleet to prepare for action when service may be intended, which is not obvious to the fleet	Three pennants One {red, white, blue} under each other	Ditto
XIV Anchor. A ship or ships to anchor immediately	A common pennant under the anchoring signal, with ship's signal	Ditto
XV Boats in chase. Boats of the squadron being in chase to leave off and return to their respective ships	Red and white flag chequered	Fore topmast head

Signification	Flags	Place where Hoisted
XVI Chase. That the chase is a friend	St. George's Ensign, Union downwards	Main top-gallant-mast head
XVII That it is a ship of the line	Dutch flag reversed	Ditto
XVIII That it is a frigate	Blue Ensign, Union downwards	Ditto
XIX That it is a transport	Red Ensign, Union downwards	Ditto
XX Ship does not gain on the chase, to be made before parting company	Red Ensign and white flag over it	Mizen topmast head
XXI Part Company. To be added Page 13, Art. XV., additional to the General Printed Sailing and Fighting Instructions ; and they are to run no hazard of parting company, unless some signal has been made which implies they may part company	Instructions	—
XXII Company. Each ship during the performance of Divine Service is to keep hoisted	Common pennant	Mizen-peak

Signification	Flags	Place where Hoisted
XXIII Distress. When any ship is in distress she will hoist her ensign only, Union downwards, but if she wants immediate assistance, she is to make it known by	Ensign, Union downwards, and white flag under it	Main topmast shrouds
XXIV Engage in the night. If at any time in the night, the fleet being in a line of battle, the Admiral should think proper to bear down and engage the enemy, he will show	Six lights, by two of equal height over each other	Mizen-shrouds
XXV If, on falling in suddenly with the enemy in the night, the Admiral would have the ships engage as they are able in the closest manner, he will hoist	Six lights as above, and burn two false fires	Ditto
XXVI Line. When in a line of battle and endeavouring to gain the wind of the enemy, the headmost ship is to make known when she can weather by hoisting	Dutch flag	Mizen topmast head
XXVII Under the like circumstances, the sternmost ships to signify the same, or when the fleet being to windward of the enemy, and on the contrary tack, to make known she is far enough astern of their rear to lead down out of their line of fire, she will hoist a	Dutch flag	Fore topmast head

Signification	Flags	Place where Hoisted
XXVIII If at any time I would have the ship that leads on the starboard tack to lead on the larboard tack, I will hoist	A red pennant, and a white pennant six feet under	Ditto
XXIX If I would have the ship that leads on the larboard tack, to lead on the starboard tack, I will hoist	The white pennant over the red	Fore topmast head
XXX If, when in line of battle, I would have the leading ship haul by the wind on the starboard tack, I will hoist	One half red, one half white flag and red under	Main topmast head
XXXI If I would have the leading ship haul by the wind on the larboard tack, I will hoist To be observed as the preceding signal	One half red, one half white flag, red pennant	Fore topmast head
XXXII *Line.* For the readier drawing the fleet into a line of battle ahead, when the case may require, if I would have the ships form promiscuously as they can come up, without attention to seniority by the prescribed order of battle, I will hoist when they are to keep at a cable's length distance asunder	Red pennant above the St. George's jack	Ditto
XXXIII If at any time in a line of battle, or otherways, I would have the fleet to close and the leading ships shorten sail for that purpose, if necessary, I will hoist	Yellow flag, with blue pennant under	Main topmast head

Signification	Flags	Place where Hoisted
XXXIV If I would have the fleet open in a line of battle, to give room for manœuvring I will hoist	Yellow flag, with red pennant under	Ditto
XXXV When I would have each ship steer for and engage his opponent in the enemy's line, I will hoist	Signal for close action, and white pennant over	Fore topmast head
XXXVI Preparatory. As a preparatory signal, the Admiral will, about five minutes previous to any general intended operation in the ships in company, occasionally hoist	Flag half white, half blue, white uppermost	Main top-gallant-mast head
XXXVII If, at any time when the signal for the line is thrown out, any ship or ships from inequality of sailing, or otherwise, cannot get into their stations in the line, I will make their signals to fall astern, and form in succession in the rear, by hoisting	Red flag with a white cross, and ship's signal	Mizen topmast head
XXXVIII Ships detached from the body of the fleet, previous to the signal for the order of battle, are not meant to be comprehended in it, until called into the fleet by the proper signal	Instruction 26	
XXXIX When I would have the fleet quit the form of battle, and resume the order of sailing, I will hoist	Yellow pennant	Mizen topmast head

Signification	Flags	Place where Hoisted
XL Engage. If I would have the enemy engaged on their starboard side, so that the enemy must fire his starboard guns, I will hoist	Red flag, white pennant over	Main topmast head
XLI If on their larboard side, and so that they may fire their larboard guns, I will hoist	Blue flag, white pennant over	Ditto
XLII Rake. If I would have any particular ship or ships make sail, and rake the van of the enemy's line, I will hoist	Yellow flag, and blue pennant over ship's signal	Ditto
XLIII ditto, to rake the enemy's rear, I will hoist	Ditto flag, and red pennant over	Ditto
XLIV Order of sailing. If I would have the ships form the prescribed order of sailing I will hoist Which order they are to preserve on all occasions, without signal, unless in line of battle, or otherways disposed of	Spanish jack, and red and white striped pennant under	Ditto
XLV Sail. If I would have any particular ship shorten sail in line of battle, or otherways, I will make her signal, and hoist	Dutch jack reversed, and ship's signal	Main top-gallant-mast head

Signification	Flags	Place where Hoisted
XLVI If I would have any particular ship make sail I will hoist	Red pennant over the striped blue, and white flag and ship's signal	Main topmast head
XLVII If any particular ship finds herself overpressed with sail, and not able to keep her station, she is to make it known to the Admiral by hoisting	Dutch jack reversed	Main top-gallant-mast head
XLVIII Close. To close up with the Admiral, and expect some alteration in the course or sail, perhaps without signal.	Blue flag and red cross	Ensign-staff
To bear up and sail before the wind	Three guns very quick and half a minute after one gun more	

Fog.—N.B. The former signal given out 2nd September, 1780, for this purpose is no longer to be observed, but in lieu thereof three guns fired very quick, and half a minute after one gun more, as the signal to bear up and sail before the wind.

To be added Page 4th, Article III., additional to the General Printed Sailing and Fighting Instructions, viz. the seconds nearest to him, the leaders on the wings, and the intermediate ships agreeable to the written order. And if the signal should be made to tack, the ships that may happen to be to windward at that time are to remain so after they shall be about on the other tack.

MEMORANDUM AND FURTHER ADDITIONAL SIGNALS FOR THE NORTH AMERICAN STATION, 1781.

[Capt. Graves's MS. Signal Book. Graves Collection.]

Signals.

Sept. 6, 1781.

To form the line parallel to that of the enemy as near as possible.

For a particular ship to lead the fleet when in line of battle or otherwise.

Sept. 8, 1781.

For the commander in the second post with his division to lead the fleet.

For the commander in the third post with his division to lead the fleet.

For the fleet to keep in more open order when in line of battle or order of sailing.

The same for closer order.

[*Note.*—Signals follow for directing more open or closer order to van, centre, or rear.]

Oct. 15, 1781.

For the van to retreat.
,, ,, centre ,,
,, ,, rear ,,

For the van to attack the enemy.
,, ,, centre ,, ,, ,,
,, ,, rear ,, ,, ,,

For the van to force through the enemy.
,, ,, centre ,, ,, ,,
,, ,, rear ,, ,, ,

To Captain Graves, commander of H.M.S. Bedford.[1]

Memorandum.

Mem°

When the signal for the line of battle ahead is out at the same time with the signal for battle it is not to be understood that the latter signal shall be rendered ineffectual by the strict adherence to the former, and the signal for the line of battle is to be considered as the line of extension, and the respective Admirals and captains of the fleet are desired to be attentive not to advance or fall back, so as to intercept the fire of their seconds ahead and astern, but to keep as near the enemy as possible, whilst the signal for close action continues out, and to take notice that the line must be preserved parallel to that of the enemy during battle without regard to a particular point or wearing. H.M.S. London, at sea, 6th Sept. 1781.[2]

To Capt. Graves,
H.M.S. Bedford.

[1] The Bedford was Commodore Edmund Affleck's flagship. The Signal Book also contains a table (the earliest at present known) for keeping station by means of quadrant observations and height of masts. The distances are calculated on the following data :—Three-deckers, height of mast 184 ft. 'above the surface.' Seventy-fours, 170 ft. Height of eye above surface, 26 ft.

[2] On the back of Hood's copy is the following note :—'It is the first time I ever heard it suggested that too strict an adherence could be paid to the line of battle ; and if I understand the meaning of the British fleet being formed parallel to that of the enemy, it is, that if the enemy's fleet is disorderly and irregularly formed, the British fleet is, in compliment to it, to form irregularly and disorderly also. Now the direct contrary is my opinion ; and I

think, in case of disorder and irregularity in the enemy's line, that the British fleet should be as compact as possible, in order to take the critical moment of an advantage opening and offering itself to make a powerful impression on the most vulnerable part of the enemy. According to Mr. Graves's Memo. any captain may break the line with impunity when he pleases.' *N.R.S.* xxxii. 127.

'Break the line' has here its ordinary contemporary meaning of a captain 'leaving his station in the line' and bearing out to windward or leeward. For the rest it would look as though Hood had wilfully misinterpreted his chief. Graves's Memo. obviously refers to cases where the enemy's line is regularly formed.

It seems impossible to acquit Hood of having written the note, though it is not in his handwriting. It is amongst the copies of his correspondence, &c., which he was in the habit of sending home to Sir Charles Middleton, and Sir John Laughton kindly informs me that 'the copy is in the same hand as the letter to Digby of Nov. 10 (which is signed by Hood)—a good clerkly hand, certainly a man in Hood's office.' (See *N.R.S.* iii. 53).

Any doubt as to the intention with which Graves issued the Memo. is removed by a note which Lieut. Graves appends to it in his Signal Book: 'N.B. The foregoing order was given the day after the action with the French fleet of 24 sail of the line, in consequence of the second in command not bearing down and engaging the enemy, which was his duty; but kept his wind, by which means a most glorious victory was lost, and with it the loss of Lord Cornwallis's army in Virginia.'

THE LAST FORM OF THE GENERAL AND ADDITIONAL FIGHTING INSTRUCTIONS

WITH MS. ADDITIONS OF RODNEY, PIGOT, AND HOOD, 1781-3

INTRODUCTORY

These instructions—the last word of the old system—are contained in what was believed to be a unique volume in the Library of the United States Navy Department at Washington. Attention was first called to them by Captain Mahan, and it is to his good offices and the courtesy of Mr. Charles W. Stewart, Superintendent of the Library and Naval War Records, that the Society is indebted for the following copy.

In a letter to the Editor, Mr. Stewart describes the book thus:—'I have to inform you that we have a volume in this office which purports to contain Rodney's fighting instructions with the title-page as follows: *Sailing and Fighting Instructions for His Majesty's Fleet.* The publication is not dated. There are about twenty-five pages (8 in MS.), size, 9 by 14 inches.' The volume contains the whole series of General and Additional Instructions with many MS. additions, but the 'Fighting Instructions' only are printed below—that is to say, the old General Instructions and the Additional Instructions, both by Day and Night, together with a new set of Instructions for landing parties added by Rodney.

At the extreme end immediately following the new 'landing instructions' are the words, 'established by Lord Rodney 20th Feb. 1782'—that is the day after his arrival at Barbadoes to take over the command. This particular copy is not signed, and, as will be seen later, was certainly not issued by Rodney. Nevertheless there was little room for doubt that the printed part of these Instructions was the long-sought set which Rodney used in his action with De Grasse on April 12, 1782. That this was indeed so was made certain by the discovery of the *Graves Collection.* For it proved to contain an identical set of instructions which had been actually issued to Capt. Graves, of the Bedford, off Barbadoes, on Feb. 19.

About the printed articles, therefore, all was clear. Still the MS. additions in the Washington copy presented considerable difficulties both as to date and authorship; but internal and other evidence now exists which enables us to determine both points with fair security, and at the same time to ascertain by whom and when the copy was actually issued.

To begin with, although these were certainly the Printed Instructions used at the battle of April 12, this particular copy must have been issued long afterwards, and certainly after July 10, when Rodney was superseded by Pigot. For Captain the Hon. Charles Phipps, of the Berwick, to whom they were delivered, was then serving with that ship in the Channel Fleet. He also was with Howe when in September he relieved Gibraltar, and after the action with Cordova sailed in a detachment of eight of the line under Admiral Hughes to reinforce the West Indian station. Moreover, a note inserted before the Fighting Instructions runs thus:—'Lord Rodney's and Admiral Pigot's Signals in 1781–82–83,' and the only MS. article specifically assigned to Rodney is the first one, No. 32, under date April 10, 1782. According to a MS. note appended later, it was the outcome of the partial action on April 9.

Next to this article comes one for inverting the line (No. 33), and then a new one for forming the fleet in two or three distinct lines of battle by divisions and for regulating their manner of sailing, both of which in a MS. signal book in my possession are assigned to Pigot. But actually they are taken direct from the 10th Article of Kempenfelt's 'Instructions and Directions for the Conduct of Ships of War when sailing or chasing by Day.'[1] They were, therefore, clearly introduced from the Channel Fleet.

Then follows (No. 35) an instruction for breaking the line with an elaboration whereby any particular ship in the line could be directed to commence the movement. This elaboration is assigned to Pigot by the contemporary MS. signal book in my possession, and also by one slightly later in the Admiralty Library.[2]

The next MS. instruction (No. 36) is for regulating the favourite form of attack by each ship steering independently for her opposite number. The Admiralty Signal Book assigns it to Hood; in my own earlier one it does not occur. A signal book in the *Graves Collection* issued by Hood to Graves, of the Bedford, proves that this signal, with some others, of which more presently, were added by Hood on April 27, 1782—that is, the day after Rodney left him in command of the bulk of the fleet to blockade Cap François. Until this time there had been no attempt to clear the obscurity of the old 17th Article which had spoiled Rodney's action of April 17, 1780. It is noteworthy that,

[1] See p. 146.
[2] *N.R.S.* xxix. (*Fighting Instructions*), 211–12.

even now, Hood did not venture to modify the old article, but added an entirely new one of his own, and we now know that it was only added after Rodney's back was turned and Hood had a free hand.

It is of course impossible to regard Pigot, any more than Sir Charles Hardy, as the actual author of the amendments officially assigned to him. By universal testimony Pigot was then incapable of any such originality. The influence may be sought in his two chief Channel men—Sir Charles Douglas, who remained on in the Formidable as his first-captain, and Commodore Affleck, who led his squadron. It may also of course have been Lord Hood. We know from his own pen that he was at this time advising Pigot freely on strategy, and that he had a very poor opinion of the admiral's staff. 'I really cannot help feeling very much for Admiral Pigot,' he wrote in a 'secret and confidential' letter to Jackson in August 1782, 'and probably have gone too far in hints I have thrown out to him, tho' I must confess he has given me no reason to suppose he has not taken all I have said in good part. . . . His situation is much to be pitied, having no one about him capable of affording wholesome advice, which . . . . as he has been so long on land and never hoisted his flag or commanded a squadron before, I should think could not be unwelcome.'[1]

Still the weight of the direct evidence is against Hood's influence. We have seen from Hood's Signal Book in the *Graves Collection* that all the principal signals attributed to him, including his special method of breaking the line, were issued the moment he was left in command by Rodney, August 27, 1782. He may well have continued

[1] *N.R.S.* iii. (*Letters of Sir Samuel Hood*), 140; cf. also *Ibid.* p. 179. 'How in God's name could the Commander-in-Chief pick up such a first-captain?' &c.

their use when, in November 1782, he was detached by Pigot from Staten Island with a squadron of thirteen of the line to cruise again off Cap François on the Jamaica station while Pigot himself took the Leeward Islands.[1]

But there is no evidence that Pigot himself adopted them. They are certainly absent from the Signal Book in my possession, which contains all Pigot's signals. They are also wanting in Phipps's copy, and his ship the Berwick was never under Hood. Hughes's squadron in which she sailed reached Barbadoes on November 8, 1782, and found Pigot there. The fleet remained in Carlisle Bay till January 10, 1783, and it must have been during this time that Phipps's copy was issued. Then under Pigot's flag the Berwick cruised till February 15, when she anchored at St. Lucia. And there she remained till the end of the war, when she went home with eleven others in April. She was paid off at Spithead in June. This copy therefore must have been delivered to Captain Phipps by Pigot; and Commodore Shirley, under whom Phipps came home, must have failed to demand its return in the usual course.[2]

The final group of articles is a MS. addition relating to landing parties. They occur also in the Graves copy dated February 19. Just before sailing, Rodney had asked for authority to make descents on the Spanish Main, and was much occupied with the idea of amphibious operations that were in contemplation. So large was the proportion of Marines in his fleet that on December 30, 1781, on the eve of sailing, he had sent up a special request that some field officers might be appointed.[3] The immediate

[1] Beatson, v. 526, vi. 334.
[2] Log of the Berwick, P.R.O. *Captains' Logs*, No. 101.
[3] See Mundy, *Life of Rodney*, ii. 177, 418.

object in his mind appears to have been the safety of Jamaica. The special object indeed of his mission was to save it. On his arrival he wrote to tell General Dalling, the governor, that he was ready to send him succour, 'being fully convinced,' he said, 'that Jamaica cannot be taken while I have the honour to command a large fleet in these seas . . . . and that numbers may not be wanted to defend so important a jewel . . I have given orders that one hundred stout seamen, with proper officers, from each of the line-of-battle ships may be disciplined and trained to small arms, to act as soldiers on shore should there be an occasion for their landing.'[1] These men are referred to in the Signals and Instruction Book as 'companies of landers' or more fully 'companies of men belonging to the fleet embodied for acting ashore.'

Rodney had no regular signal book, but relied solely, in the old fashion, upon the instruction books. There is with them, however, in the *Graves Collection* a MS. signal book which Graves apparently had made for himself. It is entitled 'Signals, &c. by Sir George Bridges Rodney, Bart. & Knt. of the Bath, Admiral of the White, Commander-in-Chief. Feb. 19, 1782. Thomas Graves.' It contains at the beginning Rodney's order of battle and his order of sailing, which is still in the old form. At the end it has Pigot's sailing order, dated July 13, 1782, in which the formation is the same. Most of Pigot's new signals are also there, but added later. So far, then, from Rodney having been in advance of his time, as has always been supposed, we are forced to regard him as the last adherent of the old system.

[1] Rodney to Governor Dalling, St. Lucia, March 5, 1782. *Ibid.* p. 192. Major-General John Dalling was one of Wolfe's men who had commanded a corps of Light Infantry at Quebec.

THE GENERAL FIGHTING INSTRUCTIONS[1]

[Sailing and Fighting Instructions for His Majesty's Fleet. Folio-printed in Library of U.S. Navy Department, Washington, with MS. additions.]

To prepare for battle—red flag at the main top-gallant-mast head, under his own flag, and fire a gun.[2]

Instruction I

Fleet to draw into a line of battle, one ship ahead of another.

When the Admiral would have the fleet draw into a line of battle, one ship ahead of another (according to the method given to each captain), he will hoist an Union flag at mizen-peak,[3] and fire a gun; and every flag-ship in the fleet is to make the same signal.

[1] These are the final form of the old General Instructions dating from the end of the seventeenth century. For the original form see *N.R.S.* xxix. (*Fighting Instructions*), pp. 188, 197. For the text as used in the War of Austrian Succession see a copy used by Captain P. Denis of the Centurion on East India convoy duty in 1747, *Admiralty Court*, *Prize Papers*, 100 (*St. Dominique*). For knowledge of this document we are indebted to the researches of Mr. Marsden, who kindly drew my attention to it. It does not contain Mathews's addition mentioned in *Fighting Instructions*, p. 188, *note*.

[2] MS. addition by Rodney. In the original the signal is painted in, a blue flag over a red. In studying the text below it should be noted that wherever MS. additions or corrections occur in the original they are given in italics.

[3] The original has 'peek' throughout.

II

Ditto abreast of another.

When the Admiral would have the fleet draw into a line of battle, one ship abreast of another (according to the method given to each captain) he will hoist an Union flag and a [*blue*] pennant [*under it*] at the mizen-peak, and fire a gun; and every flag-ship in the fleet is to do the same.

III

Admiral of the White or Blue, and their squadrons, to tack and gain the wind of the enemy.

When the Admiral would have [*him*][1] that commands in the second post, and his whole squadron, to tack, and endeavour to gain the wind of the enemy, he will spread a white flag under the flag at the main topmast head and fire a gun; and when he would have him, or he (*sic*) that commands in the third post, to do the same, he will spread a blue flag on that place and fire a gun; which is to be answered by the flag-ships in the fleet.

IV

Vice-Admiral of the Red, White, or Blue, and their divisions, to tack and gain the wind of the enemy.

When the Admiral would have the Vice-Admiral of the Red, and his division, tack and endeavour to gain the wind of the enemy, he will spread a red

[1] Up till 1780 the squadronal admirals in this article had also been designated by their colours. The article read 'the Admiral of the White or he that commands in the second post.' But in Rodney's own copies which he used in that year (*Rodney Papers*, P.R.O.) the words 'the Admiral of the White or he' have been struck out and replaced by the word 'him,' and the article made to read as it stands here.

flag from the cap on the fore topmast head downwards on the backstay; if he would have the Vice-Admiral of the White do the same, a white flag; if the Vice-Admiral of the Blue, a blue flag, at the same place, and fire a gun.

[*N.B.—These three flags to be spread from the cap, on the fore topmast head, downward on the backstay.*[1]]

V

Rear-Admiral of the Red, White, or Blue, and their divisions, to tack and gain the wind of the enemy.

When the Admiral would have the Rear-Admiral of the Red, and his division, tack and endeavour to gain the wind of the enemy, he will hoist a red flag at the flag-staff at the mizen topmast head; and if the Rear-Admiral of the White, a white flag; if the Rear-Admiral of the Blue, a blue flag at the same place, and under the flag a pennant of the same colour, and fire a gun.

VI

Fleet to bear down into the Admiral's wake, or grain, when he is to leeward of them.

If the Admiral be to leeward of the fleet, or any part of the fleet, and he would have them bear down into his wake or grain, he will hoist a blue flag at the mizen-peak and fire a gun.

VII

Ships to leeward of the Admiral, to get into his wake or grain.

If the Admiral be to leeward of the enemy, and his fleet, or any part of them, to leeward of him:

[1] MS. addition by Rodney.

that he may bring those ships into a line, he will bear up with a blue flag at the mizen-peak under the Union flag, which is the signal for the line of battle, and fire a gun; and then those ships to leeward are to use their endeavour to get into his wake or grain, according to their stations in the line of battle.

VIII

Vice or Rear Admirals, &c., and ships of the starboard and larboard quarter to come to their said tacks.

If the fleet be sailing before the wind, and the Admiral would have him that commands in the second post [*or him who sails in his station for the time being*[1]] and the ships of the starboard quarter to clap by the wind, and to come to the starboard tack, then he will hoist upon the mizen topmast head a red flag; and in case he would have him that commands in the third post [*or him who sails in his station for the time being*[1]] and the ships of the larboard quarter to come to their larboard tack, then he will hoist up a blue flag at the same place and fire a gun.

IX

Van of the fleet to tack first.

When the Admiral would have the van of the fleet to tack first, he will put abroad the Union flag at the flag-staff on the fore topmast head and fire a gun, if the red flag be not abroad; but if the red flag be abroad then the fore topsails shall be lowered a little, and the Union flag shall be spread from the cap of the fore topmast downwards; and every flagship in the fleet is to do the same.

[1] MS. addition by Rodney.

X

Rear-Admiral [1] of the fleet to tack first.

When the Admiral would have the Rear Admiral of the fleet tack first, he will hoist the Union flag on the flag-staff at the mizen topmast head and fire a gun; which is to be answered by every flag-ship in the fleet.

XI

Flag-ships to come into the Admiral's wake or grain.

When the Admiral would have all the flag-ships in the fleet come into his wake or grain, he will hoist a red flag at the mizen peak, and fire a gun; and the flag-ships in the fleet are to make the same signal.

XII

Admirals of the White or Blue to make more sail, though the Admiral himself shortens his.

When the Admiral would have [*him*] [2] that commands in the second post, and his squadron, make more sail, though himself shorten sail, he will hoist a white flag on the ensign-staff; if [*him*] that commands in the third post, a blue flag at the same place and fire gun; and every flag-ship in the fleet is to make the same signal. [*But if to shorten sail, a red pennant will be hoisted over the above flag.*[3]]

XIII

Signals for battle.

As soon as the Admiral shall hoist a red flag on the flag-staff at the fore topmast head and fire

1 The word 'Admiral' was erased by Rodney.

2 See note to Art. III. above.

3 MS. addition by Rodney.

a gun, every ship in the fleet is to use their utmost endeavour to engage the enemy in the order the Admiral has prescribed unto them.[1]

XIV

Frigates that are not in the line of battle to come under the Admiral's stern.

When the Admiral hoists a white flag at the mizen-peak, and fires a gun, then all the small frigates of his squadron that are not of the line of battle are to come under his stern.

XV

Rear of the fleet to brace their head-sails to the mast.

If the fleet is sailing by a wind in the line of battle, and the Admiral would have them brace their head-sails to the mast, he will hoist a yellow flag on the flag-staff, at the mizen topmast head, and fire a gun; which the flag-ships in the fleet are to answer. Then the ships in the rear are to brace-to first.[2]

XVI

Van of the fleet to fill their head-sails.

The fleet lying in a line of battle with their head-sails to the mast, and if the Admiral would have them fill, and stand on, he will hoist a yellow flag on the flag-staff at the fore topmast head and fire a gun, which the flag-ships in the fleet

1 This article is a return to the original form. The additions made in the middle of the eighteenth century to prevent captains opening fire at too long a range have been discarded. See *N.R.S.* xxix. (*Fighting Instructions*), p. 190, *note*. The additions there mentioned do not occur in Captain Denis's copy, 1747.

2 This article was modified by No. 12 of the Additional Instructions. See *post*, p. 290, and *supra*, p. 222.

are to answer; then the ships in the van are to fill first, and to stand on: If it happen, when this signal is to be made, that the red flag is abroad on the flag-staff at the fore topmast head, the Admiral will spread the yellow flag under the red.

XVII

Instructions to be observed in engaging the enemy.

If the Admiral see the enemy's fleet standing towards him, and he has the wind of them, the van of the fleet is to make sail till they come the length of the enemy's rear, and our rear abreast of the enemy's van; then he that is in the rear of our fleet is to tack first, and every ship one after another, as fast as they can throughout the line; and if the Admiral would have the whole fleet [*prepare*] to tack together, the sooner to put them in a posture of engaging the enemy, then he will hoist a Union flag on the flag-staves at the fore and mizen topmast heads and fire a gun; and all the flag-ships in the fleet are to do the same [*And no ship, or particular part of the fleet whatsoever, shall presume to tack, or wear, whilst in action, unless by signals, or order from the Admiral so to do*[1]]; and whilst they are in fight with the enemy, to keep within half a cable's length one of another; or, if the weather be bad, according to the discretion of the commanders.

[N.B.—*See the reference below.*[2]]

[1] This MS. alteration had been made in 1780. It is found in the copies in the *Rodney Papers* of that date. As established by Rooke in 1703 the passage had run, 'But in case the enemy's fleet should tack in their rear our fleet is to do the same with an equal number of ships.' For Howe's rule see *post*, p. 321.

[2] The reference inserted in MS. by Rodney is as follows: *In addition to the above XVII Article. Very shortly after the signal for the whole fleet to prepare to tack together, agreeable to the said XVII Article, has been repeated as above directed,*

XVIII

Ship that leads the van of the fleet when in a line, to hoist, lower, set or haul up any of his sails.

When the Admiral would have the ship that leads the van of the fleet, or the headmost ship in the fleet, when they are in line of battle, hoist, lower, set or haul up any of his sails, the Admiral will spread a yellow flag under that at the main topmast head, and fire a gun; which the flag-ships, that have flags at the main topmast head, are to answer; and those flag-ships that have not are to hoist the yellow flag on the flag-staff at the main topmast head and fire a gun: Then the Admiral will hoist, lower, set or haul up the sail he would have the ships that lead the van do, which is to be answered by the flag-ships of the fleet.

XIX

How to engage the enemy when the fleet has the wind of them.

If the Admiral and his fleet have the wind of the enemy, and they have stretched themselves in a line of battle, the van of the Admiral's fleet is to steer with the van of the enemy, and there to engage them.

XX

Not to fire till within point-blank.

Every commander is to take care that his guns are not fired till he is sure he can reach the enemy upon a point-blank; and by no means to suffer his guns to be fired over any of our own ships.

the commander-in-chief will fire a second gun (which is not to be repeated), at which instant of time the helms of the whole fleet are to be put a-lee.

XXI

Not to pursue a small number of the enemy till the main body is run or disabled.

None of the ships in the fleet shall pursue any small number of the enemy's ships till the main body be disabled or run.

XXII

When a ship is in distress.

If any of the ships in the fleet are in distress and make the signal, which is a weft with the jack or ensign, the next ship to them is strictly required to relieve them.

XXIII

The Admiral or any flag-ship in distress.

If the Admiral, or any flag-ship, should be [*hard pressed or*[1]] in distress [*in battle*[1]] and make the usual signal, the ships in the fleet are to endeavour to get as close up into a line between him and the enemy as they can, having always an eye to defend him, if the enemy should come to annoy him in that condition.

XXIV

No ship to go out of the line without leave, and the next ships to close up the line.

No ship in the fleet shall leave his station, upon any pretence whatsoever, till he has acquainted his flag, or the next flag-officer to him, with the condition of his ship, and received his direction herein ; but in case any ship shall so do, the next ships are to close up the line : and if any commander shall be wanting in doing his duty, his flag,

[1] Inserted in MS.

or the next flag-officer to him, is immediately to send for the said commander from his ship and appoint another in his room.

XXV

When a flag-ship is disabled.

If any flag-ship be disabled, the flag may go on board any ship of his own squadron or division.

XXVI

The whole fleet to chase.

If the enemy be put to the run, and the Admiral thinks it convenient the whole fleet shall follow them, he will make all the sail he can himself after the enemy, and take down the signal for the line of battle, and fire two guns out of his fore-chase; and all the flag-ships are to do the same: then every ship in the fleet is to use his best endeavour to come up with the enemy, and lay them on board.

XXVII

Any particular flag-ship with his squadron or division to chase.

If the Admiral would have any particular flag-ship and his squadron or division give chase to the enemy, he will make the same signal that is appointed for that flag-ship's tacking with his squadron or division, and weathering the enemy.

XXVIII

To give over chase.

When the Admiral would have given over chase he will hoist a white flag at the fore topmast head and fire a gun.

XXIX

Any flag to cut or slip in the day.

If the Admiral would have any flag in his division or squadron cut or slip in the day-time, he will make the same signals that are appointed for those flag-ships, and their division or squadron, to tack and weather the enemy, as is expressed in the third, fourth, fifth and sixth articles before going.

XXX

Red, White, or Blue Squadron to draw into a line of battle abreast or ahead of one another, or any Vice or Rear-Admiral to do the like.

When the Admiral would have the Red [*or centre*[1]] Squadron draw into a line of battle, abreast of one another, he will put abroad a flag striped red and white on the flag-staff at the main topmast head, with a pennant under it, and fire a gun. If he would have the White Squadron, or those that have the second post in the fleet to do the like, the signal shall be a flag striped red, white and blue, with a pennant under it, at the aforesaid place. And if he would have the Blue Squadron [*or those that have the third post*[1]] do the like, he will put on the said place a [*white flag with a red cross*[2]] together with the pennant: but when he would have either of the said squadrons to draw into a line of battle ahead of one another, he will make the aforesaid signals without a pennant; which signals are to be answered by the flag-ships only of the said squadrons, and be kept out till the Admiral takes in his. And if the Admiral would have any Vice-Admiral of the fleet, and his division,

[1] Inserted in MS.
[2] Substituted for 'Genoese ensign.'

draw into a line of battle, as aforesaid, he will make the same signals at the fore topmast head that he makes for that squadron at the main topmast head; and for any Rear-Admiral of the fleet, and his division, the same signals at the [*mizen*] topmast head; which signals are to be answered by the Vice or Rear-Admiral to whom the signal is made.

XXXI

Fleet to draw into a line of battle, one astern of another.

When the Admiral would have the fleet draw into a line of battle, one astern of another, at the distance of two cables' length asunder, with a large wind, and would have [*him lead who commands in the second post, he will hoist a red and white flag at the mizen-peak, and fire a gun; and if he would have him lead who commands in the third post, he will at the same time make the established signal for inverting the line of battle; all which is to be answered by the flag-ships of the fleet. If at the distance of one cable's length asunder, a red pennant will be hoisted under the flag.*[1]]

[1] This MS. alteration is obviously the outcome of Keppel's action, and the subsequent court-martial on him. It may have been made by the Admiralty, for Admirals as a rule were not allowed to alter the General Instructions materially. In any case the alteration must have been recent, for the original form appears in all copies up to 1780. Before the alteration the article ran, 'and if he would have those lead who are to lead with their starboard tacks aboard by a wind he will hoist (*signal as above*), and if he would have those lead who are to lead with their larboard tacks aboard by a wind he will hoist a Genoese flag at the same place and fire a gun which is to be answered by the flag-ships of the fleet.'—*N.R.S.* xxix. (*Fighting Instructions*), p. 199. The Third Article of the charge against Keppel accused him of not having made this signal as it then stood in the old form established by Rooke in 1703.

XXXII

Signals made by the Admirals to be repeated by the flags.

When the fleet is in the line of battle, the signals that are made by the Admiral, for any squadron, or particular divisions, are to be repeated by all the flags that are between the Admiral and that squadron, or division, to whom the signal is made. *And when at any time the signal for inverting the line of battle (or any other signal, the fleet being in line of battle, or otherwise) shall have been made, though hauled down, after having been duly repeated and acknowledged, its operation is still to continue in force until it be annulled by the annulling flag, or until it be naturally superseded by the purport of some subsequent signal. But the signals for the line of battle, ahead or abreast, and for engaging the enemy, are to be (respectively) kept flying so long as the commander-in-chief shall judge proper to have the ships continue in line, or to continue engaging the enemy. Sailing in two or three lines, according to the 34th Article of the Additional Fighting Instructions, being considered as a kind of sailing order, the signal for the fleet so to form itself is to be hauled down, when acknowledged, but to continue in force until annulled by the annulling flag, or until superseded by the meaning of some subsequent signal.*

N.B.—The foregoing is referred to in Manuscript in the 58th Article (being with regard to annulling) of the Additional Sailing Instructions.[1]

[1] This is all a MS. addition to the original article of 1703. It is probably again official. Presumably it was the outcome of Rodney's action of April 17, 1780, which was spoiled by his captains believing his signal of intention to attack the rear was annulled by subsequent signals, whereas Rodney regarded it as remaining in force.—See Beatson, v. 59. The allusion to the

FINAL FORM OF THE REGULAR ADDITIONAL INSTRUCTIONS

(*Lord Rodney's and Admiral Pigot's signals in* 1781, 82, & 83 [1])

Formidable

Memo.[2]

Some examples and observations, &c. &c., with regard to the triangular flags hereby established, for the purpose of particularly denoting the squadrons of the fleet. To be pre-fixed to the Book of Additional Sailing and Fighting Instructions.

In order to facilitate the carrying on service, each squadron of the fleet is in future to be denoted, as occasion may require, by a triangular flag, signifying in any situation of the fleet, when hoisted wheresoever sufficiently conspicuous, that any signal

34th Article of the Additional Fighting Instructions would tend to show that at least the latter part of the above addition was not made by Rodney. The 34th Article was one of those added in MS. later than Rodney's issue of April 10, and in my own MS. Signal Book it is attributed to Pigot, though by some change in the numeration the article in question had become No. 33. No. 34 was a new instruction for breaking the line on contrary tacks.

[1] MS. note of later date.

[2] All in MS. The triangular flags for distinguishing squadrons were suggested by Kempenfelt as part of his new system in March, 1780—*N.R.S.* xxxii. (*Barham Papers*, i.), p. 314—but he had been using them apparently the previous year. They occur in his Signal Book of 1779 and the subsequent editions: and cf. *ibid.* p. 343. Rodney, however, did not adopt them. This memo. was subsequent to his retirement, and is not found in the copy he issued to Graves.

at the same time displayed regards only the squadron thereby denoted. A blue triangular flag, with a white horizontal stripe, displayed as above, denotes the Blue or Centre Squadron. A red one, having a white horizontal stripe, denotes the Red, or Van Squadron. And a white one, having a red horizontal stripe, the White or Rear Squadron.[1]

Example the 1*st. When the Admiral would have the Van or Rear Squadron go into port before him, instead of denoting such squadron with the respective pennant hoisted at the mizen-peak over the anchoring flag, as expressed under the* 20*th Article of the General Sailing Instructions and Signals by Day, a triangular flag as above described, being more convenient, will, in future, be used to signify such the purpose of the commander-in-chief and to denote the squadron.*

Example the 2*d. When the Admiral would have any squadron (or division) of the fleet chase to windward, to leeward, or on any particular quarter of the compass, as expressed in the* 59*th,* 60*th, and* 61*st Articles of the Additional Sailing Instructions, instead of signifying his purpose by hoisting the flag, or broad pennant of him who commands such squadron (or division) as therein mentioned, the respective triangular flag being more convenient, will in future be hoisted wheresoever sufficiently conspicuous, at the same time that the chasing flag is displayed.*

Example the 3*d. If at any time being in line*

[1] In Kempenfelt's latest book the arrangement differed. The one he adopted was as follows :—

First or Centre Squadron—red with yellow stripe.
Second or Van Squadron—white with blue stripe.
Third or Rear Squadron—blue with white stripe.
Detached Ships Squadron—yellow with red stripe.
Corps de Réserve or Flying Squadron...........—yellow with red flag.

of battle, or otherwise, the Union jack be hoisted, where it serves as a signal for the fleet to tack, or if the signal be made to wear, and come to the wind on the other tack and at the same time a triangular flag be displayed as above directed, such signal to tack or wear then regards the squadron only which is thereby denoted, which is then to tack or wear accordingly, its headmost or sternmost ship tacking or wearing first, or so doing altogether, as the signal for tacking or wearing shall have expressed.

Nevertheless, the signal for any particular ship or ships chasing, or for any particular ship otherwise sailing, to tack continues to be a Dutch flag at the fore or mizen topmast heads, respectively, which will also be sometimes there used, as more conspicuous than an English jack, as a signal for a squadron being at any considerable distance from the fleet to tack, the triangular flag denoting such squadron being at the same time displayed wherever best seen.

FIGHTING INSTRUCTIONS AND SIGNALS BY DAY

I

To draw into a line of battle, one ship ahead of another, and keep two cables' length asunder—To keep only a cable's length asunder—When in a line ahead, the course to be taken from the leading ship.

When the signal shall be made for the squadron to draw into a line of battle, one ship ahead of another, by hoisting an Union flag at the mizen-peak and firing a gun, the ships are to make all the sail they can into their respective stations, and keep at the distance of two cables' length asunder; but if the commander-in-chief would have them keep only a cable's length asunder, he will hoist a blue flag with a red cross under the Union flag at the mizen-peak and fire a gun; and it is to be observed that whenever the squadron shall be in a line ahead, the course is to be taken from the leading ship; the others in succession being always to be guided therein by their seconds ahead.

II

To draw into a line abreast.

When the commander-in-chief would have the squadron draw into a line of battle, one ship abreast of another, and keep *either of*[1] the distances

[1] MS. insertions and additions are indicated in italics throughout. This one is not in the copy which Rodney issued to Graves.

asunder directed in the aforegoing article, he will hoist a blue pennant under the *respective flag or* flags therein mentioned at the mizen-peak and fire a gun.

III

To draw into a line of battle and bear on particular points of the compass from each other.

When the commander-in-chief would have the squadron draw into a line of battle *at the distance of two cables' length asunder*, and regulate themselves by bearing on some particular point of the compass from each other, always steering *with precision while so formed* the same course as the commander-in-chief, he will make the signal expressed against the points of the *compass in the following table and fire a gun; and if he would have them keep at the distance of one cable's length asunder, a yellow pennant, with a blue fly, will be hoisted at the mizen-peak over the respective flag; if at three cables' length asunder, a white one with a red fly; and if at half a mile asunder, a blue one.*[1]

If to bear from each other	Signals
North and South . . .	A flag striped blue and white at the mizen-peak.
N. by E. and S. by W. . .	A red } pennant under the said flag.
NNE. and SSW. . . .	A white } pennant under the said flag.
NE. by N. and SW. by S. .	A blue } pennant under the said flag.
NE. and SW. . . .	A blue flag pierced with white at the mizen-peak.
NE. by E. and SW. by W. .	A red } pennant under the said flag.
ENE. and WSW. . . .	A white } pennant under the said flag.
E. by N. and W. by S. . .	A blue } pennant under the said flag.

[1] In Graves's copy (Rodney) the article ends, 'fire one gun, but if he would have them only a cable's length asunder he will fire two guns; *if half a mile*, 3 *guns; if one mile*, 4 *guns* (MS. addition).

If to bear from each other	Signals
East and West	A red flag with a white cross at the mizen-peak.
E. by S. and W. by N.	A red pennant under the said flag.
ESE. and WNW.	A white pennant under the said flag.
SE. by E. and NW. by W.	A blue pennant under the said flag.
SE. and NW.	A yellow flag at the mizen-peak.
SE. by S. and NW. by N.	A red pennant under the said flag.
SSE. and NNW.	A white pennant under the said flag.
S. by E. and N. by W.	A blue pennant under the said flag.

IV

When in a line of battle, for all the ships to alter their course and preserve the same bearings and distance from each other as before—To starboard—To port.

When sailing in a line of battle (either ahead, abreast, or in any other position) and the commander-in-chief would have all the ships *prepare to* alter their course at one and the same time, still preserving their bearings and distance from each other as before, always taking it from the centre; if to starboard, he will hoist a blue flag with a red cross at the main top-gallant-mast head and fire a gun; if to port, a flag half blue half red at the same place and fire a gun; and after the signal has been repeated, he will, for every point of the compass he would have the course altered *haul down the respective flag and then rehoist it once, after which a second gun will be fired* (*which is not to be repeated*).[1] Whereupon every ship in the line is immediately to alter her course accordingly.

[1] This alteration of the old signal is not in Graves's copy. It must have been made very late, for it is not in my MS. Signal Book. Rodney used one gun for every point.

V

When in a line of battle ahead for the leading ship to alter her course, and the rest of the ships to get into her wake, still preserving the line ahead.

When sailing in a line of battle ahead, and the commander-in-chief would have the ship that leads alter her course, and the rest of the ships get into her wake, still preserving the line ahead, he will hoist a white pennant under the flags mentioned in the aforegoing article, at the main top-gallant-mast head and fire a gun ; and after the signal has been repeated he will, for every point of the compass he would have the course altered, *haul down the respective flag and then rehoist it once, after which a second gun is to be fired, which is not to be repeated;*[1] whereupon the leading ship is immediately to alter her course accordingly, and the rest of the ships in the line are *in succession* to get into her wake as fast as possible.

VI

If the signal should be made for the headmost ship to tack whilst in a line of battle, the ship that then leads is to continue leading on the other tack.

If the signal should be made for the headmost ship to tack first, whilst in a line of battle, the ship that then leads is to continue leading on the other tack after she shall be about, and the rest of the ships in the line are to follow her in the same order they did on the former tack.

[1] Both the MS. alterations in this article are subsequent to Rodney. He used a gun for every point, as above.

VII

If the signal should be made for the whole squadron to tack together whilst in a line ahead, for the ships to preserve the same bearing from each other as before.

If, when sailing in a line of battle ahead, the commander-in-chief should make the signal for the whole squadron *to prepare* to tack together, and at the same time hoist a red pennant under the signal for the line ahead, every ship when about is carefully to preserve the same bearing as before the signal was made. For instance, if they were drawn up in a line N.E. and S.W. all their mainmasts when about are to bear on those points of the compass from each other, taking it from the centre, and making or shortening sail so as to preserve their stations with the distance prescribed by the signal; but in case the wind should shift, their mainmasts are to bear from each other on the points of the compass whereon they will lie on the other tack (always allowing twelve points) so that whenever they put about again they may be in a direct line ahead.

N.B.—*Very shortly after the above signal shall have been duly repeated he will fire a second gun (which is not to be repeated), at which instant of time the helms of the whole fleet are to be put a-lee.*[1]

VIII

When in a line of battle, to keep the same distance asunder those ships do that are next the commander-in-chief. For the ships ahead, or on the starboard beam, to close to the centre.

In sailing in a line of battle, every ship is to keep at the same distance those ships do that are

[1] This MS. addition is subsequent to Rodney.

next the commander-in-chief, always taking it from the centre; and if at any time the commander-in-chief shall think the ship next ahead of him, or next on his starboard beam, is at too great a distance, he will make the same known to her by putting abroad a common pennant at the jib-boom-end, which will be kept flying till she is closed to the proposed distance; and if that ship shall find the next ahead of her, or the next on her starboard beam, is at a greater distance from her than she is from the ship of the commander-in-chief, she is to make the same signal and keep it flying till the other shall be closed to the proper distance; and so on to the van, or the outermost ship of the starboard wing of the line. *If he thinks her too near, he will show a Spanish jack on the bowsprit where best seen, or in his starboard mizen-shrouds, which signal if necessary is to be communicated on as above.*[1]

IX

For the ships astern, or on the larboard beam, to close to the centre.

But when the commander-in-chief shall think the ship next astern of him, or the next on his larboard beam, is at too great a distance, he will make it known to her by putting abroad a common pennant at the mizen top-sail yard-arm, which will be kept flying till she is closed to the proposed distance; and if that ship shall find the next astern of her, or the next on her larboard beam, is at a greater distance from her than she is from the ship of the commander-in-chief, she is to make the same signal, and keep it flying till the other shall be closed to the proper distance; and so on to the rear, or the outermost ship of the larboard wing

[1] This MS. addition is subsequent to Rodney.

of the line. *And if he thinks her too near, he will show a common pennant at the cross-jack yard-arm, which signal when necessary is to be communicated on as above.*[1]

X

For any particular ship to close her second.

And if at any time the captain of any particular ship in the line shall think the ship without him at a greater distance than the ships which are next the centre, he is to make the same known to her by the signal appointed for that purpose in either of the two aforegoing articles ; whereupon such ship is immediately to close to the proper distance.

XI

If the squadron should be in two divisions, for them to form in separate lines of battle.

If the squadron should happen to be in two divisions, and the commander-in-chief would have them form themselves into separate lines of battle, one ship ahead of another at the distance of a cable's length asunder, and each division to be abreast of the other, when formed, at the distance of two cables' length asunder, he will hoist a flag quartered blue and white at the mizen-peak and fire a gun.

XII

Bringing-to in a line of battle.

If the commander-in-chief should make the signal appointed by the 15th Article of the General Printed Fighting Instructions for bringing-to in a line of battle, the ships are to bring-to with the

[1] This MS. addition is subsequent to Rodney.

main top-sail to the mast, instead of bracing their head sails to the mast as is there prescribed.

XIII

To change stations in the line.

If at any time the commander-in-chief shall think it necessary to alter the disposition of the ships in the line of battle, and would have any two of them change stations with each other, he will make the signal for speaking with the captains of such ships, and hoist a flag quartered red and white at the main top-gallant-mast head.

XIV

The whole squadron being in chase,[1] to engage the enemy in succession as they may happen to get up.

If the commander-in-chief should chase with the whole squadron, and would have those ships that are nearest attack the enemy, the headmost opposing their sternmost, the next passing on under the cover of her fire and engaging the second from the enemy's rear, and so on in succession as they may happen to get up, without respect to seniority or the prescribed order of battle, he will hoist a Dutch flag at the main top-gallant-mast head and fire a gun, keeping at the same time the signal for chase flying. When each ship as they get up are to engage their opponents, and on no pretence quit them, until they are so disabled that they cannot get away or submit; if to engage to windward the above flag as specified; if to leeward a blue pennant under the same flag.

[1] The original has 'chace' throughout.'

XV

The whole squadron being in chase, for some of the headmost ships to draw into a line of battle ahead and the rest to strengthen that line as they get up.

If at any time, when the whole squadron shall be in chase, the commander-in-chief would have a certain number of ships that are nearest the enemy draw into a line of battle ahead, in order to engage the ships in their rear, endeavouring at the same time to get up with the van, he will hoist a red flag with a white cross at the main top-gallant-mast head and fire

one gun	if he	five ships	draw into a line ahead of each other.
three guns	would have	seven ships	

Whereupon those ships are immediately to form the line without any regard to seniority, or the general form delivered, but according to their distances from the enemy, viz. the headmost and nearest ship to the enemy is to lead, and the sternmost to bring up the rear, that no time may be lost in the pursuit; and the rest of the ships are to form and strengthen that line as they get up, without paying any respect to the prescribed order of battle.

XVI

When turning to the windward on the enemy, the headmost and sternmost ships to make known when they can weather them.

If the squadron should be turning to windward on the enemy in a line of battle, the headmost ship is to make known when she can weather them by hoisting a common pennant at the mizen top-mast head, which is to be repeated by every ship between her and the commander-in-chief, until he make the same signal, and if he should think proper to stand on till the sternmost ship can weather them, she is to make the same known by hoisting a common pennant at the fore top-gallant-mast head, which is to be repeated as before. The sternmost ship is likewise to do so whenever the squadron shall be to windward of the enemy and her commander shall think himself far enough astern of their rear to lead down out of their line of fire.

XVII

When in a line of battle ahead to windward of the enemy, to lead down to them, and every ship to steer for her opponent.

If the squadron should be sailing in a line of battle ahead to windward of the enemy, and the commander-in-chief would have the course altered in order to lead down to them, he will hoist an Union flag at the main top-gallant-mast head, and fire a gun. Whereupon every ship in the squadron is to steer for the ship of the enemy, which, from the disposition of the two squadrons, it must be her lot to engage, notwithstanding the signal for the line ahead will be kept flying ; making or shortening sail in such proportion as to preserve the distance assigned by the signal of the line, in order that the whole squadron may, as near as possible, come to action at the same time.

XVIII

The headmost ship to attack the enemy's rear, and so on in succession till the sternmost become the leader and opposed to the enemy's van.

If the squadron should be to windward of the enemy (or in any other position that will admit of it) and the commander-in-chief would have the headmost ship lead down out of their line-of-fire and attack their rear, he will hoist a Dutch flag at the main top-gallant-mast head and fire a gun. The second from the leader is then to pass on under the cover of her fire, and attack the second ship from the enemy's rear; and so on until the sternmost ship become the leader and opposed to the enemy's van. If to engage to windward, the above flags as mentioned; if to leeward, a blue pennant under it.

N.B.—You are referred to the latter part of the 14th Article respecting your opponents when up with them.

XIX

To come to a closer engagement.

If at any time, whilst engaged with the enemy, the commander-in-chief shall judge it necessary to come to a closer engagement, he will hoist a flag half blue and half white under the signal for engaging at the fore top-gallant-mast head; whereupon every ship is to engage the enemy as close as possible.

XX

Upon meeting with an enemy of inferior force, for some of the smallest ships to quit the line.[1]

In case of meeting with an enemy inferior to his Majesty's squadron, if the commander-in-chief would have any of the smaller ships quit the line, that those of the greatest force may be opposed to the enemy, he will put abroad the signal for speaking with the captains of such ships as he

[1] Note that the similar article (No. 26) which Rodney had cancelled in 1780 is wanting, and that his MS. addition to the old Article 24 has been established. See *supra*, pp. 226–7.

would have quit the line, and hoist a flag striped yellow and white at the main top-gallant-mast head; whereupon the next ships are immediately to close up the line, and those that have quitted it are to hold themselves in readiness to assist any ship that may be disabled or hard pressed, or to take her station if she should be obliged to go out of the line, in which case the strongest ship that is withdrawn from the line is strictly enjoined to supply her place and fill up the vacancy. If he engage to windward of the enemy, the ships are to draw out of the line, to lay-to to windward; if to the leeward of the enemy, they are to draw out ahead or to the rear.

XXI

Upon meeting with an enemy with merchant ships under convoy, for some of the ships to fall upon the convoy.

And in case of meeting with a squadron of the enemy's ships of war, with merchant ships under their convoy; if the commander-in-chief (though the signal for the line of battle should be out) would have any of the frigates that are out of the line or any of the ships in the line, fall upon the convoy whilst the others are engaged, he will hoist a flag striped yellow and white at the main top-gallant-mast head, with a white pennant under it, and make the signal for speaking with the captains of such ships as he would have perform that service.

XXII

For the fire-ships to prime.

When the commander-in-chief would have the fire-ships prime, he will hoist a flag half yellow half blue at the main top-gallant-mast head and fire a gun ; but if the squadron should at any time be in chase of the enemy's fleet, the fire-ships are to prime as fast as possible, whether the signal be made or not.

XXIII

The ships to be held in constant readiness for action ; and in case of engaging, a boat to be kept manned and armed, &c., on the off-side from the enemy.

Every ship in the squadron is to be held in constant readiness for action ; and in case of coming to an engagement, a boat is to be kept manned and armed with hand and fire-chain grapnels, &c., on the off-side, to be ready to assist, as well as any ship that may be attempted by the fire-ships of the enemy, as our own fire-ships, should they be ordered on service.

XXIV

For the three-decked ships to form in the van or rear.

If the commander-in-chief would have three-decked *or other* heavy ships, *to be distinguished by their respective pennants in succession and to form accordingly*, draw out of their places in the line-of-battle and form in the van of the fleet, he will hoist a white flag pierced red at the fore top-gallant-mast head ; but if he would have those ships draw out of the line and form in the rear of the fleet, he will put out the above flag and a red pennant under it. In both the above cases the ships who preceded and followed those ships who have quitted the line, to form in the van or rear, are immediately to close the line and fill up their places. *In the former case the ship for which the signal is last made is to be the headmost in the van, and the latter case the sternmost in the rear. To annul in whole either of the above signals, when it is re-displayed therewith, will be hoisted the annulling flag only. To do so in part, pennants for particular ships will be added. Each is accordingly to resume her former station.*[1]

XXV

To close in order in line of battle.

If the commander-in-chief would have the ships to close in order in line of battle, or otherwise, he will hoist a flag half red half blue at the main top-gallant-mast head under his own flag; but if he would have the ships to open in line of battle, or otherwise, to give room for manœuvring, he will hoist a red pennant under the above flag.

XXVI

To attack the enemy's centre.

When the commander-in-chief means to make an attack upon the enemy's centre, he will hoist a *Spanish jack* at the fore top-gallant-mast head *with a red pennant over it.*

XXVII

Ditto on the enemy's rear	Ditto flag and a *white* pennant over it.

XXVIII

Ditto on the enemy's van	Ditto flag and a *blue* pennant under it.

1 By this and the next four articles Rodney's special method of concentration by massing his heavy ships is officially adopted. The passages in italics are his final MS. amendments. See *Introduction*, *supra*, p. 13. They all occur in the Graves copy.

XXIX

For the line of battle ahead, and the Admiral who commands in the second post, &c.

If at any time the Admiral should make the signal for the line of battle ahead, and would have the Admiral who commands in the second post lead with his division, he will hoist a flag half white half red at the fore top-gallant-mast head; and if he would have the Admiral who commands in the third post and his division do the same (*without inverting the order of the other divisions*)[1] he will hoist a flag half white half red at the mizen top-mast head, when he is to form accordingly.

XXX

When the commander-in-chief thinks the van at too great a distance from the centre.[2]

Whenever the commander-in-chief thinks the van of the fleet are at too great a distance from the centre, he will hoist a red flag pierced with white at the fore top-gallant-mast head, when the van are immediately to close, and upon no account to be more than two cables' length from each other, or the distance prescribed by the signal for the line; and when he thinks the rear of the fleet are at too great a distance from the centre, he will hoist the above-mentioned flag at the mizen top-mast head, when they are immediately to close with all despatch possible, and no ship whatever to chase from the fleet during action, before the main body of the enemy's fleet are beat, or a particular signal or order for that purpose.

[1] This MS. addition is subsequent to Rodney.

[2] This article is new—the outcome obviously of Rodney's experiences in handling his fleet in 1780.

XXXI

Whereas, from the separation of the ships under my command, it may be necessary from time to time to form a temporary line of battle with the ships who may be in company with me.[1]

That the captains may know the stations they are to take in such line, I will, at the time of making the signal for the line of battle ahead, or abreast, or on any bearing as I shall see occasion, hoist the established preparative flag, which being answered by all the ships, their answering flags are to be hauled down: I will then throw out the captain's signal who is to lead on the tack I am on, who is to answer as soon he can; immediately after his answering, another captain's signal will be made, who is to answer and form next to the ship whose signal was first made, and so on in succession until the line of battle ahead is formed, and the last ship's signal that is made is to bring up the rear, and be the leading ship on the other tack, should the signal for that purpose be made; or if sailing large or before the wind, and I should see it necessary to form the line of battle abreast, the signal for the line and the preparatory flag will be hoisted as before-mentioned, and the first captain's signal which is made is to be the wing ship on the starboard side, the second ship's signal which is made, next to him, and so on in

[1] The whole of this instruction except the MS. insertions is Captain Young's, who established it while he was Rodney's flag-captain in 1780. He sent it home for approval on September 22 of that year, with his own approval of Kempenfelt's new signals.—*Barham Papers*, i. 76. It will be seen that the final words in MS. increase the difficulty raised by Sir J. K. Laughton in his note (*ibid.*). He suggested the Red Ensign order must have been cancelled, because on April 12 squadron colours seem to have been used. Here, however, the Red Ensign is clearly established, but possibly only for the 'temporary' line of battle.

succession until the line is formed, and the last captain whose signal is made is to be the wing ship on the larboard side.

N.B.—The ship thus appointed to lead is to lead on both tacks, according to established order.[1]

And this order is to be considered and noted as the disposition of the line of battle, and the ships are to take their stations accordingly until such dispositions are altered by any other signal.

Each ship to be prepared with a blank form to put down in writing each ship's station in those temporary lines of battle, as it shall be signified by the above mode; and when the signal for the line is taken in the captains are to fall into their stations with the commanders of the divisions, as established by the regular line of battle delivered to them.

And likewise to observe, that when forming the line as before-mentioned, to distinguish the last ship of each division to the officers commanding them, and to the captains reciprocally, that they may know the ships of their division and the division they are in: a pennant striped blue and white will be hoisted at the fore top-gallant-mast head at the time the captain's signal is out, to point out to the officers commanding divisions, and the captains that that ship is last of that division.

In action all ships are to wear RED ENSIGNS *and proper English pennants.*[1]

XXXII

If at any time from baffling winds or other cause I think it expedient for my division to lead the fleet in line of battle for attacking the enemy, I will previous to the signal for the line at making it or

[1] This MS. addition is subsequent to Rodney.

while in line as shall be proper hoist a yellow flag with a blue fly at the fore top-gallant-mast head and fire one gun. And if I would have the van division then become the centre, a red pennant will be hoisted under the said flag. And for the rear division to become the centre, a blue pennant. The leading ship of my division is then to lead the fleet, and the leading ship of the division next to follow is, as above alluded to, of course to be next to the sternmost of mine and so on.

N.B.—To be hauled down when acknowledged, but to operate until annulled by the annulling flag. Established by Lord Rodney 10*th April*, 1782.[1]

FINAL MS. ADDITIONS BY PIGOT AND HOOD.

XXXIII

To invert the order of battle, a Dutch ensign reversed at the main topmast head, or if necessary, where best seen.

XXXIV

When sailing by the wind or large for the divisions of the fleet (whether it consists of two or three divisions) the flag officers keeping their places therein, to form in as many distinct lines of battle ahead (which is a good order of sailing) one ship two cables' length astern of another, keeping the distance of half a mile between the wakes of such divisions, and the sternmost ships of the division leading for the time being keeping right

[1] All this article except the last paragraph is in Graves's copy, and therefore Rodney's. The Washington copy has the following MS. note of later date: *April* 9. *Partial engagement of Van Division with French owing to light airs, hence Article* 32.

abreast of the commander-in-chief's second ahead,[1] and the headmost ship of the division following him keeping abreast of his second astern, a white flag with a red fly will be hoisted at the mizen-peak. If at the distance of one cable's length astern of each other, a red pennant under the said flag; and if at the distance of three cables' length, a blue one. When formed as above the frigates, sloops, fire-ships, &c., are to follow in straight lines astern of their respective repeaters at the distances from each other as above mentioned, on the weather, starboard or larboard quarters (respectively) of their divisions, and at the distance of two cables' length from the wakes of said divisions. N.B.—To invert the above order, the Dutch ensign reversed as for inverting other lines of battle will be hoisted.[2]

XXXV

When standing towards the enemy in line of battle, on a contrary tack, for the leading ship to lead through his line in order to cut off his van or rear, a flag chequered blue and yellow will be hoisted at the fore top-gallant-mast head; and when so standing towards an enemy or being actually in battle, for any particular ship to lead through his line, and all the rest stationed astern of that ship to follow in due and close succession to support her for the same purpose, a flag quartered red and

[1] The Commander-in-Chief's station was in the centre of his division. From the wording of this article it will be seen that the new sailing order was based on the conception of squadrons or divisions in separate lines of battle.

[2] In the editor's Signal Book this article is cited as No. 33, and it is assigned to Pigot. Kempenfelt had introduced it into the Channel Fleet as early as 1779, but Rodney had never adopted it. As a Channel Fleet man Sir Charles Douglas probably approved of it, and induced Pigot to sanction it as soon as Rodney's back was turned.

white (with such particular ship's signal displayed) will be hoisted at the fore or mizen top-gallant-mast head respectively. If at the mizen top-gallant or mizen topmast head, a red pennant will be hoisted over the said flag.[1]

XXXVI

If at any time the more surely and speedily to bring on, or with the greater efficacy to continue an engagement, the commander-in-chief would have his ships (independently of each other) steer forand respectively engage those of the enemy happening to be opposed to them for the time being, he will hoist a flag half blue half yellow at the fore top-gallant-mast head with or without firing a gun as may be proper.[2]

XXXVII

When at any time being in line of battle (or otherwise) the Admiral would have the whole fleet prepare to wear together, and come to the wind on the other tack, he will hoist a white flag with a red fly under the usual broad pennant at the ensign-staff[3] and fire a gun; and after the said signal shall have been duly repeated, he will fire a second gun (which is not to be repeated), at which instant of time the helms of the whole fleet are to be put a-weather. And when all the ships are come to the wind after wearing, they are, until

[1] In my Signal Book this article is No. 34. It is not assigned to Pigot, and was certainly the Instruction corresponding to Hood's signal issued April 27, 1782.

[2] This and the following articles are later than the editor's Signal Book. No. 36 corresponds to Hood's signal for engaging independently, issued April 27, 1782.

[3] The signal for wearing was a white broad pennant at the ensign staff.

otherwise directed by signal, to keep at the same bearings and distance they were at from each other on the former tack, agreeable to the intent and meaning of the 7th Article of these Additional Fighting Instructions. But, if after so wearing or tacking together in line, or after the rear shall have tacked first, the signal for inverting the order of battle should be made, the ships are then as fast as they can to get into the wake of him who then becomes the leader. If the fleet was then in an inverted order, previous to having so wore or put about, after the signal for annulling or discontinuing such inversion shall have been made (the signal for the line of battle ahead in either case being either made afresh or kept flying) the ships are then also as fast as they can to get into the wake of the leading ship.

Supplementary MS. Article.

Formidable.

Mem. To be added to the Additional Fighting Instructions and Signals by day, making the 38th Article altogether.

XXXVIII

When at any time being in line of battle ahead, the Admiral would have the fleet prepare to wear in succession, the headmost ship wearing first, and come-to the wind on the other tack, which from sundry causes may become expedient, he will hoist a flag half blue half white at the ensign-staff, under the usual signal for wearing, and fire a gun, and shortly after such signal shall have been duly repeated and acknowledged, he will fire a second gun, which is not to be repeated; at which instant of time the helm of the leading ship is to be put a-weather, and she is to run under an easy and governing sail to leeward of the line, at the distance of two cables' length therefrom, and parallel thereto, until she passes under the lee quarter of the sternmost ship of the fleet, when she is to haul close to the wind and, continuing to lead the fleet, to carry the same sail she was under at the time the signal was made for wearing. When after having put her helm a-weather as above directed the stern of such leading ship shall be right abreast of the stern of her immediate follower, the follower is then to put her helm a-weather and follow at the distance of two cables' length astern of the leader, hauling also by the wind after having passed the lee quarter of the sternmost ship of the fleet, and so on in due succession through the whole line; the sternmost ship wearing last, and all proceeding after having hauled up at the same distance from each other which they were at upon the former tack. The repeating frigates, other frigates, fire-ships, sloops, &c., &c., still keeping themselves to windward of the line, are to wear in like manner and as fast as safely may be to assume their respective stations after wearing.

To the Hon. Captain Phipps
of His Majesty's Ship Berwick.

FIGHTING INSTRUCTIONS AND SIGNALS BY NIGHT

I

To draw into a line of battle ahead.

If the commander-in-chief would have the squadron draw into a line of battle ahead, he will show two lights (*to be kept abroad while in line*) in the main topmast shrouds, one above the other, with or without a gun, as there may be occasion. *For the signal to form the order of sailing when in line of battle or otherwise, see the 17th Article of the Additional Sailing Instructions and Signals by night. N.B.—To invert the order of battle, one light in the mizen topmast shrouds besides the two above-mentioned.*[1]

II

To tack in a line of battle ahead.

When the squadron shall be in a line of battle ahead, and the commander-in-chief would have them tack, and preserve the same order of battle after they shall be about, he will, in addition to the usual signal for tacking, show two lights, one under the other, at the bowsprit end; whereupon the headmost ship is to tack first and continue to lead, the rest of the ships tacking in her wake, and forming a direct line after her. *And when he would have them wear in succession and sail in the same order of battle after coming to the wind on the*

[1] The MS. parts of these articles are all subsequent to Rodney and do not occur in Graves's copy.

other tack, he will hoist one light at the mizen-peak and fire two guns, and also show two lights, one under the other at the bowsprit end, whereupon the sternmost ship is to wear first and to lead the fleet, and the rest of the ships wearing in succession are to get into her wake as fast as possible, forming a direct line astern of her. Although in the latter case the line of battle should become inverted, the signal for inverting (being herein superfluous) is not to be expected.

N.B.—When the signals in question are made each ship of the fleet is of course to show, as usual, a light at her mizen-peak.

III

To know our ships when in action in the night.

In case of engaging the enemy in the night, the better to know our ships, and prevent their firing into each other, every ship in action is to hoist three lights in a triangle at the mizen-peak, and two at the bowsprit end, one over the other ; the admiral will hoist the same signals exclusive of his usual lights.

IV

To know what course the enemy may steer in the night.

For the better ascertaining what course the enemy may steer in the night, the headmost ship in chasc (while she keeps sight of the enemy) shall carry one light in her middle poop lanthorn, and one at her main topmast head.

V

In case of engaging the enemy's King's ships.

In case of engaging any King's ships of the enemy the ships are to form the line of battle ahead in the closest manner they can, taking it from the headmost ship without paying attention to the form of the line of battle, and to pass on in succession, the headmost opposing their sternmost, the next passing under cover of her fire, and engaging the second ship of the enemy's rear, and so on as they may happen to get up; and on no pretence whatever to pass by the ship they ought to engage, but to stay by her until she submits, or is so disabled that she cannot get away.

VI

In case the enemy should disperse.

In case of meeting a squadron of King's ships of the enemy, and they should disperse, and take different courses on purpose to get away, the ships as they get up are to engage the first ship they meet with, and not to quit her (except distressed) on any account whatever until she strikes, or is so disabled that she cannot get away.

VII

If the ship should be disabled.

When in battle, should any ship in the squadron be disabled or in distress, the captain of the said ship is to show four lights one above the other where best seen, and fire two guns, when the ships nearest to the ship who made the signal, are to give her immediate assistance with boats, &c. &c.

VIII

To bear up and sail large.

If the commander-in-chief, when in battle *or while in line of battle*, should think it necessary to bear up and sail large or before the wind *still preserving the line in its former direction according to compass*, he will hoist two lights, one under the other at the mizen-peak, and two ditto, one under the other at the ensign-staff, and fire one gun ; if to *come to* the wind and sail on the starboard tack, he will put abroad four lights in a square 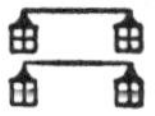 where best seen, and fire one gun ; if to do the same to port, four lights in a lozenge  where best seen, and fire one gun; and when the Admiral fires a gun after the signal guns have been fired, the ships are to alter their course accordingly.

N.B.—While sailing large in the order above alluded to, two lights of equal height, as low down, and as far asunder as may be well (after bearing up), [to] be kept abroad in the main topmast shroud.

IX

To lie-by on the starboard tack.

If the commander-in-chief should bring to and lie-by on the starboard tack, he will show triangular lights inverted thus: 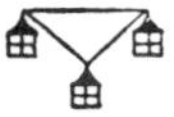 where best seen, and fire two guns (*the sternmost ships and so on in succession bringing-to first*) ; if to bring-to on the larboard tacks, three lights one over the other where best seen, and fire two guns. To make sail after lying-by two lights at the ensign-staff, one at the mizen-peak, and two guns, whereupon the headmost ship is to fill and make sail first, and so on in succession.

N.B.—The lights at the ensign-staff to be further asunder than for tacking.

X

For the transports and convoys to disperse.

If the Admiral would have all the transports and vessels under convoy disperse and shift for themselves, he will hoist two lights one under the other at the fore and main topmast heads, and fire two guns quick, and two minutes after two guns more quick.

Articles added in MS.

XI

For the fleet when in line of battle, or otherwise, to form itself in three lines according to the 34th Article of these Additional Fighting Instructions, three lights in the mizen topmast shrouds, one over the other, and two lights of equal height as far asunder as may be in the mizen shrouds, with or without a gun, as shall be proper.

XII

When being in line of battle the Admiral would have the rear of the fleet tack first and in succession (the sternmost ship consequently putting about first) he will in addition to the usual signal for tacking, put abroad two lights, one over the other in the mizen shrouds, and the ships when about are in succession to get as fast as they can into her wake, forming a direct line astern of her.

[*MS. note as to repeating frigates.*]

N.B.—Anything heretofore signified to the contrary notwithstanding. When the signal is made to form the line, as also when other signals are made while the fleet is in line of battle, either ahead or abreast during the night, the repeating frigates are so far to repeat as to show the respective lights, but are not to repeat the guns fired, which are to be repeated by the flagships only. Nevertheless, when a division of the fleet is stationed ahead of the Admiral at the distance of one, two, three or more leagues, the repeating frigate belonging to such division is, during the night, fully to repeat all such signals, whether made with false fires, firing of guns, or lights as shall be made by the flag-officer commanding such division, or by the commander-in-chief, and such repeating frigate when so sailing by the wind or laying-to, is for that purpose (as also for the purpose of repeating signals in the day-time while her respective division is so situated) to be stationed four points upon her said flag-officer's weather quarter, and when sailing large four points upon his starboard quarter, so as to be at the same distance from him as from the commander-in-chief.

N.B.—In manner and under circumstances as above-mentioned only, unless otherwise particularly required, signals are to be repeated by the repeating frigates during the night.

ADDITIONAL SIGNALS RELATIVE TO THE LANDING OF MARINES AND COMPANIES OF LANDERS[1]

I

For all the Marines of the fleet to prepare for landing, a yellow flag with a blue fly at the mizen topmast head and one gun.

II

For the Marines of the centre division to prepare for landing, a yellow flag with a blue fly, at mizen topmast head, with a red pennant under it and one gun.

III

For the Marines of the van division to prepare for landing, a yellow flag with a blue fly at the mizen topmast head, with a white pennant under it and one gun.

IV

For the Marines of the rear division to prepare for landing, a yellow flag, with a blue fly at the mizen topmast head, with a blue pennant under it and one gun.

V

For the Marines in whole or in part (having been previously directed to prepare themselves for landing as above expressed) *to get into the boats*,

[1] These eleven articles are a MS. addition by Rodney. See *supra*, p. 266.

a flag red, white and red at the fore top-gallant-mast head and one gun; actually to land, a blue pennant under the said flag and one gun.

VI

For the companies of men belonging to the fleet embodied for acting on shore and called Landers, to prepare for landing, a white flag with a red fly at the fore top-gallant-mast head and one gun.

VII

For the companies of Landers of the centre division to prepare for landing, a white flag with a red fly at the fore top-gallant-mast head, with a red pennant under it, and one gun.

VIII

For the companies of Landers of the van division to prepare for landing, a white flag with a red fly, at the fore top-gallant-mast head, with a white pennant under it, and one gun.

IX

For the companies of Landers of the rear division to prepare for landing, a white flag with a red fly at the fore top-gallant-mast head, with a blue pennant under it and one gun.

X

For the Landers (in whole or in part) having been previously directed to prepare themselves for landing as above expressed *to get into the boats*, a flag red, white and red at the main top-gallant-mast head and one gun. Actually to land, a red pennant under the said flag, and one gun.

XI

If at any time, after the signal shall have been made for Marines or embodied Landers to prepare themselves for landing, the Admiral should think proper to land a lesser number of each or of either, for example, those belonging to one division only, the preparative signal for those of such division (respectively) as shall be then destined to land will be made afresh. N.B.—When at any time the signal for Marines or Landers is made to get into the boats, they are forthwith to repair to the flag-ships of their respective divisions, on the signal being made for Marines or Landers to prepare for landing. Each man is to be furnished with two days' ready dressed provisions of beef, pork, and bread, and every eight men with a four-gallon keg of water. The Landers are to be armed with muskets and bayonets, or (some of them) with pistols and pole axes as occasion may require, for which purpose the weapons last mentioned are to be kept in readiness for being with them landed in the following proportion, viz. :

For every two Landers, one pair of pistols and one pole axe, to the end that the most active half thereof (sustained by the muskets and bayonets of the other) may be suitably armed for the purpose of scaling walls or heights by the means of ladders or otherwise.

For every Marine so landing, besides what his cartouch box contains, twenty-six full musket cartridges are to be landed, and for each Lander, besides what his cartouch box contains, eighteen full musket cartridges are to be landed. N.B.—In two distinct boxes, and each Marine or Lander is to be furnished with two spare flints.

For every pair of pistols which are to be distributed as above, before or after landing as occasion may require, one cartouch box filled with the proper cartridges is to be given out on board or sent on shore.[1]

Given under my hand on board His Majesty's Ship Formidable.

For Captain of His Majesty's Ship——

By command of the Admiral——

[1] Here has been written in another hand 'Established by Lord Rodney 20th Feby. 1782,' with the following footnote appended:—'*Rodney arrived at Barbadoes February* 19, 1782, *having left England five weeks before* (*Mundy's Life of Rodney*, *Vol. II.* 190). *It is therefore evident that these were prepared on the passage out, and issued immediately upon arrival.*'

LORD HOWE'S ADDITIONAL INSTRUCTIONS, 1790–1794

With the exception of the 'Explanatory Instructions' which are taken from 'Lord Howe's Signal Book (1793?)' in the Admiralty Library, all these Instructions are printed from the original copies in the *Bridport Papers*, as they were issued by Lord Howe to Vice-Admiral Sir Alexander Hood, the junior squadron-commander of his fleet at the time of the 'Nootka Sound' armament. The first three sets were issued on July 10, when Howe was about to sail in search of the Spanish fleet. They are on loose folio sheets — printed, with the usual blanks for signals and some MS. amendments. The rest are in MS. and were issued on October 19, after his return to Spithead and when he was under orders to sail again at a moment's notice. The signal numbers have been filled in by hand, and tally with the Walsh Signal Book of 1790–1. From the reference in Article V. of the second set to 'Art. 2nd, page 9 . . . in the Signal Book,' it would appear there was a printed Signal Book.[1] The code used was practically identical with that of 1793 referred to above, but the signals were arranged in a different order. It was entirely different from the Howe-Kempenfelt book of 1782, but closely resembled that of the MS. book in the editor's possession signed 'R. C. (? Roger Curtis) 1789.'

[1] In this book each signal with its signification is called an 'article,' e.g. Art. 2=Numeral 2, the single flag signal 'to form order of sailing by divisions.'

The first group of orders are a revival of the Additional Instructions which Howe had used on the North American station thirteen years before. Those of October 19 are clearly the outcome of his experience during his summer cruise in the Soundings. Between August 19 and September 12 he was constantly exercising his fleet in tactical evolutions, but not entirely to his satisfaction. He records in his Journal that on one occasion he ordered the fleet repeatedly to tack, 'but neither the distance of the ships from each other, nor of the columns, with no more sail abroad than might be requisite on service, were properly observed.' Later he tried it again, but he says, 'it did not appear they had acquired the facility or correctness in these essential movements that is to be desired.'[1] The excellent results which were the eventual outcome of his efforts have been sufficiently dealt with in the General Introduction.

The 'Explanatory Instructions' which follow are found at the beginning of Howe's printed 'Signal Book' in the Admiralty Library, conjecturally assigned to 1793. The last article goes to confirm that conjecture: for the Signal Book he used in 1790 did not contain it, and it occurs in the *Bridport Papers* as a MS. addendum issued on August 26 of that year.

The whole group is worth careful study. It will be found to contain a final formulation of the doctrine of the Howe-Kempenfelt school, to which Howe brought all that was best in the British tradition and practice and Kempenfelt the essence of French theory, and so produced that potent blend which made the school of Nelson possible. We need read no further than the first two articles to see that for Howe tactics were once more a living

[1] Barrow, *Life of Howe*, p. 202.

thing, having for their sole end to do the enemy as much injury as possible with the least risk to yourself—to enable captains to develop the utmost fighting energy of the fleet. From this point it was but a step to the direct and drastic methods of Nelson, and it is easy to understand how the young admiral, when he came to appreciate what Howe's work really meant, was moved in his enthusiastic way to call him 'the first and greatest sea-officer the world has ever produced.'[1]

[1] Nelson to Howe, Jan. 8, 1799. *Nicolas*, iii. 230. Four years earlier Nelson had expressed an opinion that Hood was the greater officer. Same to Hoste, June 22, 1795. *Ibid.* ii. 46.

LORD HOWE. 1790

[Bridport Papers IV. Add. MSS. 35194 f. 41. Printed.]

Additional Instructions respecting the Conduct of the Fleet preparatory to and in action with the Enemy.

I

Limitation to place and distance in order of battle in some occasions dispensed with.

The chief purpose in the establishment of a regular disposition of the ships limited to place and distance in a stated order of battle has been that they may remain as little as possible exposed in their approach to the fire of more than the particular ships corresponding in station to them in the enemy's line, or be subject to injury from each other. But as a strict adherence thereto may sometimes be found prejudicial to the service, by restraining the captains from taking advantage of the favourable incidents which may occur in the progress of a general action, it is the object of these instructions to facilitate the means of improving similar opportunities by an authorised deviation from such restrictive appointments occasionally.

II

The van to be extended to the length of the enemy's van, and the same of the rear; though they consist of a greater number of ships—Of the ships of the enemy to be less regarded when engaged with a superior force thereof.

It is meant that the British van should most frequently be extended to the headmost ships of the enemy's van preparatory to a general action in regular order of battle, though they consist of a greater number of ships. And it is equally desirable under such circumstances that the same care should be taken in the rear, to engage more particularly the sternmost ships of their rear, that no unoccupied ships may be left at either extremity of their line to facilitate any attempt to double upon some part of the British fleet; though it is judged that such use of their superiority proposed to be made by an unexperienced Enemy will be proportionally guarded against, as the ships of the fleet subject to be affected thereby shall be more closely engaged with their immediate opponents in the enemy's line.[1]

In respect to the limitation and rule for the government of the captains, with whom the option must remain in these cases with reference to the particular parts of the enemy's line, wherein it may be advisable to leave such unoccupied ships in the meantime; it is recommended to those commanding ships of greater force to disregard or pass the weaker and worst sailing ships of the enemy, and confine their first endeavours solely to disable the stronger or more active, as their accidental situations in the line may afford opportunity.

III

When weathering the enemy on different tacks—When ships in the enemy's rear should tack a proportion of the rear of the fleet to do the same.

In case of weathering the enemy preparatory to a general action, and being then approaching each

[1] This cumbrous sentence may be paraphrased thus:—'Don't trust to the above tactical disposition to prevent the enemy using his superiority by doubling. The only sure way is

other on different tacks, the fleet will most probably be to continue standing on as before. And as soon as the Admiral has judged the van of the British Fleet is advanced far enough towards the rear of the enemy to allow sufficient space to form and bring up properly against those opposed to them in the enemy's line, respectively, when come to the wind on the other tack, he may be expected to make the signal for the rear to tack first, or for the whole fleet to tack together, as he sees most convenient for forming upon the line of bearing best suited to the position of the enemy.

But if any number of the ships of the enemy's rear should at this time tack it will be proper for the commander in the rear of the British Fleet to direct such a proportion of his division as he sees requisite to do the same in succession after that which will then become the leading ship. And being thereby formed in line ahead parallel to those of the enemy tacking as aforesaid they will be to engage them in that situation unless otherwise by signal directed.

IV

When coming up with the enemy and having the wind of them on the same tack.

When arriving up with the enemy on the same tack, having the wind of them, and they are observed to be lying-to or waiting under an easy sail by the wind in line ahead, but in such distance to leeward that the fleet is not liable to be materially injured by their fire; the Admiral will then most probably choose to continue on upon the same course until

closely to engage the units, in whose favour he would execute the manœuvre.' The objection to doubling an enemy was the danger of injuring the friend with whom he was engaged, and the closer the engagement, the greater the danger.

the van of the fleet appears to be advanced within a sufficient distance of the extent of the enemy's van. He may be thereupon expected to make the signal for shaping a course to join the enemy and come to action with them on bringing up: each ship of the fleet opposed to that of the enemy corresponding in situation as before expressed.

V

When arriving up with the enemy as before, and meaning to attack their rear previous to a general action.

But if the Admiral should think proper under the same circumstances in respect to the enemy to attempt upon their rear previous to the commencement of a general action and makes the signal 44,[1] provided for that occasion; the leading ship of the van division so appointed is to open to a convenient distance, and upon arriving up with the enemy to give their sternmost ship her fire upon the quarter; then tack or wear as the circumstances of the case render most suitable, and fall into the rear of the detachment appointed for this service: in order to repeat this mode of attack successively, with the rest of the ships sent on this service, until countermanded.

VI

When to desist from such partial attack for bringing on a general action.

When from any movement of the enemy it is thought inexpedient to continue the manner of attack specified in the preceding article, and that the Admiral would have the ship next in preparation

[1] See signal 218 of his code of 1782, *supra*, p. 171.

for the same movement and the succeeding ships to take their stations with the purpose of bringing on a general action; he may possibly make the signal for inverting the line in succession primarily instituted for the circumstance of arriving up at a small distance to windward of the enemy upon the same tack. The then headmost ship of the British line is thereupon to be placed against the sternmost ship (not before disabled) in the enemy's line; the ship her second astern is to pass without her to attack the next ship of the enemy; and the others to do the same in order throughout the enemy's line.

VII

When more in number than the enemy, how the supernumerary ships of the fleet are to proceed.

On meeting with a fleet of the enemy, inferior in number of ships to that under the Admiral's command, or if by the early desertion of their posts in battle the British Fleet should become superior to them in the line; the ships in the van or rear, in either case over and above the number of the enemy, will be at liberty to quit their stations in the line when the attack has commenced, without waiting for further signal or instruction to that effect. The captains thereof are to endeavour to distress and annoy the nearest ships of the enemy, in conjunction with the ships of the fleet particularly opposed to them, or otherwise to assist or relieve any disabled ships of the fleet, as they can be employed with most advantage.

VIII

When directed to steer for and engage independently the ships respectively opposed to those of the fleet in the enemy's line.

As it may be requisite on some occasions to leave the ships of the fleet at liberty to steer for those opposed to them in the enemy's line, independent of the necessary regard to uniformity of distance, course, and movements to be at other times observed; when the signal 42 is made for that purpose, it will be incumbent on the captains of the fleet to keep those ships of the enemy to which they are thus separately directed upon the same constant bearing if possible as they advance towards them. Suitable care is, however, to be taken by them mutually not to cross upon or otherwise subject themselves to any hazard of falling on board each other in execution hereof. In which view, when they are so straitened or confined in their situations by the ships near them, that they have not sufficient space to shape or vary their course correspondent to the alterations in the enemy's position made, as it may happen, they will best remedy that inconvenience *by a suitable increase or decrease of sail carried (or even throwing-to for a short time when going down large upon the enemy)* [1] so as to be assured of effecting the intended junction as nearly together as may be, with all convenient despatch. They are permitted in bringing up against the enemy *to take their stations on either part, to windward or to leeward of their opponents, as they see most suitable for closing with them to advantage and to disable them most speedily.* [2] They

[1] Blank filled in MS.

[2] This is the first appearance of Howe's famous manœuvre. With a view to secrecy, or because he had not fully decided on his form of attack, a blank was left in the print after the words 'against the enemy.' It was filled in as above in MS.

must nevertheless be mindful that they are not drawn away by any impression feigned or actually appearing to be made upon the enemy so far that they cannot have assistance from the fleet occasionally; being, in such circumstances, to consider wherein they may render the most effectual service against the enemy, and to govern themselves accordingly.[1]

IX

Preparations to be made when necessary to anchor for attacking the enemy's ships, &c., in port.

The purpose of the signal 54 being to have timely preparation made in the ships or division referred to, when it is proposed to attack any ships of the enemy protected by their batteries in port, or otherwise obliged to anchor in shore for their security; and when neither the time nor the circumstances of the case may admit of giving earlier notice of the Admiral's intentions therein. It is therefore deemed expedient to specify some of the most necessary provisions to be made for the services thence likely to ensue.

[2] *The captains of the ships so pointed out are to prepare for such service in due time, by having springs fixed upon their lower cables; and the end of their sheet cable taken into their stern ports, for stopping short without winding, when they are to sail to their answering stations against the works of the en·my with the wind aft.*

Their boats are to be hoisted out, and hawsers coiled in their launches or longboats, with their

[1] This last proviso may have been added by Howe in consequence of the representation which Sir Charles Knowles had recently made to him concerning what he believed to be a regular manœuvre of the French for meeting an attack from the windward. See *N.R.S.* xxix. (*Fighting Instructions*), p. 258. In fact the French had no such manœuvre.

[2] All that follows is a MS. addition.

stream or coasting anchors; in readiness to transport their own ships to their destined stations, or to assist other ships of the fleet when requisite, on the same occasion.

Their spare topmasts and yards (wind and weather permitting) will be best secured from injury in action by being lashed alongside, under their lower deck ports, or towed astern in smooth water, when no opportunity offers for leaving them in the care of any other ships or vessels attending on the fleet. And similar precautions in respect to the topmasts and yards may be often advisable for action at sea.

It is recommended while advancing (in either case) under the fire of the enemy to keep their men (not necessarily employed in working the ship) laid close down upon their decks, on the offside from the enemy's ships or works; to prevent disorder amongst them by untimely accidents, and that they may be less exposed to the enemy's fire, until the ships are duly placed.

Given on board His Majesty's ship the 'Queen Charlotte' at Spithead, the 10*th day of July*, 1790.

To Sir Alexander Hood, K.B.
Vice-Admiral of the Blue Squadron
of his Majesty's fleet.

By Command of the Admiral.
JOSH. DAVIES.

[Ibid. f. 43. Printed.]

Separate Instruction

Respecting the signal {*with a white flag* / *with a blue cross*}

Page 9 of the Signal Book.

I

General purpose of the signal.

The general purpose of this signal is to give timely notice of the Admiral's intentions meant to take effect at, or after, the close of day; that the division or ships to which they may relate may be suitably prepared when it is thought expedient, later in the evening or course of the night, to make the different signals expressive of those intentions.

II

When a disposition of the ships different from the prescribed order of battle is to be made in presence of a superior enemy.

If the preparation so required refers to a fleet or squadron of the enemy present, either greater in force and number of ships than the British fleet, or which the Admiral may for other reasons mean to defer bringing to action till at, or after, the close of day, when he judges it may be done with greater advantage in two or more divisions acting independent of each other; and it then happens that the circumstances of the case do not admit of a more leisurely communication of his plan; he will signify the form (if to be different from any before delivered) in which he would have the ships drawn up for conducting the attack after dark; by showing the flags expressive of the different divisions, in succession at proper intervals and putting abroad with each divisional flag the signal pennants distinguishing the several ships of which he would have (in such succession of place) each of the two or more divisions to consist. The commanders and captains are thereupon to take their stations accordingly; and to keep their ships in readiness for proceeding to engage the enemy in the order so pointed out when the proper signal is made for engaging the enemy at or after the close of day. But the divisions of the fleet, for the purpose of this signal, will be to remain as in the established form of battle expressed if no such change is to be made in the disposition thereof as in this article provided.

III

Of the conduct to be observed in coming to action with the enemy.[1]

The van division of the British Fleet is, on these occasions, to be placed against the van of the enemy, and the rear division against their rear, each to each, for engaging independently the same number of the enemy, computing from their outer or leading ships at each extremity of their line inwards towards their centre; and without reference to the Admiral's motions with the ships of his centre division (if the order be for forming in three divisions) except in the instance of suffering him to get with that division into action nearly at the same time. The ships of the centre division, or that in which the Admiral shall have taken his station, are respectively to engage, on each part, the ships of the enemy, equally distant ahead and astern of their commander-in-chief.

[1] That is a superior enemy. Here Howe, like Nelson at Trafalgar, assigns to himself the containing function.

IV

Ships of the van or rear not otherwise appointed as before are to act with the centre division—The commanders to act as they can most effectually disable the enemy.[1]

When such change in the disposition of the ships more correspondent to the respective force of the two fleets has been thought necessary as aforesaid; and that the van or rear division so constituted is composed of a less number of ships than that appropriated for either of those divisions according to the original disposition of the fleet in the established order of battle; the ships of either division, omitted in these occasional arrangements, are to close to the centre, and to act as a part of the centre division thereafter for the purpose of such temporary appointment.

The commanders and captains of the different divisions must necessarily be left at liberty to conduct themselves in operations of this kind as they see they can most effectually distress the enemy; without regard to any stated intervals of distance respectively, when come to action with the enemy, or having other relative attentions requisite to be generally observed on similar occasions in the day time.

V

When it is meant to confine the attack to any particular part of the enemy's line. Ships to repair to join the Admiral, as they are able, in the morning.

If from any injudicious position of the enemy or irregularity observed in their line, the Admiral would confine the intended attack to any particular

[1] See note on p. 328.

parts or division of their fleet, or would have it conducted in any other manner, as provided for by the day signals; the proper signal will be made for that purpose, and the '*flag, white bordered with red,*' *art. 2nd, page* 9, shown at the same time, as appointed in the Signal Book; and on these and all other occasions when coming to action with an enemy of superior force during the night, the several commanders and captains of the fleet are to repair to join the Admiral in the morning; forming in line of battle ahead and astern of him as nearly in equal numbers, and with as much regularity as the state of their ships will permit, or otherwise holding them in readiness to proceed on further service against the enemy, as he shall then see occasion from their situations by signal to direct. It is to be further observed, that after they have taken such suitable stations they will be consided in the Admiral's future signals as being of such division (starboard or larboard) of the fleet in which they may so happen to be placed for the further service to be then expected.

VI

When meant to countermand any signal before made for an operation to take place at or after the close of day.

Lastly—When it is meant, from some change of circumstances, to supersede these or other similar dispositions of the ships appointed to take place, for coming to action near to or after the close of day, either in order to substitute some more reasonable arrangement instead thereof, or entirely to annul the same; notice of that determination will be given by repeating the signal for the particular appointment to be revoked, and hoisting [*the flag white bordered with red, together with the annulling flag, white with a blue cross. Page* 11.][1]

After which the ships are to be continued in such order of battle or of sailing as had been previously in force; and to proceed in all other respects as if no change in their former disposition or signal for revoking such appointment has been made.

Given on board H.M.S. 'Queen Charlotte' at Spithead, the 10*th day of July*, 1790.[2]

To Vice-Admiral Sir Alexander Hood, K.B.

[Ibid. f. 47. MS.][3]

Instruction respecting the formation of the order of battle.

I

The squadron under the commander in the second post is generally to lead on either tack—But each squadron is to retain the relative station wherein it may be eventually placed.

The squadron under the commander in the second post will be generally meant to lead, when the line of battle is to be formed, whether the fleet is then sailing on the starboard or larboard tack. But as it may be necessary at times for the squadron under the commander in the third post (in that which may be to leeward in the order of sailing) to take

[1] Added in MS. The signal to be hoisted with the annulling flag was 'to be carried into execution after the close of day.'

[2] This paper is followed by a set of Printed Instructions entitled 'Of the Order of Sailing.'

[3] Collated by kind permission of Mr. John D. Enys, of Enys, with a copy in his possession issued October 9 to 'Sir James Barclay, captain of H.M.S. Windsor Castle.' It is identical except for the numbering of the ships.

such leading station, it is to be noticed, when that squadron is to institute the van, that the ship No. 25 will be to lead the said squadron, and the fleet; and the ship No. 35 to be the sternmost of that squadron. And if the squadron under the commander in the second post is then to form the rear in this temporary disposition of the fleet, the ship No. 11 will be the sternmost of the said squadron, and of the fleet on the same occasion.

Nevertheless when any change of wind, or situation of the fleet, by tacking, wearing, &c., whereby the squadron which was first formed in the rear is brought into the van, or which leading before on one tack becomes the leading squadron on the other tack, such leading squadron is to retain that station, and continue to lead the fleet until some further change takes place by signal or otherwise in the relative situation thereof.

II

When the Admiral is withdrawn from the line.

Though the Admiral is withdrawn from the line with the ship in which he embarked, for being better situated to direct the movements of the fleet, or otherwise, the same course and relative bearing of the ships remaining in the order of battle are to be continued as before, the alterations which may be afterwards to take place in the arrangement of the fleet will be directed by further signal or instruction. And the signals addressed to the centre squadron under such circumstances will apply to the senior commander and remaining ships of that squadron, until the admiral has resumed his station in the line.

III

Frigates, fireships, &c., how to take their stations.

The several frigates, fireships, and other attendant vessels assigned to the different squadrons or divisions of the fleet, will be to act (when not otherwise particularly appointed) as the several commanders of those squadrons or divisions shall direct. And the said commanders will order any change of situation in the line, between the ships of their respective divisions, which they judge necessary in service, at a suitable opportunity.

Given on board H.M.S. Queen Charlotte at Spithead, 10th July, 1790.

HOWE. (Autograph.)

To Sir Alex. Hood, K.B.

[Ibid. f. 96. MS.]

Instruction respecting the disposition of the fleet in order of sailing by divisions, denoted by the signal flag, half black, half white. Page 11, *art.* 15.

The several squadrons being formed in two divisions as signified in the order of sailing delivered herewith, they are to be kept about half a mile asunder ; the divisions nearly at the same distance ; and the ships of each division respectively about three cables' length from each other, in fair weather.

When sailing by the wind in this order the signal 80 (*to tack in succession*) is made, and the triangular flag, page 8, signal 6, is shown therewith : the commanders of the different squadrons will be to put in stays together ; they are to be followed in like manner by the ships in each division respectively of the several squadrons : and the leading ship of the lee division (when tacking as aforesaid) is to pass astern of the last ship (supposed to be in her proper station) of the weather division of her particular squadron. But when the signal 82 (*to tack together*) is made, and the triangular flag, page 6, signal 6, is shown therewith: the whole fleet is to tack together, and preserve the line of bearing of the former tack, until that tack is again resumed, or a different appointment of the fleet is to take effect.

The order of sailing denoted by the signal flag No. 3 will be readily formed from this disposition of the fleet; the first, starboard or weather division of each squadron being (when that signal is made) to fall in ahead of the second or larboard divisions respectively; or by the ships of the larboard or lee division, *tacking together* by signal when so directed and changing again to the former tack, astern of the first division: the ships of each division not failing to regulate the proportion of sail carried, so as best to forward the speedy arrangement of the ships of each squadron in the order intended. The centre and rear squadrons will be afterwards to pass on, and bring up to leeward of the weather squadron or column at the proper distance from each other, for perfecting the movement.

The line of battle will be soon formed in the same manner in the wake of the squadron under the commander in the second post; or otherwise as at the same time specially appointed.

When the signal is made for the leaders of divisions to wear together, the several leading ships (preceded by the commanders of squadrons) will be to wear at the same time, followed by the ships of their respective divisions as before.

The signals 24 or 25 for forming the fleet on either line of bearing, being made with the flag appropriated to denote this order of sailing; those signals will be then meant as for forming on such bearing, in order of sailing only. When they are made alone, they regard the disposition of the fleet in order of battle ahead, on such bearing respectively.

Given on board H.M.S. Queen Charlotte at Spithead, the 19th of October, 1790.

HOWE. (Autograph.)

To Sir Alex. Hood, K.B., Vice-Admiral of the White.

By command of the Admiral.

ROB. MARSH,
for the Secretary.

[At back of an 'Order of Battle,' Ibid. f. 99. MS.]

Observation.

The several flag officers are to have the particular superintendence and conduct of the divisions respectively, in which their ships are placed in the order of battle; but subject to the general direction of the commanders of the squadron to which they belong. The ships are to close to the proper distance from the next leading ships ahead of them, in place of those detached or not present with the fleet in order of battle or of sailing. And the senior flag officer remaining with either division or squadron is to have the charge thereof for the time being, in the absence of any other divisional commander.

Spithead, Oct. 19th, 1790.

HOWE. (Autograph.)

EXPLANATORY INSTRUCTIONS

[From Lord Howe's Signal Book, 1793. Admiralty Library. Printed.]

I

The signals are to be complied with by the ships of the fleet, *generally*, unless they are specially addressed to particular ships, squadrons, or divisions, denoted by their proper distinguishing signals shown at the same time, and to which such signals are meant *then only* to relate.

II

The signals will be generally made without gun, when it may be done with the same effect, unless when it happens that two or more guns are necessary to contribute a part of the signal, or that it does not appear to have been timely observed.

III

The observance of signals made to the fleet, or any ships, squadron, or division thereof, is to be denoted in the ships to which they are addressed, by the signal 2, page 72, which answering signal is to be kept abroad until the admiral's signal is taken in.

IV

When it happens that a signal made by the Admiral, or any divisional commander, is not sufficiently distinct, notice thereof is to be given by the ships concerned, by the signal 49, page 67; and when such signals not perfectly comprehended, respect ships detached or distant from the fleet, besides the indication thereof to be given as above mentioned, the ships are to stand back towards the admiral, or other flag-officer making the signal, until the purport of it is fully understood. The answering flag is then to be hoisted, and the ship to proceed as before, or as any subsequent appointment may express.

V

Distant ships to which it is denoted in reply that the signal made to the Admiral is indistinct, are to return in like manner nearer to the Admiral, until he has made known by the proper answering flag that the signal is then understood. The distant ships will be thereupon to resume the station, or service, on which they were before employed, if not otherwise directed.

VI

When either on account of the distance of the ships to which the Admiral's signals are addressed, the view of them being intercepted, or otherwise that they do not appear to have been timely regarded, notice thereof should be given from any private ship happening to be better situated for observance from the ship referred to, either by a repetition of the signal, or by the distinguishing pennant of the ship thrown out to denote inattention to the Admiral's signal in that ship.

VII

When the Admiral tacks, wears, lies-to, makes or shortens sail, &c., whether in consequence of the signal put abroad for such purpose, or otherwise, the ships of the fleet are to be regulated in the timely conforming thereto, as may best correspond with the means to preserve, or regain their appointed stations, with suitable expedition.

VIII

When the signal has been made for forming in the order of battle, for engaging the enemy, or for any other purpose, whereof it has been usual to keep the signal flying as an indication of the time the appointment was only to remain in force, such signals are to be deemed of equal validity for regulating the conduct of the fleet, until annulled or countermanded by some subsequent signal for a different purpose, although taken in when duly notified, as is generally intended.

IX

All general signals made by the Admiral are to be repeated by the different flag-ships in the fleet; and those made to the particular ships, also, whenever it appears that the Admiral's intentions may be thereby more expediently communicated to the ships concerned. But when such signal respects any squadron or division of the fleet *separately*, it will be sufficient for the commander thereof to indicate his notice of the signal by showing the answering flag; being at liberty, on such occasions, to postpone the repetition of the Admiral's signal, until he deems it expedient to direct the immediate execution of the specified movement or purpose of the signal, by the ships under his direction.

X

Particular care is to be taken by the several commanders furnished with these signals, that they may be timely destroyed, with every other signal and instruction given for the conduct of the fleet for his information, so that they may not fall into the hands of the enemy, by the capture or loss of their ships.

XI

Flag officers to regulate their squadrons or divisions.

When it is meant of the appointment in this Signal Book, as for ships to chase, to keep their stations in order of sailing or of battle, or any other service the Admiral may have occasion to signal to denote ; and it is intended that any particular flag officer of the fleet should direct the same ships in his squadron or division ; the proper distinguishing signal (p. 52), as for speaking with such officer, will be made herewith.[1]

[1] This article was originally issued by Howe as an addendum to the corresponding instruction of the Signal Book of 1790. See *Bridport Papers*, *Add. MSS.* 35194, f. 76, August 26, 1790.

LORD HOWE'S FURTHER INSTRUCTIONS, 1794

[Bridport Papers, iv. f. 294. MS.][1]

Instruction to be entered in the Additional Instruction Book, page 12, *art.* 17, *relative to the signal* 166.

Station of the divisional commanders when the order of sailing has been discontinued. Sig. 166, pa. 39.

When the signal has been made for the ships to take their stations as most convenient at the time without regard to any established order of sailing; the flag officers and other divisional commanders are nevertheless to keep their appointed stations with reference to the commander-in-chief in the succession to each other as by the order of sailing directed. Both for the more effectual communication of his signals throughout the fleet; and for enabling them to keep the ships of their several squadrons or divisions in the more regular order necessary to prevent separation, by making such timely signals for their government as they see needful in that respect.

HOWE. (Autograph.)

To Vice Adml. Sir Alex. Hood.

[1] This and following paper must be assigned to 1794. See General Introduction, pp. 72–4.

[Ibid. f. 298. MS.]

Order of sailing with convoy by the wind.

Advanced frigates or other ships of war to lead the fleet.

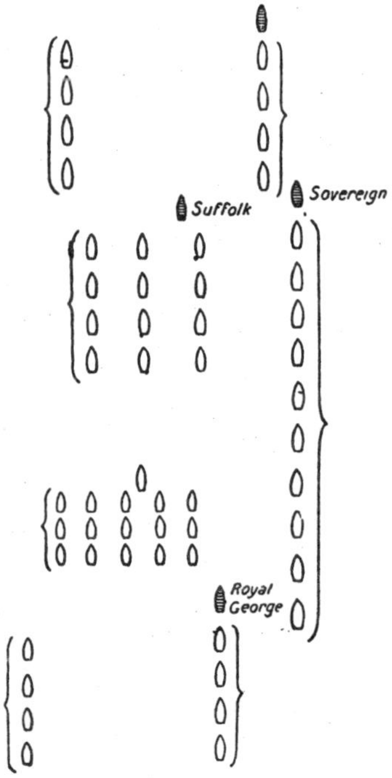

Suffolk

Sovereign

Royal George

[Ibid. ff. 301–3. MS.]

The Charlotte, at Spithead, 20th April, 1794.

SIR,—Deeming it expedient when the fleet consisting of the number of ships as at this time assembled is to be formed in order of sailing in two columns, that a detachment of ships, more or less in number, as shall be occasionally requisite should be appointed under the direction of a divisional flag officer to a station separate from the body of the fleet; and having nominated Rear-Admiral Pasley in the 'Bellerophon,' with the other ships named in the margin [Russell, Marlborough, Thunderer], for the conduct of that service; I transmit, enclosed, a copy of the orders by which he is to be governed, for your more particular information and occasional interposition, as the benefit of His Majesty's Service therein may require.

I have the honour to be, Sir,
Your most obedient Servant,
HOWE. (Autograph.)

To Adml. Sir Alex. Hood, K.B.

[Ibid. f. 301. MS.]

By the Earl Howe, Admiral and Commander in Chief of His Majesty's Fleet employed, and to be employed in the Channel, Soundings, &c. &c. &c.

Whereas it may be on many occasions expedient, when the fleet is to be formed in order of sailing in two columns, that a detachment of ships more or less in number should be appointed under the conduct of a divisional flag officer to a station separate from the body of the fleet: and Rear-Admiral Pasley is nominated for having the conduct of that detachment, whereof the ship under your command is to make a part: When therefore the signal 3, page 7 of the Signal Book, is hoisted with a WHITE pennant OVER, as provided in the order of sailing delivered, you will be to take your station on either quarter most to windward of the weather column of the fleet, or as by the signals or example of the Rear-Admiral pointed out; and to act under his orders for intercepting any ships of the enemy which may be crossing ahead of the fleet, or otherwise as he shall appoint.

When in presence of any considerable force of the enemy with a prospect of bringing them to action, and that you have not previously been directed to take your proper station in the order of battle (or of sailing as provided by the signal 74, page 23, to form the fleet in two columns, consisting of the general starboard and larboard divisions of the fleet, be the numbers more or less) the Rear-Admiral will make known to you the manner in which he would have you to proceed on service against the enemy (or you will be yourself so to do when he may have been already engaged with them, or is otherwise not in a situation so to advise you) for most effectually promoting their defeat, and assisting the rest of the fleet in their operations for that purpose.

Your most particular attention will be at all times requisite (and on this service more particularly) so to close with the Rear-Admiral or fleet before night, and in thick weather to profit by your best endeavours for noticing the movements and signals made for regulating the conduct of the fleet, and preventing your separation from it.

Spithead, 20th of April, 1794.

HOWE.

To Rear-Adml. Pasley.

By Command of the Admiral (Copy).

Signed

N.B.—When the signal 3 with a *red* pennant *over*, or signal 74, as above mentioned, are made, the said detached ships are at all times to take their proper stations in either order of sailing, as the particular signal imports.

[Ibid.]

Arrangement of the fleet in order of battle and of sailing.

Whereas it is intended that a squadron of Portuguese ships of war under the command of the Rear-Admiral Senhor Antonio Januario should be to co-operate with the Channel Fleet on the present occasion; the order of battle and arrangements of the united force are to be regulated as undermentioned.

The body of the fleet will be to consist of the British ships; the reserve or advanced detachment of the Portuguese squadron.

The commander-in-chief will remain for the most part with the body of the fleet, and lead the starboard or weather column, in order of sailing; and the reserve or advanced squadron, conducted by the Rear-Admiral Senhor Antonio, be stationed on the quarter to windward (as the course of the fleet is varied) of the weather column when sailing by the wind or large, and without the body of the fleet, on either part, when sailing before the wind. The advanced squadron is proposed to be kept about three miles distant from the body of the fleet, more or less according to the state of the weather. But to be sufficiently closed to the fleet always before night (and in thick weather more especially) for better assurance of being able to notice the movements and signals made for the conduct of the fleet, and preventing separation from it.

The commander-in-chief will most probably take his station, when to come to battle with the collected force of the enemy, for directing the service of the body of the fleet. The Portuguese or advanced squadron will be (for supporting the operations of the British squadrons) to act on such occasions of general engagement against the unoccupied ships of the enemy's rear, or to attack any of their separated ships as circumstances render advisable, in the judgment of Senhor Antonio; when not in any different manner, by signal or other notification, from the commander-in-chief appointed.

Dated on board the 'Charlotte' at Spithead, August 11th, 1794.

HOWE. (Autograph.)

To the Admiral Lord Bridport,
'Royal George.'

APPENDIX A

ADDITIONAL INSTRUCTIONS OF THE SEVEN YEARS' WAR.

I.

As the present volume was going through the press the papers of Captain Robert Duff, Hawke's favourite cruiser commander, and Commodore Howe's most valued colleague, were placed in my hands by the kindness of his descendant, Mr. Robert Fraser Duff, of Mapledurham. They proved to contain a whole series of additional instructions, issued by various squadron and fleet commanders between 1756 and 1761, which go far to elucidate the technical obscurity of this period of naval warfare.

For the most part they relate to chasing, fleet cruising, and the conduct of combined expeditions. They are clearly a development of Norris's 'Chasing Instructions,' and show that as yet no distinction had been made between additional sailing and additional fighting instructions. For this reason they do not seem worth printing in full. The headings of the various articles in one typical set are sufficient to show their nature, and only those articles which relate to fleet tactics are given below verbatim.

The first of the series is a set of articles in MS. issued by Captain Richard Howe, in June 1756, when, at the age of 31, he was placed in command of a cruiser squadron of eight sail for the protection of the Channel Islands. They consist of 'Signals by day,' 'by night,' and 'in a fog.' The day signals are as follows :—

Signals by Day.

1. Upon seeing a strange sail.
2. To pass within hail under the Dunkirk's stern (*Howe's flagship*).
3. For particular ships to examine strange ships standing into the fleet.
4. Upon discovery of danger.
5. For particular ships to keep ahead during the night.
6. For the whole squadron to chase.
7. For ships in chase to tack.
8. Ships in chase to signify they come up with the chase.
9. For ships to keep between the Dunkirk and ships in chase, to repeat signals or direct them back to the squadron.
10. To signify the chase is an enemy and may be spoke with, without losing company.
11. To signify the chase is of superior force to the chasing ships.
12. For ships stationed between the squadron and chasing ships to signify the signal being made to call them in.
13. For ships of the squadron to look out in any quarter of the compass.
14. Upon joining the squadron after separation (*private signals*).

Art. 15. 'Upon discovery of a fleet of the enemy's ships under convoy by ships in chase, they are to make known the number of ships of the line the convoy may consist of by hoisting a Dutch flag . . . . to be lowered and hoisted so many times according to the number of ships so discovered.'

Art. 16. 'If at any time when in chase with the whole squadron, or otherwise, I would have the ships nearest the enemy to draw into a temporary line of battle, and engage according to the order in which they may happen to come up, without regard to the general form of battle appointed; I will hoist, &c.

Art. 17. "If on meeting a lesser number of the enemy's ships I would have any particular ship or ships to quit the line and keep a station so as to be best able to succour any of the squadron needing her assistance, the signal will be &c."

18. For the boats from the ships of the squadron to tow a 'particular ship.'

19. For particular ships to attack the enemy's convoy (*transports or merchant ships*).

20. For particular ships to change their places in the line.

21. For ships leading on one tack to continue to lead on the other.

22. For the smaller ships to put into port though the commanding officer keeps the sea.

'Given on board his Majesty's ship the Dunkirk, in Guernsey Road, the 23rd day of June, 1756.

RICH. HOWE (*autograph*).'

'To Capt. Robt. Duff, of his Majesty's ship, Rochester.'

II.

The second of the series is a MS. set of 'additional signals' issued by Captain the Hon. Augustus Keppel, when, in October 1756, he was ordered off Finisterre in command of a small cruiser squadron. Though differently arranged, they are on the same lines as those of Howe; and the only articles which call for special notice, and which are not in Howe's set, are as follows:—

Art. I. 'Every ship that chases from the squadron is not to wait for the signal from the Torbay (*Keppel's ship*) to engage, but is to begin when she is at a proper distance, except the enemy is equal or superior to the ships with me. In that case you are not to venture engaging till my force is collected. Then if no signal is made for the line of battle every ship is to take the nearest her own size and engage her as near as possible.'

Art. II. For closer action.

III.

The third is a similar set of articles, also in MS., issued by Captain Charles Proby of the Medway of 60 guns on December 8, 1757, in which ship he had been serving under Hawke at Rochefort. The articles relate, as before, mainly to chasing and squadronal cruising, and at the end he has this direction:

> 'For all other signals I refer you to the general printed sailing and fighting instructions, and Sir Edward Hawke's additional instructions.'

The only additional instructions of Hawke's that are known are those printed in *Fighting Instructions*, p. 217. (*N.R.S.* xxix.) Proby's articles, however, are noteworthy as containing three separate 'Additional fighting instructions':

1. A new signal 'To engage'—a Union jack at the main top-gallant-mast head.
2. To pursue the enemy's convoy.
3. Ship leading to lead more to starboard or to port.

IV.

A very similar set of articles in MS. was issued on December 19, 1757, by Captain Samuel Cornish, of the Stirling Castle, then serving in the Channel and afterwards commander-in-chief in the East Indies. This set also includes the 'Additional fighting instructions' used by Proby.

V.

Next in date is a rearrangement by Howe of his instructions of 1756 with some additions, issued by him at Spithead, May 25, 1758, for his operations against the French coasts. During June he issued several supplementary orders relating mainly to the management of the transports and the flat-boats, and the landing operations and re-embarkations generally. All these are in MS. However, under date 'Spithead, July 24, 1758,' that is, after his return from St. Malo and Cherbourg, when he was about to renew his operations under Pitt's orders, we have a long printed set of 'Additional signals and instructions to be observed by the ships of war.' In these he embodied all the articles he had been using, with four prefatory ones and certain alterations and extensions, as the result of his recent experience.

This set of articles is remarkable as being the first instance of an attempt to give the instructions signal book form for ready reference. The printed day articles are 54 in number, and of these, 40, including the whole of his previous code, are tabulated in three columns, one for the flag, one for the 'place where,' and one for the article, corresponding to the later signification column, as in Arbuthnot's instructions of 1781 (see *supra*, p. 249). Sailing and fighting instructions are not separated but are intermingled with chasing, transport and landing orders in no logical sequence. Beyond the above interesting arrangement they contain nothing new of importance.

VII.

Seventhly, we have a unique copy, so far as is known, of the additional instructions issued by Saunders for the Quebec expedition, all in MS.

They begin with 32 articles, entitled 'Additional signals by day,' and dealing, like their predecessors, with control of chasing ships, fleet scouting and the like. The last one only is a fighting article—'For particular ships to attack the enemy's convoy while the rest are engaging or in pursuit of the men-of-war.' Then follow the usual night and fog signals.

Separate from all these articles is an elaborate set of instructions issued at Louisbourg, on May 15, 1759, for the conduct of the expedition in the approach through the Gulf of St. Laurence and up the river to Quebec. Most of them naturally relate to the organisation and control of the transports, and are beyond the scope of this work. At the beginning, however, is a group of tactical signals, designed for the protection of the convoy in case of attack. 'From Louisbourg,' he says, 'the fleet will sail in three divisions, in such order as I shall direct by the signals hereafter mentioned, each division to have a commanding officer and to be distinguished by different colours.' Each division of the fleet sailed with its own division of transports. Then follow 15 signals for controlling each division separately and relatively to the others, two signals for all the transports to keep to leeward or to windward, and for all transports to make the best of their way back to Louisbourg, and for the men-of-war of (his own) the Red Division only to weigh, and one 'for the ships of the line only in the white and blue divisions to weigh.' But of actual battle signals there are none, nor is there any sign that he adopted those used by Boscawen the same year.

The whole of these orders will be found printed in Captain John Knox's *Historical Journal of the Campaigns in North America 1759–60* (i. 260 *et seq.*).

VIII.

Here the direct evidence at present ends, and the inference is that no regular additional tactical instructions were issued. There are, it is true, in the naval papers of the time allusions to printed additional instructions. For instance on May 28, 1757, Commodore Moore, in sailing for the Leeward

Islands Station, with the trade, issued to his captains 'The sailing and fighting instructions with the printed additional signals, and further additional signals' (*Moore's Journal, Admirals' Journals,* P.R.O.) But the title shows that these were something corresponding to the printed articles and MS. additions issued by Howe in 1758.

Again, on May 18, 1759, Hawke issued to Captain Hood, as additions to the 'Additional fighting instructions,' his own article of 1756, and Lord Anson's of 1747 (*Bridport Papers, Add. MS.* 35193 f 82); but there is no evidence they were used by Boscawen.

In Boscawen's Journal for 1760, when his headquarters for the blockade of the French coast were at Quiberon Bay, there are many entries of his having issued to frigate captains going on a cruise, and to others joining the fleet, 'The general and additional printed sailing and fighting instructions and private signals (or day and night signals).' The first entry is April 17, and they continue into June.

These 'Additional sailing and fighting instructions' must have been something different from any of those mentioned above, which make no distinction between sailing and fighting articles. It would look as though Boscawen had had his fighting instructions of 1759 printed in one book with the usual chasing instructions, which thenceforward always appeared as 'Additional sailing instructions.' The only other allusion to new instructions during the war that has yet come to light is an order of Rodney's in the Duff Papers dated March 20, 1762. It runs as follows :—

'Whereas, I have observed that the third article of my additional signals has not been properly regarded by some of the ships under my command, and that several of them in sailing do not make the necessary sail to keep up with me:

'You are hereby directed to give the strictest orders to all your lieutenants that the said article is punctually complied with, and that the ship under your command is always in her proper station assigned her for forming the line of battle.

'You are likewise . . . . to add the signals I send you herewith to the other additional signals you have already received.'

The additional signals were for a particular ship to make more sail, and a change in the flag for a particular ship to come within hail.[1]

From this it is clear that Rodney had issued his additional signals in the old form, and not like Hawke and Boscawen as separate sailing and fighting instructions.

So far, then, as the evidence goes we have still to credit Hawke and Boscawen with the introduction of a regular set of additional fighting instructions.

We must also conclude that, as the nature of the war would lead us to expect, battle tactics made little progress beyond the instructions of these two officers; but that fleet cruising, convoy protection, and combined operations made great strides, and that their conduct became thoroughly systematised.

[1] At this time Rodney was on very bad terms with his captains. Hollwall wrote to Duff, who had just had a serious quarrel with Rodney, that he was 'a man without friendship or any principle that adorns a gentleman and an officer.' Augustus Hervey, he says, called Rodney 'the Superior of the Jesuits.' He was bent on turning both Duff and Hollwall out of their ships. (Hollwall to Duff, June 5, 1762; *Duff Papers.*)

APPENDIX B

RODNEY'S LANDING INSTRUCTIONS, 1761–2

INTRODUCTORY

THESE instructions are contained in a printed form, with blanks unfilled, amongst the Rodney Papers at the Record Office. It is without date, but from the fact that Rodney's rank is given as Rear-Admiral, and that his flagship was the Marlborough, it can be assigned with certainty to the end of the Seven Years' War, when Rodney, having recently received his flag, was in naval command of the expedition against Martinique. Though not falling within the period of the present work, they are printed here as embodying the rich experience of landing operations which the war had furnished and as completing our view of Rodney as a commander.

Amongst the Duff Papers is a corresponding set of transport instructions entitled 'Regulations respecting the conduct of the transports and disembarkation of the troops.' It has the blanks filled in MS. and was signed and issued by Rodney to Captain Duff of the Foudroyant from the Marlborough, on January 3, 1762, together with other supplementary orders on the 4th, 5th, 9th, and 11th. Rodney arrived off St. Pierre, Martinique, on the 8th. There can therefore be little doubt that it was under this set of instructions that the highly successful landing at Fort Royal was conducted.

[Rodney Papers, Bundle XIX. Printed. Record Office]

RULES

To be observed by that part of His Majesty's Fleet under the command of Rear-Admiral Rodney in Landing and Re-embarking the Troops.

When I make the signal to prepare to land or re-embark the troops, you are to send a few men for the flat-bottomed boats according to the directions you receive herewith, and to take them on board your own ship, and to man each with twenty rowers; when they are so manned they are to return on board the transports they are to receive the troops from; and when the troops are in, to repair under the stern of the rendezvous ship according to the brigade, and there to wait till I make the signal for landing, which you are immediately to put in execution. When the boats are sent to receive the troops, a lieutenant is to be sent to command the whole detachment you are to receive, and a careful petty-officer in each boat, with directions to obey the orders of any of the captains of the men-of-war whom I shall send on shore to command the landing or re-embarking.

Several guns are be mounted in the long-boats, which are also to attend to take the troops in, and those ships of war that have General Officers on board are to have their pinnaces to attend them whenever they shall request it.

The rendezvous-ship for the First Brigade is the which for distinction sake will hoist close under the flag at the main top-gallant-mast head in the day, and in the night wear at the main top-mast cross-trees one under the other.

The rendezvous-ship for the Second Brigade is which will hoist under the flag at the fore top-gallant-mast head in the day, and in the night wear at the fore top-mast cross-trees one under another.

The rendezvous-ship for the Third Brigade is the which will hoist under the flag at the mizen topmast head in the day, and in the night wear at the mizen topmast cross-trees, one under the other.

The transports you are to send on board of for the flat-bottomed boats, besides the one you have on board, are the

Upon the debarkation, you are to attend the Second Brigade, and as soon as they are landed to return to the Third Brigade, as per their signal.

Additional Signals and Instructions to be observed by the Ships of War

I

For the advantage of despatch and the more convenient distribution of orders occasionally, the captains of the squadrons are to direct their lieutenants in chief to provide themselves accordingly, and copy off from the day-book of the Marlborough such orders as are intended then to be issued, to which they are to subscribe their names in the said day-book respectively in acknowledgment of their receipts of such orders, if so required.

Colour	Place

II

For officers by land and sea and all other persons belonging to the fleet to repair on board their respective ships, after which signal is made no boat is to be suffered to go on shore from ships of war or transports, on any account whatsoever, without leave first obtained from the Commander-in-Chief.

III

For the ship or ships whose signals are made therewith to remain by, or accompany into the nearest port, ships making signals of distress. These attendant ships, after having seen such disabled ships in safety, to return in quest of the fleet, agreeable to the appointed rendezvous.

IV

For the ships to prepare for battle.

V

For the ships whose signal is made therewith to take in tow any disabled ship of war, transport or tender whose signal (to distinguish the same) will be made after the first signal is judged to have been observed.

VI

When it is meant that the captain of a ship whose signal is made therewith should endeavour to keep the trans-

Colour	Place

ports or other ships under convoy then nearest to him, within the circle of the ships of war.

VII

For all the boats in the squadron to go to the assistance of, or tow the particular ship whose signal is made therewith.

VIII

When the Commander-in-Chief means anchoring with a stream anchor.

IX

When lying-by, though not in order of battle, to fill and stand on.

X

For the fleet to bring-to, and lie-by when sailing either in line of battle, or otherwise, upon a wind.

XI

For the ships of the line to form in order of battle ahead, for the guard of the convoy, at half a mile distance of each other.

XII

For the ships of the line to form as above in a line abreast.

XIII

For the ships in the rear of the fleet to make more sail.

Colour	Place	
		XIV For the fleet to gather nearer round the Commander-in-Chief, when judged to be too much extended. XV For the flat-boats to be manned and sent on board the ship of the Commander-in-Chief. XVI If the barges or pinnaces or other boats proper to assist in the disembarkation are wanted there at the same time. XVII For the convoy to lie-by, shorten sail, or keep their wind, though the Commander-in-Chief on the contrary makes sail ahead, or bears away with any of the ships of war. XVIII For the convoy to make sail ahead or bear away though the Commander-in-Chief on the contrary shortens sail, lies-by, or otherwise, with any of the ships of war. XIX To be made by ships having occasion, in bad weather, from the accident of springing a leak, or other disaster, to part company with the fleet; the

Colour	Place

which will be answered from the Commander-in-Chief by a French jack at the ensign staff and firing one gun.

XX

If such disabled ship needs likewise the company of another ship to see her in safety to the nearest port.

XXI

In case you perceive a strange ship standing into the fleet during the night you are to endeavour as much as possible to prevent the same, and upon discovery of such ship to be an enemy, to lay them on board, upon knowledge of which the ship of war situated nearest to you is required immediately to assist you, without waiting for any further directions.

XXII

It is to be observed that the order of sailing delivered herewith is not meant to confine the frigates stationed on either quarter of the fleet to keep always on that same quarter, particularly on the change of tack when working to windward; but that division of them happening to be then to windward when the signal is made for tacking are to remain still to windward of the body of the fleet till an opportunity offers, by change of wind or otherwise, to regain, without inconvenience or loss of time, their destined stations; the

Colour	Place

intent of this distribution of the ships of war in sailing order being only to secure the transports, &c., against any hazard of insult from the sudden arrival of the enemy on either quarter of the fleet during the night.

XXIII

For the artillery transports to move up to the van of the fleet.

XXIV

For the artillery transports to move from the place of their then present anchorage nearer to the part of the shore at which their stores are to be disembarked.

XXV

When action shall be ordered for covering the descent of the troops, by signal from the Commander-in-Chief, the ships proceeding on that service are to continue firing from time to time only whilst the signal for battle remains abroad; but everything is to be kept in readiness for beginning the action again as soon as the signal shall be repeated, and when a   shall be hoisted at the fore top-gallant-mast head, the whole detachment, or the ships whose signal is made therewith, are to retire back from the shore to a proper place of anchorage.

Upon the descent of the troops, the several flat-boats, where manned from the men-of-war, are to be commanded by lieutenants who will receive and are to obey orders for their proceedings from the senior captains appointed to conduct the descent, and the boats of the different divisions placed in the order as underwritten.

From what ships manned	Mark of boats	Division

N.B.—It is the Admiral's directions that the ships that man the flat-boats do send so many lieutenants and inferior officers in them as they can conveniently spare.

Colour	Place

When it is intended the boats should advance, the signal will be made by a when to halt a and when to retire from the shore in order to deceive the enemy or otherwise a shown from the boats in which the senior sea officer is embarked; and the several inferior officers, commanding in the other boats, are strictly required to be watchful for and act conformable to these signals.

APPENDIX C

ADDENDA TO THE SOCIETY'S VOL. XXIX. 'FIGHTING INSTRUCTIONS, 1530–1816'

INTRODUCTORY

I. *Instructions issued to William Wynter, March* 31, 1558.—This was in the period of panic which followed the loss of Calais. The country, with great difficulty, was being placed in a state of defence, the local levies were mutinous, and the same day these instructions were signed an order was sent to the Governor of the Isle of Wight to discharge a portion of the garrison, as a fleet would arrive for the protection of the island. The main fleet was then under the command of Sir William Wodehouse, Vice-Admiral of England. He had been recalled to the Thames after the belated attempt to save Calais, and now Wynter, who was both Surveyor and Master of the Ordnance to the Navy, was to be detached to Portsmouth where the whole fleet was about to gather under the new Lord Admiral, Lord Clynton.

The instructions were probably the standing form. They show little or no advance on those in the *Book of Orders for the War* drawn up by Thomas Audley for Henry VIII. about 1530, the tactical articles of which are given in *Fighting Instructions*, p. 15. That document appears to have held the field till well into Elizabeth's reign. For in the Admiralty

Library there is a transcript of it made by James Humphreys in the year 1568, that is, at the time of the first stir which led directly to the Elizabethan naval revival. But no great reliance can be placed upon this; Humphreys appears, for some reason, to have been collecting precedents of this nature. (See 'Domestic Calendar,' 1547 8vo. p. 414.)

II. *Parliamentary and Commonwealth Orders* 1648–50.—In *Fighting Instructions*, p. 87, is an extract from some Parliamentary orders dated 1648. It now appears that Mr. Penn, in his 'Memorials of Sir William Penn,' was correct in assigning their origin to 1647. For a copy of them has been found in the Admiralty Library dated '6 April 1647,' and signed 'Warwicke; Fra. Dacre; Wal. Erle; Alex. Bence; John Rolle.'

In the same place another copy of them has come to light, which shows that with very little alteration they continued in force till 1650. This copy is signed by Blake and Popham, and dated April 13 of that year. The title and fighting article are extracted below, and it will be seen that the latter is only verbally altered from the form issued in 1647. Consequently, we may be sure that the 'Supplementary Instructions' (*ibid.* p. 88) which were assigned conjecturally to 1650, cannot have been earlier than that date. We can fix them, therefore, to the years 1650–3.

I

INSTRUCTIONS OF MARY 1558

ORDERS TO BE OBSERVED AT THE SEAS IN THE QUEEN'S MAJESTY'S SHIPS

[MS. Admiralty Library]

The last day of March 1558. Instructions made by Wm. Wynter, Esq., presently Admiral of the Fleet of Ships appointed by the Queen's Majesty, the Lord Admiral, and the rest of the Honble. Council to be transported to Portsmouth, for the captains and masters having the charge of the vessels of the said fleet, as follows :—

To praise God once in a day

First and before all things that every captain and master having charge of any vessel shall take an order that God may be praised, and honoured, with such service as is appointed, once a day in the ship.

No mariner, gunner, nor soldier to go on land without licence

Item : That no mariner nor soldier be suffered to go to land except he be licensed by his captain or the master, nor the master nor the master-gunner without the licence of his captain, provided that neither the master nor the master-gunner shall give any licence, the captain being in place.

Lights to be kept very close by night

Item : That very straight warning be given that the lights in every ship be kept very close, so that the enemy may not discover you by the same, whereby ofttimes the service is greatly hindered.

How the ships shall ride at anchor

Item : That all ships of war do ride as near the Admiral as they may conveniently, and the ship laden with provisions, by himself apart ; so as when occasion serveth that we shall counsel together, we be not so far asunder as that we cannot easily come one to another.

The victuals to be carefully looked unto

Item: That every captain do admonish the officers having charge of the victuals that the same may be carefully looked unto, and that there be not waste made thereof: And also to know from time to time of the pursers and other officers aforesaid the state that the victuals is in.

No ordnance to be shot, but by the captain's licence, and that not in vain

Item: That charge be given to the gunner of the ship that no piece of ordnance, except hackbutters [1] for the exercise of the soldiers, be shot off but when he doth receive order or commandment from the captain, and then that he be appointed not to spend it in vain.

To speak with the Admiral twice a day

Item: That every man do all that he may to keep company with the Admiral and twice every day to speak with him, that is to say, in the morning and at evening.

Good heed to be taken that victuals stolen ashore be not brought aboard

Item: That charge be given to the master, boatswain, and the cook that there be no kind of fresh victuals brought into the ship, by any suspected person, not dressed; but that he be examined how he came by the same to the end no such be encouraged to steal from the shore to bring it aboard.

An order for bearing of the flag.

Item: That every ship of war do set up a flag of St. George upon her bonaventure-mizen,[2] except Mr. Brook,[3] captain of the Red Galley,[4] who is appointed to wear the

[1] MS. 'Haccabutrs' = Arquebuses.

[2] The fourth and aftermost mast of four-masted ships.

[3] Probably the Richard Brooke who commanded the French prize, the Galley Blanchard, in 1546.—Oppenheim, *Administration of the Royal Navy*, p. 78.

[4] MS. 'reed gally.' There were three galleys in the Navy at this time: viz. the Black galley, the Red galley, and the

Flag of Vice-Admiral for this present journey; and the victualling hoys and others for to wear their flag between the mizen and the aftermost shroud.

An order for the boarding of the enemy that every man shall choose his match

Item: If it chance to meet with any ships of war enemies having an admiral and vice-admiral, and so fortune to join with them, then no man shall offer to board the admiral and vice-admiral of the said enemies, before Wm. Wynter and Richard Brook, Admiral and Vice-Admiral of our Fleet; but to give place if they should be able to fetch them. And when not, every man to choose his match as nigh as he can, and to have a good regard one to another that succours may be given as occasion serves.

Powder not to be carried about the ship in barrels or bags at the time of fight

Item: Before ye shall deal with your enemy that there may be straight charge given that the master-gunner do suffer no barrel, budge-barrel, or bags of powder to be carried about the ship, because there be many fortunes of evil belonging to it; but if he shall need to lade his brass, or cast pieces, to do it by cartridge which may be covered in mantells, or some other thing out of hazard of fire; and as for the lading of his chambers[1] that it be done in the cook room, the fire being all quenched, and not upon the overlops, or decks, or any cabin.

That the captain ought to comfort his men at the time of the boarding, and to put his things in order for the same

Item: Before you deal with your enemies, ye shall call before you the officers, and company of your ship, not only to encourage them in words of comfort, but likewise to know, and also to feel it yourself, the state and readiness

Brigantine. See 'Ships thought worthy by my Lord Admiral to repair to Portsmouth and presently remaining in the Narrow Seas.' May 22, 1558. *State Papers Domestic, Mary*, xiii. 11.

[1] The movable powder chambers that fitted into the breech of breech-loading guns. Brass and cast pieces were muzzle-loading.

of your things, which may serve for the annoying of the enemy and defending of yourself, which being cared for in time do make the victory, by God's help, the more certain.

Warnings to be given in sudden leaks or fire

If a sudden leak or chance of fire should happen, as God defend, in such sort that help were required, then they being in that peril shall shoot off the great pieces, and all to the end she may be relieved by the rest.

What orders to be observed in the time of mists

Item: If there do happen any great mists, in such sort that one cannot discern another, then, according to the weather or place we be in, we must order ourselves, that is to wit, if there be sea room. The Admiral will strike his sail and shoot one piece then, whereby every man may be warned to do the same; and if the Admiral will anchor, then he will shoot off two pieces, one after another, and strike the sail incontinent upon the same; but if it so fortune that he can neither drive nor ride at anchor, then every man mark well at the beginning of the mist what course the Admiral keepeth, and to do the same. And the said Admiral will within every glass-running shoot one piece for a knowledge, and because one may be the better warned of another, ye shall make noise with trumpets, drums, or knocking.

No wrong to be done in taking

Item: That no man do take from the Queen's Majesty's subjects, or other being in amity with her Grace, any kind of victual or other goods, without he do agree with the party from whom it is taken, so that he hath no cause to think himself injured.

To stay such ships as can give knowledge

Item: If any do fortune to meet with any vessel that can give intelligence he shall cause the same to be brought with speed to the Admiral, to the end he may understand their knowledge.

Ships separated to know the place for them to resort to

Item : If by mist, tempest, or other fortune it chance that any of our ships be separated from the company of the Admiral, the ships so separated shall with all speed consider by the weather and the wind that had indeed blown, where the said Admiral might be, and there to make his repair with speed, and not finding them, then he or they shall themselves to Portsmouth.

Ships separated how they shall know one another if they do come in fight

Item : If any be separated, as before said, and that they descry by fortune one another, to the end they may be assured that they are of one company, the one shall strike his foresail, and a yaw, and to house it and strike it in that sort, until he do think that the same be seen unto the other, and then shall the other answer him by striking of his foresail, and shooting of one good piece, so that by the signs they shall be certain the one of the other.

For the fetching of the enemies being chased ashore

Item : If it shall chance our enemy's ships or vessels be aground, so as they are not to be fetched off but by boats, then if you shall see the Admiral man his boat for the doing thereof, you shall do the same, and cause that every of your boats have in them their boat anchors, a grapnel of iron, with a small warp, and the ships drawing little water, to ride as near the enemy's vessel as maybe, for the succouring of the said boats.

What is to be done when a prize is taken

If God shall fortune us to take any ship or ships of our enemies, that they be straightly commanded and charge given that that which remaineth under the overlop be not spoiled nor touched, being the Queen's Majesty's ; and for that which is upon the overlop and decks, and belonging to the captain, master, and company, it be so used as every man of the takers may receive thereof according to his deservings.

The bearing of the lights in the night by the Admiral

Item : If in the night we do change our course, then the Admiral will bear a light in his cresset for the space of one hour, whereby every man may know what he ought to do ; and all the night after, none ; and then he will show out a lanthorn with a candle-light in the mizen-shrouds.

The sign to know when the captains be willed to come aboard the Admiral

Item : When there is a warning piece shot off, and the flag of council set up, then shall the captains and masters resort aboard the Admiral, and the captains to bring the masters and pilots with them.

And thus endeth the good orders to be observed at the seas.

II

COMMONWEALTH INSTRUCTIONS 1650

[MS. Admiralty Library. Extract]

Instructions given by Edward Popham, Robert Blake, and Richard Deane, Esqrs., Admiral and General of the Fleet, appointed by Parliament for this present expedition ; to be duly observed by all commanders and officers whatsoever and common men respectfully in this fleet, provided to the glory of God, the honour and service of the Parliament and Commonwealth of England.

If any fleet shall be discovered at sea which may be probably conjectured to have a purpose to encounter, oppose, or affront the fleet in the service of the Parliament and Commonwealth, you are in that case to proceed in such sort as shall be most for the honour and safety of this Commonwealth, taking notice that in case of joining battle, you are to leave it to us, or the chief of your squadron, to assail the enemy's admiral and to match yourself, as equally as you can, to succour the rest of the fleet, as cause shall require, not wasting your powder nor shooting afar off, nor till you come side to side.

Given under our hands the 13th of April 1650.

ROBT. BLAKE.
EDWARD POPHAM.

To Capt. Wm. Haddock,
Capt. of the Ameria.

APPENDIX D

BREAKING THE LINE

I

AN ENGLISH VIEW OF THE MANŒUVRE (CIRCA, 1750)

[O'Bryen's 'Naval Evolutions, or a System of Sea Discipline,' 1762, p. 65]

WHEN Lieutenant O'Bryen published his partial translation of Hoste, under the above title, he included in the volume '*An Essay on Naval and Military Discipline in General, by a late experienced Sea Commander,*' in which occurs the following passage, showing how prominent a place the idea of breaking the line then held in tactics:—

'The chief judgment of an Admiral is to form his line in a proper disposition and strength, from the van throughout to the rear, in doing which particular regard must be had to make the centre strong, for if that is forced or broke through the battle is looked on as lost.'

II

CONTEMPORARY CRITICISM OF RODNEY'S MANŒUVRE, APRIL 12, 1782

[Beatson's 'Naval and Military Memoirs,' 1790, Vol. V. p. 470]

'THE whole success of the battle on the 12th of April has been sometimes attributed to this measure, which has, of course, been deemed a masterly evolution, worthy of imitation. The British Admiral has also been supposed to break through a connected line of the enemy's ships. These representations, however, appear to proceed from mistakes; for the French line was completely deranged by the change of wind *alone*; and so far was the measure of sailing through the enemy's line with six ships, unconnected with the rest of the fleet, from being decisive of victory, that it may be doubted whether it was a fortunate evolution. If Admiral Rodney's fleet had kept a connected line of battle sailing large across the bows of the French ships, which were necessarily forced towards the broadsides of the British by the wind and totally disordered, it is highly probable that the French must, upon the whole, have sustained much more damage than it did from the six ships attached to Admiral Rodney, which had an opportunity of attacking three or four of the French collected in a confused manner, and forced to leeward of the British Admiral. And this is the only real advantage which has been supposed to arise from Admiral Rodney's weathering the French rear with six ships.'

III

THE MANŒUVRE IN THE TEXT-BOOK OF 1797

['A System of Tactics . . . with the Present Practice of the British Navy,' 1797, pp. 113-123 [1]**]**

To force or traverse the enemy's line

THIS is a manœuvre the lee fleet may execute to gain the advantage of the wind. It is performed by the van ship, if within gun-shot, tacking when she and the centre ship of the weather line are on a perpendicular to the direction of the wind; then all the lee fleet tack in succession, and thus may pass through the enemy's line, or perhaps a little more towards the enemy's van, and go about in succession to windward of him. But as he will not be long without doubt before he performs the same manœuvre he will thus be able to regain the wind, if you do not force him to give way under your fire before his evolution is finished. The enemy to windward may even cause his van ship to tack, as well as the rest of the vanguard to follow in succession, as soon as the leading ship

[1] All this part of the work is a reprint of the tactical part of Sauseuil's translation of Villehuet, though in the Preface it purports to be a new translation of Morogues.

of the lee fleet shall have passed through his line and be ready to go about; by which means he will bring them between two fires. This manœuvre, well executed, might perhaps give no little trouble to the ship attempting to force the line.

This evolution may be performed with advantage if, by some accident or fault in manœuvring, the centre division of the weather line be separated from their van or rear. For example, when the centre division to windward is encumbered with disabled ships, then those of the centre division to leeward are with all sails set to tack in succession and force with promptitude through the weather fleet to augment their disorder, leaving their own van division to engage that of the enemy on the other tack.

To prevent the line being forced

When the lee fleet go about in succession in order to traverse the enemy, the whole line to windward are to tack together, and at the same time, to get upon the same board as the enemy, who will neither be able to join nor to traverse them.

To perform this evolution with advantage you must let some of the van ships of the traversing fleet pass to windward, then go all rapidly about, in order to put and keep them between two fires. Thus you may succeed in destroying them without their own fleet being able to give them any effectual assistance.

It is easy to perceive, from what has been said, that there is little occasion to fear being traversed, as such a manœuvre may turn to be more prejudicial than advantageous to those who perform it. Nevertheless, it may and ought to be put in practice when the weather fleet leave such vacancies between their divisions as to allow some ships of the lee fleet to be inactive. In this case the ships that are without opponents abreast of them are made to tack with all sails set in succession and pass through the intervals of the weather line in order to double the centre division, or any other part of it, and bring it between two fires; while the other ships which are abreast and on the other side of it cannonade from to leeward.

To bear down on the enemy and force him to action

. . . . . .

If the lee fleet bear away four points to move their order of battle on the other tack and avoid an action, filing off in succession in the wake of the van ship ; the weather line, by bearing away all together eight points, cannot fail (both fleets being supposed to sail equally) to pass through the middle of the line, and force them to fight at a disadvantage, if their extent be double the distance between the two fleets.

. . . . . .

If the lee fleet bear away four points all together . . . in that case . . . if the van ship and the rest of the weather fleet have a sufficient velocity to keep the centre ship of the lee line on the same point of bearing, the leading ship may break through the enemy's line about the middle ship of the centre division. . . .

APPENDIX E

ENGLISH WORKS ON NAVAL TACTICS 1750–1850

1. *Naval Evolutions or a System of Sea Discipline*, by Lieutenant Christopher O'Bryen, R.N., 1762.

Dedicated to the Duke of York. It is a partial translation of Hoste's *L'Art des Armées Navales* 1697 ; but it also contains an earlier English essay entitled *An Essay on Naval Discipline in General by a late Experienced Sea-Commander.*

2. *Naval Tactics or a Treatise of the Evolutions and Signals . . . . by Monsieur de Morogues . . . . and translated by a sea officer* 1767.

Dedicated to Hawke, a partial translation of Morogues' *Tactique Navale*, 1763. It also contains an earlier English essay on tactics written *circa* 1750. (See *supra*, p. 4.)

3. *An Essay on Naval Tactics*, by John Clerk, Esq., of Eldin, 1782. Privately printed.

This was Part I. of the complete work. Only a few copies were printed 'not for sale, but to be given away.'

4. *The Manœuverer or Skilful Seaman* . . . . Translated by the Chevalier de Sauseuil 1788.

Dedicated to H.R.H. Prince William Henry. It is a translation of Bourdé de Villehuet's *Le Manœuvrier* 1765. (See *supra*, p. 5.) Sauseuil describes himself as Knight of the most noble order of St. Philip ; captain of infantry in the French service ; late captain and major-adjutant of the Legion of Tonnerre and member of the English Society for the encouragement of arts, manufactures, and commerce.

5. *The Art of War at Sea, or Naval Tactics reduced to new principles, with a new order of battle.* Translated from the French by the Chevalier de Sauseuil, London, 1788.

A translation of the Vicomte de Grenier's *L'Art de la Guerre sur Mer*, 1787. (See *Fighting Instructions N.R.S.*, xxix. pp. 285-6.)

6. *Essay on Naval Tactics* (*First Part*), by John Clerk, Esq., of Eldin, Edinburgh, Jan. 1790.

This was the original essay of 1782, now first published 'with additions and improvements.' It subsequently became Part I of the complete work. Parts II and III were not published till 1797.

7. *Elements of Rigging and Seamanship.* Printed for David Steel. London 1794, 4to.

A treatise on naval tactics extends from p. 347 to p. 425, *i.e.* 79 pp. with 18 plates. It purports to be a compendium of Morogues, Villehuet, and Grenier. It adopts Grenier's curious sailing formation in a three-sided figure, styling it 'the order of circumvallation.'

8. *A System of Naval Tactics combining the Established Theory with general practice and particularly with the present practice of the British Navy.* Anon. 1797.

In three parts. Parts I and II are a *réchauffé* of Morogues and Villehuet. Part III is 'the present practice of the British Navy.' (See *supra*, p. 75.)

9. *An Essay on Naval Tactics, systematical and historical, with explanatory plates; in Four Parts*, by John Clerk, Esq., of Eldin. London, 1797.

This was the first edition of the complete work. It contains Part I, as issued in 1790 (not reprinted), and Parts II, III, and IV, with a separate title-page dated 1797.

10. *The same.* Edinburgh, 1804.

11. *Treatise on Naval Gunnery*, by General Sir Howard Douglas, F.R.S. First edition, 1820.

Part V of this treatise is *Observations on some recent naval operations and on the tactics of single actions.* The author was the son of Admiral Sir Charles Douglas, Rodney's first captain in 1782. Other editions appeared in 1829, 1851, and 1860.

12. *Naval Battles from* 1744 *to* 1814 *critically reviewed and illustrated by Rear-Admiral Charles Ekins.* 4to. 1824.

This work is of special value, as reproducing much tactical criticism current in the service at the time.

13. *Naval Researches, or a candid inquiry into the conduct of Admirals Byron, Graves, Hood, and Rodney in the action off Grenada, the Chesapeake, St. Christophers, and of the* 9*th and* 12*th of April,* 1782, *being a refutation of the plans and statements of Mr. Clerk, Admiral Ekins, and others,* by Captain Thomas White, R.N. 8vo. 1830.

14. *Naval Evolutions: a Memoir, by Major-General Sir Howard Douglas, Bart., K.S.C., C.B., F.R.S., &c., containing a review and refutation of the principal essays and arguments advocating Mr. Clerk's claims in relation to the manœuvre of the* 12*th April,* 1782, *and vindicating by tactical demonstration and numerous authentic documents, the professional skill of the British Officers chiefly concerned on that memorable occasion.* London, 1832.

It is in this work that he claims for his father the honour of originating the movement for breaking the line on April 12, 1782. The book was suggested in a conversation with Sir Walter Scott, at Abbotsford. (Lockhart, *Life of Scott*, p. 365.)

15. *An Essay on Naval Tactics, systematical and historical, with explanatory plates, in four parts, by John Clerk, Esq., of Eldin, &c. Third Edition, with notes by Lord Rodney, and an introduction by a naval officer.* Edinburgh, 1827.

This was the third edition of the complete work. The 'naval officer' states that Rodney's notes were made in the margin of a copy of the original (privately printed) edition of 1782, that is, Part I, which belonged to General Robert Clerk. (See *supra*, pp. 13–15.)

16. *Naval Battles of Great Britain from the accession of the illustrious House of Hanover to the battle of Navarino*, by Admiral Charles Ekins. Second edition, 1828.

17. *A Treatise on Navigation by Steam, comprising .... an essay towards a system of the naval tactics peculiar to steam navigation ....* by Captain Sir John Ross, R.N. London, 1828.

Dedicated to the Duke of Clarence, Lord High Admiral. This was the first treatise on steam tactics.

18. *A Treatise on Naval Tactics*, by Paul Hoste, 1697; translated by Captain J. D. Boswall, R.N., F.R.S.E. Edinburgh, 1834. With appendices by Boswall.
    (i) The passage of the Dardanelles, 1807.
    (ii) Notes relative to breaking through an enemy's fleet.
    (iii) Explanations of the battles on the 9th and 12th April, 1782.

19. *The Principles of Naval Tactics exemplified with tables for facilitating the several evolutions*, by Capt. C. R. Moorsom, R.N. 32 pp. and 6 plates. London, 1843.

20. *An Essay on Naval Operations*, 1849, by Vice-Admiral William Bowles.

Contained in his *Pamphlets on Naval Subjects*, 1854.

21. *Naval Tactics and Trials of Sailing*, by George Biddlecombe, Master, R.N., of H.M. Yacht 'Victoria and Albert.' London, 1850.

Dedicated to the Lords Commissioners of the Admiralty. This was the last handbook on sailing tactics. In 1855 he published his *Steam Tactics*. (See *supra*, p. 79.)

APPENDIX F

INSTRUCTIONS AND SIGNAL BOOKS 1650 to 1830

NOTE

The dates in the date column are those of the printing or writing of the documents. Where such dates appear within parentheses, they are conjectural or approximate. Where no date appears in the document, except the date of issue, it is marked 'no date' (n.d.). The abbreviations in the 'Where Found' column are as follows:—

P.R.O. = Public Record Office.
A.L. = Admiralty Library.
B.M. = British Museum; MS. Department if MSS. are specified.
R.U.S.I. = Royal United Service Institution.

Date (approximate date in parentheses)	—	Description	Where Found
1653	1	Instructions for the better ordering of the fleet in fighting, 29 March, 1653, and instructions for sailing. **MS.** *Printed N.R.S. xxix. p.* 99.	Duke of Portland's MSS. and A.L.
1665	2	'Orders given by direction of the Earl of Sandwich to Captain Hugh Seymour,' 1 February, 1665. **MS.** *Printed Ibid. p.* 108.	Duke of Somerset's MSS.
1665	3	Duke of York's 'Instructions for the better ordering of H.M. fleet in time of fighting,' 10 April, 1665. **MS.** *Printed Ibid. p.* 122.	Earl of Dartmouth's MSS.
1665	4	Duke of York's 'Additional instructions for fighting,' 18 April, 1665, and sailing, 24 April, 1665. **MS.** *Printed Ibid. p.* 126.	B.M. Harl. MSS. 1247
1665	5	Encouragement for the captains and companies of fire-ships, small frigates and ketches. **MS.** *Printed Ibid. p.* 149.	B.M. (Harleian 1247) and A.L.

Date (approximate date in parentheses)	—	Description	Where Found
1665	6	Duke of York's 'Additional instructions for fighting,' 27 April, 1665. **MS.** *Printed N.R.S. xxix. p.* 128.	B.M., Sloane MSS. 3232
1666	7	Prince Rupert's 'Additional instructions for fighting.' **MS.** *Printed Ibid. p.* 129.	Earl of Dartmouth's MSS.
1672	8	Duke of York's 'Instructions for the better ordering of H.M. fleet in fighting.' **MS.** *Printed Ibid. p.* 146.	Earl of Dartmouth's MSS. and A.L.
1672	9	Encouragement for the captains and companies of fire-ships, &c. *See No.* 5.	Earl of Dartmouth's MSS.
(1672)	10	Duke of York's sailing and fighting instructions (1672) and indices of signals. **Folio. n.d.**	R.U.S.I.
1673	11	Duke of York's sailing and fighting instructions 1673, with an abstract and index of the signals. **MS. Folio. n.d.** *Printed in Penn's Memorials of Penn and N.R.S. xxix. p.* 152.	A.L., B.M.
1678	12	Sir John Narbrough's 'Instructions for all commanders to place their ships for their better fighting and securing the whole fleet if a powerful enemy sets upon us,' 4 May, 1678. **MS.** *Printed Ibid.* 165.	B.M. Egerton MSS. 2543
1688	13	Lord Dartmouth's 'Instructions for the better ordering H.M. fleet in fighting,' October, 1688. **MS.** *Printed Ibid.* 170.	B.M. Sloane MSS. 3650
1691	14	'Instructions made by the Rt. Hon. Edward Russell, Admiral, in the year 1691, for the better ordering of the fleet in sailing by day and by night and by fighting.' **Folio. n.d.** *Printed Ibid.* 188.	R.U.S.I.
1703	15	'Instructions for the directing and governing H.M. fleet in sailing and fighting, by the Rt. Hon. Sir George Rooke, Kt., Vice-Admiral of England, &c., Admiral and Commander of H.M. fleet, &c. in the year 1703.' **Folio. n.d.** *Printed Ibid.* 197.	R.U.S.I.

Date (approximate date in parentheses)	—	Description	Where Found
(1714)	16	'The sailing and fighting instructions and signals as they are observed in the royal navy of Great Britain,' by Jonathan Greenwood. **$5\frac{3}{4}$ in. by 3 in. n.d.**	R.U.S.I., B.M., and A.L.
(1740)	17	Admiral Vernon's 'Additional instructions to the fighting instructions.' *N.R.S. xxix.* 214.	Matthews and Lestock Pamphlets
1746	18	Signals for the royal navy, &c., with additional signals by Admiral Vernon, and day and night signals for the squadron under the command of the Duke d'Anville, 1746. **12mo. 1746.**	R.U.S.I., B.M., and A.L.
(1747)	19	'Lord Anson's additional fighting instructions' (in signal-book, 1756). **MS.** *Printed Ibid.* 216.	R.U.S.I.
(1756)	20	Day and night signals with additional fighting instructions and signals. **MS. 8vo. n.d.**	R.U.S.I.
1756	21	'Signals by day and night and in a fog,' issued by Captain Richard Howe (Lord Howe), 23 June, 1756. **MS. Folio. 11 pp.** *See supra, p.* 348.	R. F. Duff, Esq.
(1756)	22	Sailing and fighting instructions for H.M. fleet, with additional signals aud instructions in MS. **Folio. n.d.**	A.L.
1756	23	'Additional signals' for day, night, and fog, issued by Captain the Hon. Augustus Keppel, 7 September, 1756. **MS. Folio. 11 pp.** *See supra, p.* 349.	R. F. Duff, Esq.
1757	24	Additional signals and instructions issued by Captain Charles Proby, 8 December, 1757. Chasing and fighting. **MS. Folio. 8 pp.** *See supra, p.* 350.	R. F. Duff, Esq.
1757	25	Additional signals issued by Captain Samuel Cornish, 19 December, 1757. Chasing, fog, fighting and night. **MS. Folio. 6 pp. 1757.** *See supra, p.* 350.	R. F. Duff, Esq.

Date (approximate date in parentheses)	—	Description	Where Found
1758	26	'Instructions respecting the disposition of flat boats in the disembarkation of the troops' and 'Regulations respecting the sailing, anchoring and guard of transports on the enemy's coast,' issued by Commodore Howe, 25 May, 1758. **MS. Folio. 10 pp.** *See supra, p.* 350.	R. F. Duff, Esq.
1758	27	Additional signals and instructions to be observed by the ships of war, issued by Commodore Richard Howe, 24 July, 1758, day, night and fog. **Folio, printed. 12 pp. and 3 pp. MS.** *Partly in Signal-book form.* *See supra, p.* 351.	R. F. Duff, Esq.
1759	28	'Additional instructions and signals by day,' issued by Boscawen, 27 April, 1759. **Folio. n.d.** *Printed N.R.S. xxix. p.* 219.	A.L.
1759	29	'Additional signals and instructions' issued by Admiral Charles Saunders at Louisbourg, 15 May, 1789, for the Quebec expedition; also 'Sounding signals.' **MS. Folio. 22 pp.** *See supra, p.* 351. *Printed in Knox's Journal, vol. i. p.* 260.	R. F. Duff, Esq.
(1760)	30	Signals and instructions for H.M. fleet. (A revised edition of the sailing and fighting instructions, embodying many of the additional instructions. Possibly never issued to the fleet.) **Folio. n.d.**	A.L.
1760	31	'Instructions for the better keeping of company.' Convoy instructions with signals. Issued by Captain Wm. Payne, 5 August, 1760. **Folio. 2 pp. with MS. additions.**	R. F. Duff, Esq.
(1760)	32	Unfinished signal-book. **MS. 4to. n.d.**	R.U.S.I.
1761–2	33	'Rules to be observed . . . in the landing and re-embarkation of the troops.' Issued by Rodney for the Martinique expedition, circa 1761–2, in signal-book form. **Folio, printed. n.d.** *See supra, p.* 356.	P.R.O. Rodney Papers, Bundle 19.

Date (approximate date in parentheses)	—	Description	Where Found
1762	34	'Regulations respecting the conduct of the transports and disembarkation of the troops.' Issued by Rodney, 3 January, 1762. **Folio. 14 pp. printed with MS. additions.**	R. F. Duff, Esq.
—	35	Sailing and fighting instructions for H.M. fleet. **Folio. n.d.**	R.U.S.I.
—	36	Sailing and fighting instructions for H.M. fleet, with MS. alterations. **Folio. n.d.**	R.U.S.I.
—	37	Sailing and fighting instructions for H.M. fleet, with references in MS. **Folio. n.d.**	R.U.S.I.
1776	38	Instructions and standing orders issued by Lord Howe, 12 July, 1776, for the North American station. With additional instructions respecting the conduct of the fleet preparative to and in action with the enemy, dated July 1777. (Copy.) **MS. Folio. n.d.** *Supra, p.* 37.	R.U.S.I.
1777	39	'Instructions for the conduct of the ships of war, explanatory of and relative to the signals contained in the signal-book herewith delivered.' Copy of sailing and fighting instructions issued by Howe, 30 July, 1778. **MS. 4to. n.d.** *Supra, p.* 93.	R.U.S.I.
(1777)	40	'Signal-book for the ships of war,' day, night and fog signals, presumably drawn up by Howe in 1777. Corresponds to Howe's additional instructions of 1777. **4to. n.d.**	R.U.S.I.
(1777)	41	'Signal-book for the ships of war.' (Copy of the above signal-book.) **MS. 4to. n.d.**	R.U.S.I.
1778	42	'Sailing and fighting instructions for H.M. fleet.' Official copy issued by Admiral Byron, 26 October, 1778. **Folio. n.d.**	R.U.S.I.
(1778)	43	General signals for the officers of the army to assemble on board the Admiral, and night signals to the troops. **MS. Folio. n.d.**	R.U.S.I.
1778	44	Day and night signals to the sailing and fighting instructions of 1778. **MS. Folio.**	R.U.S.I.
(1778)	45	Sailing instructions and signals by day and by night for transports and ships under convoy (by Lord Howe). **4to. n.d.**	R.U.S.I.

DATE (approximate date in parentheses)	—	DESCRIPTION	WHERE FOUND
1778	46	'Night signals for the conduct of frigates or other ships of war appointed to observe the motions of a strange fleet, by Lord Viscount Howe, commander-in-chief North America. 21 August, 1778.' (Copy.) **MS. 4to. 1778.**	R.U.S.I.
—	47	Night signals for the fleet commanded by le Comte d'Orvilliers. (Translation.) **MS. 4to. n.d.**	R.U.S.I.
1779	48	Orders &c. given by Sir Charles Hardy to the grand fleet 1779 (order of sailing, &c.). **MS. 4to. 1779.** *Supra, p.* 124.	R.U.S.I.
1779	49	'Signals and instructions in addition to the general printed sailing and fighting instructions.' Issued by Admiral Byron, 3 March, 1779; with comments by Lieut. Thomas Graves. **Folio. n.d.** *Supra, p.* 190.	R.U.S.I.
1779	50	'Sailing and fighting instructions for H.M. fleet.' Official copy signed by Admiral Arbuthnot, 2 April, 1799, with alterations and additions. Headed, 'The book by which others are to be examined and filled up for service before being signed.' **Folio. n.d.** *Supra, p.* 236.	R.U.S.I.
1779	51	'Sailing and fighting instructions for H.M. fleet.' Official copy issued by Admiral Arbuthnot, 25 August, 1779. **Folio. n.d.**	R.U.S.I.
1779–80	52	'Signals and instructions in addition to the general printed sailing and fighting instructions.' Issued by Arbuthnot, 25 August, 1779, with additions dated 17 June and 19 August, 1780. **Folio. n.d.** *Supra, pp.* 244 *and* 246.	R.U.S.I.
1779	53	'Signals and instructions in addition to the general printed Fighting Instructions.' Apparently an official publication. Issued by Admiral Arbuthnot, 25 August, 1779. **Folio. n.d.**	R.U.S.I.
1779–80	54	Day and fog signals for the general and additional fighting instructions. Two vols. arranged by flags in one and by signals in the other. (The references agree with the additional instructions of 1779-80.) **MS. Folio. n.d.**	R.U.S.I.

Date (approximate date in parentheses)	—	Description	Where Found
(1779–82)	55	Copies of additional signals, lines of battle, orders of sailing, &c., by Admirals Hyde, Parker, Graves, and Rodney. **MS. Folio. n.d.**	R.U.S.I.
(1780)	56	Night signals extracted from the general and additional sailing and fighting instructions. **MS. 4to. n.d.**	R.U.S.I.
1780	57	'General and additional sailing and fighting instructions,' together with private ship signals, issued by Admiral Sir George B. Rodney for his campaign of 1780. Various copies with MS. alterations. **Folio. n.d.** *Supra, p.* 190.	P.R.O. (Rodney Papers, Bundles 15 and 19)
1780	57*a*	Another copy issued by Rodney 29 March, 1780. **Folio. n.d.**	R.U.S.I.
(1780)	58	Signals of the general and additional sailing and fighting instructions, arranged under headings. **Folio. n.d.**	R.U.S.I.
(1780)	59	Private code of signals. (Tabular system.) **MS. 12mo. n.d.**	R.U.S.I.
(1780)	60	'Signals and instructions in addition to the general printed sailing and fighting instructions.' (Day, night and fog.) **Folio. n.d.**	R.U.S.I.
1780	61	Fighting and sailing instructions drawn up by Admiral Sir Charles H. Knowles. (*Printed in* 1798.) **Folio. n.d.**	R.U.S.I. & A.L.
(1780)	62	Unfinished MS. signal-book. **MS. 8vo. n.d.**	R.U.S.I.
1780	63	Signals made by private ships by day and night. **MS. 12mo.**	R.U.S.I.
1780	64	Admiral Arbuthnot's private signals. 10 January, 1780. **MS. Folio.**	R.U.S.I.
1780	65	'The general and additional sailing and fighting instructions, together with those additions and alterations made by Admiral Sir Charles Hardy, Kt., Vice-Admiral Arbuthnot, and Rear-Admiral Thomas Graves. Arranged and digested for the ready and immediate making of signals.' **MS. 4to.** *Supra, p.* 47.	R.U.S.I.
1781	66	'Lord Howe's signals received from Captain Orde 1781.' (Day, night and fog.) **MS. 4to. n.d.**	R.U.S I.

Date (approximate date in parentheses)	—	Description	Where Found
1781	67	A private code of signals (tabular system) issued by Captain Charles Hudson, 8 January, 1781. **MS. Folio.**	R.U.S.I.
1781	68	'Additional signals for the North American station,' by Vice-Admiral M. Arbuthnot. (Dated in MS. 1781.) **Folio n.d.** *Supra, p.* 249.	R.U.S.I.
1781	69	'Signals by Thomas Graves, Esq., Rear-Admiral of the Red.' 1781. **MS. 8vo.** *Supra, p.* 259.	R.U.S.I.
1781	70	'The sailing and fighting instructions, or signals, as they are observed in the Royal Navy of Great Britain.' MS. signal-book to the general printed sailing and fighting instructions presented by Rear-Admiral Digby to Prince William Henry, 17 August, 1781. **MS. Sm. 8vo.**	Julian Corbett, Esq.
1781–2	71	'Signals &c. by Rear-Admiral Richard Kempenfelt.' Day, night and fog. (Combined old system and tabular numerary system.) **MS. Folio. n.d.**	R.U.S.I.
1781	72	Signals arranged under headings, with a line of battle, issued by Admiral Arbuthnot 31 May, 1781, and a code of signals on the simple numerary system. **MS. 8vo. n.d.**	R.U.S.I.
1781	73	Copy of the signal-books taken from the Comte de Grasse 12 April, 1782. (Tabular system.) **MS. 4to.**	R.U.S.I.
1781	74	Admiral Digby's private signals by day, 2 December, 1781. **MS. Folio sheet.**	R.U.S.I.
1781	75	Admiral Digby's private signals by night, 2 December, 1781. **MS. Folio sheet.**	
1781	76	Ordres de marche et de bataille de l'Armée du Roi commandée par M. le Comte de Grasse. MS. copy. **MS. Folio, 1781.**	R.U.S.I.
1781	77	'Instructions for the conduct of the ships of war, explanatory of, and relative to the signal-book herewith delivered.' Issued by Vice-Admiral G. Darby, 11 February, 1781, and marked 'Admiral Kempenfelt.' **Folio, n.d.** *Supra, p.* 135.	R.U.S.I.
1781	78	Another copy unsigned. **Folio, n.d.**	R.U.S.I.

Date (approximate date in parentheses).	—	Description	Where Found
1781	79	'General instructions for the conduct of the ships of war, explanatory of, and relative to the signals contained in the signal-book herewith delivered by Rear-Admiral Richard Kempenfelt. **MS. 4to. n.d.** *Graves's transcript, supra, p.* 136.	R.U.S.I.
1781	80	'Signal-book for the ships of war.' Day, night, and fog signals by Admiral Kempenfelt corresponding to above instructions. Combined old system and tabular system. **Folio, n.d.**	R.U.S.I.
1781	81	Instructions and signals by Captain R. Fanshawe for ships under his convoy. 14 February, 1781. **MS. Folio.**	R.U.S.I.
1781	82	'Instructions for the better keeping company with H.M.S. . . .' Issued by Captain T. Symons of H.M.S. Charon, 4 May, 1781. **Large sheet, n.d.**	R.U.S.I.
1781	83	General and additional sailing and fighting instructions &c. for His Majesty's fleet, as used by Rodney on 12 April, 1782; with MS. additions by Rodney and Pigot, and Rodney's instructions for Naval Brigade (MS.) **Folio, n.d.** *Supra, p.* 268.	U.S.N. Library, Washington.
1782	84	'Signal-book for the ships of war.' Issued and signed successively by Admirals Samuel Barrington and Richard Kempenfelt, in April and May, 1782, with MS. additions by Kempenfelt dated 6 May 1782. Old system combined with tabular numerary system. **Folio, n.d.** *Supra, pp.* 135–9.	Julian Corbett, Esq.
(1782)	85	'Signals by Rear-Admiral Kempenfelt 1780' (*sic*). The Channel Signal Book of 1782 with Howe's General Instructions for the ships of war. **MS. 4to.** *Transcript by Admiral Page. See supra, p.* 137, 140 *et seq.*	R.U.S.I.
1782	86	Sailing and fighting instructions, probably compiled by Lord Howe in conjunction with Kempenfelt in 1782. **Folio, n.d.** *Supra, p.* 140.	A.L.
1782	87	Day, night, and fog signals, corresponding to the instructions attributed to Lord Howe, 1782. Tabular numerary system. **Folio, n.d**	A.L.

Date (approximate date in parentheses)	—	Description	Where Found
1782	88	Copy of above attributed to Admiral Kempenfelt. **4to. n.d.**	R.U.S.I.
1782	89	Day, night, and fog signals as used by Rodney in 1782, with additional signals by Hood and Pigot. Old system. **MS. Folio, n.d.** *This and No.* 90 *are in one volume formerly belonging to Lieut. Waters, R.N. See supra, p.* 37.	A.L.
1782	90	Day, night, and fog signals of Admiral Kempenfelt, 1782. (Old system and tabular numerary system combined.) **MS. folio, n.d.** *Same as No.* 84.	A.L.
1782	91	Sir S. Hood's private signals by day, 27 January, 1782. **MS. Folio sheet.**	R.U.S.I.
1782	92	Sir S. Hood's private signals by night, 12 January, 1782. **MS. Folio sheet.**	R.U.S.I.
1782	93	Private signal to be made at Barbados. Sir S. Hood, 23 January, 1782. **MS. Folio sheet, 1782.**	R.U.S.I.
1782	94	Line of battle issued by Admiral Pigot, 13 July, 1782. **MS. Large sheet.**	R.U.S.I.
1782	95	Signals for speaking with officers. Issued by Admiral Pigot, 13 July, 1782. **MS. Folio sheet.**	R.U.S.I.
1782	96	Line of battle issued by Admiral Pigot, 19 July, 1782. **MS. Folio sheet.**	R.U.S.I.
1782	97	Admiral Digby's private signals by day, 5 October, 1782. **MS. Folio.**	R.U.S.I.
1782	98	Day signals and fighting instructions. Copy of signals issued by Digby, 5 October, 1782. Old system and tabular system. Apparently a private composition. **MS. and print. 4to. n.d.** *Probably drawn up by McArthur. See supra, p.* 58.	R.U.S.I.
1782	99	Admiral Digby's private signals by night, 5 October, 1782. **MS. Folio.**	R.U.S.I.
1782	100	Night and fog signals issued by Admiral Digby, 5 October, 1782. **4to. n.d.**	R.U.S.I.

Date (approximate date in parentheses)	—	Description	Where Found
1782	101	Captain Knell's signals, 6 December, 1782. Tabular system. **MS. 12mo.**	R.U.S.I.
1782	102	A private code of signals by Captain Swiney, H.M.S. Assurance, 1782. **MS. 8vo.**	R.U.S.I.
1782	103	'Signals': a MS. signal-book corresponding to the above, with Hood's and Pigot's additions. After April, 1782. **Sm. 8vo. n.d.**	Julian Corbett, Esq.
1782	104	'Signals and instructions by Sir George Bridges Rodney, Bart., &c. &c., being alterations and additions to the general and additional sailing and fighting instructions (1782), day and night.' **MS. 4to. n.d.**	R.U.S.I.
1782	105	An alphabetical index to the signals by day contained in the general and additional sailing and fighting orders. **MS. 13 in. by 4 in. n.d.**	R.U.S.I.
1784	106	Day, night, and fog signals and instructions. (Howe, 1782.) **MS. 4to. n.d.**	R.U.S.I.
—	107	Admiralty instructions for the captains of H.M. ships and masters of merchant ships under convoy. Day, night, and fog signals. **Folio, n.d.**	R.U.S.I.
—	108	Signals by night and in fog. **MS. Folio, n.d.**	R.U.S.I.
1789	109	General index to the signals by day. 'R. C. 1789.' (? Sir Roger Curtis.) **MS. Sm. 8vo.**	Julian Corbett, Esq.
1790	110	Additional fighting and sailing instructions issued by Lord Howe between 10 July and 19 October, 1790. **Folio sheets, partly MS.** *Supra, p.* 319.	B.M. Add. MSS. 35194.
1790	111	'Earl Howe's signals, by which the grand fleet was governed, in 1790, 1791, and 1794.' Admiral's signals on simple numerary system. Private ship-signals, tabular system. **MS. 8vo. n.d.** *Copy by Lieut. John Walsh, R.N. The dates* '1791 and 1794' *have been added on the title-page at a later date. This book was not used by Howe in* 1794. *See supra, pp.* 62–3.	R.U.S.I.

DATE (approximate date in parentheses)	—	DESCRIPTION	WHERE FOUND
1791	112	'Lord Howe's signals classed under general heads, alphabetically subdivided and adapted for a commander-in-chief's ship. The whole arranged for Lord Hood in the Russian armament, summer 1791, by John McArthur, secretary.' **MS. 6½ in. by 4¾ in. n.d.** *Supra, pp.* 66–9.	Admiral Sir Wilmot Fawkes.
(1792)	113	Index to signals by day and night. (c. 1792.) **MS. 4to. n.d.**	R.U.S.I.
(1793)	114	'Signal-book for the ships of war,' as used by Lord Howe June 1, 1794. **4to. n.d.** *Supra, pp.* 63, 316–7.	A.L.
1794	115	Capt. Schomberg's copy of same (Admiral's signals only). *See N.R.S. xvi.* (*Great Sea Fights*), *and supra, p.* 69 *n.*	Arthur Schomberg, Esq.
(1794)	116	Signals for ships of war, compiled by Wm. Goddard. **4to. n.d.**	A.L.
1794	117	Supplementary instruction by Lord Howe issued 1794. **Folio sheet. MS.** *Supra, p.* 340.	
(1795)	118	Mediterranean signal-book (much mutilated). Numerary system, and tabular private ship signals, as used at the Nile and St. Vincent. **8vo. n.d.** *Copy used by Capt. George Grey, Jervis's flag-captain* 1794–7.	A.L.
1796	119	'Day signals for the fleet in the Mediterranean under the command of Admiral Sir John Jervis, K.B. &c.' **MS. 4 in. by 3¼ in.**	R.U.S.I.
(1797)	120	Copy of Lord Howe's 'Signal-book for the ships of war.' (1793 edition, but each signal number advanced by 5.) *See No.* 114.	Commander C. N. Robinson & R.U.S.I.
1797	121	Standing orders &c. (compiled by Admiral Sir C. H. Knowles 1797 and printed 1798.) **Folio, n.d.**	R.U.S.I., B.M., and A.L.
1797	122	Signaux Généraux de jour, de nuit et de brume à la voile, et à l'ancre, à l'usage des armées navales de le République Française. (Autograph—Jean Bart.) (Tabular system.) An. VI. **4to. 1797.**	R.U.S.I.

Date (approximate date in parentheses)	—	Description		Where Found
1798	123*a*	Day signal-book compiled by Admiral Sir Charles Knowles, 1798. (Tabular system.) (*This and the next three items were never used or established.*)	**Folio, n.d.**	R.U.S.I., B.M., and A.L.
1798	123*b*	Convoy signal-book compiled by Admiral Sir Charles Knowles, 1798.	**Folio. n.d.**	R.U.S.I., B.M., and A.L.
1798	123*c*	Night and fog signal-book compiled by Admiral Sir Charles Knowles, 1798.	**Folio, n.d.**	R.U.S.I., B.M., and A.L.
(1798)	123*d*	Sir Charles Knowles's fighting and sailing instructions and standing orders. Printed in 1798. *See No.* 61.	**Folio, n.d.**	A.L.
1799	124	Signal-book for the ships of war.	**4to. 1799.**	R.U.S.I. and A.L.
1799	125	Signal-book for the ships of war, 1799, with MS. additions.	**4to. 1799.**	P.R.O. and B.M.
1799	126	Night signals and instructions for the ships of war.	**4to. 1799.**	A.L. and R.U.S.I.
1799	127	MS. copy of the signal-book for the ships of war, 1799.	**MS. 5 in. by 3½ in. n.d.**	R.U.S.I.
1799	128	Additional instructions for the ships of war. Issued by Vice-Admiral Sir Roger Curtts, 1 September, 1799.	**4to. n.d.**	R.U.S.I.
—	129	Signals to be made by one man by day or by night and by ships at a great distance.	**5 in. by 4 in. n.d.**	R.U.S.I.
—	130	Night and fog signals, etc.	**MS. 4to. n.d.**	R.U.S.I.
1800	131	MS. copy of signal-book for the ships of war.	**MS. 4 in. by 3½ in.**	R.U.S.I.
1800	132	MS. copy of the signal-book for the ships of war.	**MS. 8vo.**	R.U.S.I.
1801	133	Signaux généraux de jour, de nuit et de brume—à l'usage des armées navales de la République Française. (Fructidor an IX.)	**4to. 1801.**	A.L.
(1801)	134	Thoughts on several plans combining a system of universal signals by day and night. (J. McArthur.)	**4to. n.d.**	A.L.

Date (approximate date in parentheses)	—	Description	Where Found
1803	135	Telegraphic signal vocabulary, by Sir Home Popham. MS. additions. **4to.**	A.L.
1803	136	Telegraph signals or marine vocabulary, by Sir Home Popham. **4to.**	R.U.S.I.
(1804)	137	Copy of day and night signals. **MS. $4\frac{3}{4}$ in. by $3\frac{3}{4}$ in. n.d.**	R.U.S.I.
(1804)	138	Appendix to the signal-book for the ships of war. **4to. n.d.**	R.U.S.I.
(1804)	139	Appendix to the signal-book for the ships of war, with MS. additions. **4to. n.d.**	R.U.S.I.
(1804)	140	MS. index to the signal-book for the ships of war. **12mo. n.d.**	R.U.S.I.
(1804)	141	MS. copy of signal-book for the ships of war. **MS. 8vo. n.d.**	R.U.S.I.
1804	142	'Commercial and military signals for the ships in the service of the Hon. East India Company.' (By Sir Home Popham.) **Large 4to. 1804.**	A.L.
(1804–8)	143	'Signal-book for the ships of war, 1799.' With flags and signals corrected to 1808. **4to.**	A.L.
(1805)	144	Copy of day and night signals, order of battle, pennants, &c. **MS. $6\frac{1}{2}$ in. by 4 in. n.d.**	R.U.S.I.
1805	145	Telegraphic signal vocabulary, by Sir Home Popham. **8vo. 1805.**	P.R.O.
1806	146	Telegraphic signal vocabulary, by Sir Home Popham. MS. additions. **8vo. 1806.**	P.R.O.
1806	147	Night signals and instructions for the ships of war. **4to. 1806.**	A.L.
(1806)	148	MS. copy of day and night signals and of telegraphic vocabulary. **MS. $4\frac{1}{2}$ in. by $3\frac{3}{4}$ in. n.d.**	R.U.S.I.
(1808)	149	Copy of the signal-book for the ships of war 'used on board H.M.S. Excellent, 1808.' **12mo. n.d.**	R.U.S.I.
1808	150	'Signal-book for the ships of war, 1808.' *New edition of the official signal-book, superseding that of* 1799.	A.L., R.U.S.I., and B.M.
1809	151	Telegraphic signal vocabulary, by Sir Home Popham, and Addenda. **8vo. 1809.**	A.L.

DATE (approximate date in parentheses)	—	DESCRIPTION	WHERE FOUND
1809	152	Telegraphic signal vocabulary, by Sir Home Popham. MS. additions. **8vo. 1809.**	P.R.O.
(1809)	153	Signals for cutters, tenders, &c., not supplied with general signal-book. **8vo. n.d.**	A.L.
1812	154	Telegraphic signal vocabulary and observations on signal flags, by Sir Home Popham. **8vo.**	A.L.
1816	155	Telegraphic signals for the use of H.M. fleet. **4to.**	A.L.
1816	156	A book of signals and instructions for the use of H.M. fleet. **4to. 1816.** *The regular signal-book which superseded that of* 1804. *See N.R.S. xxix. p.* 342.	R.U.S.I., P.R.O., A.L., &c.
1827	157	General signals for the use of H.M. fleet. **4to. 1827.** *The new signal-book which superseded that of* 1816.	A.L.
1827	158	Vocabulary signals for the use of H.M. fleet. **4to. 1827.**	A.L.

ADDENDA

Date (approximate date in parentheses)	—	Description	Where Found
1782	159	'Signals and Instructions in addition to the General Printed Sailing and Fighting Instructions.' With MS. additions. Issued by Rodney, 19 Feb., 1782. **Folio, n.d.**	R.U.S.I.
1782	160	Private signals by day and by night. Issued by Rodney, 19 Feb., 1782. **Large sheet, n.d.**	R.U.S.I.
1782	161	'Sailing and Fighting Instructions for H.M. Fleet.' With MS. additions. Issued by Rodney, 19 Feb., 1782. **Folio, n.d.**	R.U.S.I.
1782	162	'Signals by Sir George Bridges Rodney, Bart., 19 Feb., 1782.' Day, night, and fog signals, lines of battle, and order of sailing. **MS. 8vo. 1782.**	R.U.S.I.
1782	163	Additional signals issued by Sir S. Hood, 27 April, 1782. **MS. Folio, 1782.**	R.U.S.I.
1782	164	'Signals by Rear-Admiral Sir S. Hood, Bart., 12 Jan., 1782,' with additional signals dated 27 April, 1782. Lines of battle and coloured sketch of action with De Grasse, 26 Jan., 1782. **MS. 8vo. 1782.**	R.U.S.I.
1782	165	Signals by Capt. C. Mason, 1 June, 1782. (Numerary system.) **MS. Folio, 1782.**	R.U.S.I.

INDEX